FOR GOODNESS SAKE

FOR GOODNESS SAKE
Bravery, Patriotism and Identity

Coline Covington

PHOENIX
PUBLISHING HOUSE
firing the mind

First published in 2021 by
Phoenix Publishing House Ltd
62 Bucknell Road
Bicester
Oxfordshire OX26 2DS

British Library Cataloguing in Publication Data

A C.I.P. for this book is available from the British Library

ISBN-13: 978-1-912691-35-7

Typeset by Medlar Publishing Solutions Pvt Ltd, India

www.firingthemind.com

To
those whose bravery has no witness
other than their own heart

Only in the conduct of our action can we find the sense of mastery over the Fates.

—Joseph Conrad, *Nostromo*

Contents

Acknowledgments

I'm very grateful to friends and colleagues who have been my readers and my sounding board for my book as it has developed. Their encouragement and thoughts have kept me going and their contributions have been invaluable. I would especially like to thank Richard Carvalho, Owen Renik, Ted Jacobs, Patricia Williams, Graeme Taylor, Armand D'Angour, and Richard Johnson. Thanks also to Norma Percy, Katia Glod, and Anatoly Golubovsky for their help with Russian liaisons.

Finally, I couldn't have wished for a more dedicated and helpful editor than Kate Pearce, who has been a great pleasure to work with.

Permissions

I would like to thank the following for their permission to reproduce material within my work:

Excerpts from *Boys in Zinc* by Svetlana Alexievich, translated by Andrew Bromfield (Penguin Books, 2017). Text copyright © Svetlana Alexievich, 1989, 2013. Translation copyright © Andrew Bromfield, 2017. Reproduced with the kind permission of Penguin Random House UK.

Excerpts from *The Plague* by Albert Camus, translated by Robin Buss (Penguin Books, 2002). Translation copyright © Robin Buss, 2002. Reproduced with the kind permission of Penguin Random House UK.

Eva Hoffman for her kind permission to reproduce an excerpt from her lecture at the Hubert Butler Annual Lecture, 2017, Kilkenny, Ireland © Eva Hoffman.

Excerpt from *The Mighty Dead: Why Homer Matters* by Adam Nicolson. Reprinted by permission of HarperCollins Publishers Ltd © Adam Nicolson (2014).

"FOR WHAT IT'S WORTH" Words and Music by Stephen Stills © 1966 Springalo Toones (BMI), RICHIE FURAY MUSIC (BMI), Cotillion Music Inc. (BMI) and TEN EAST MUSIC (BMI). All rights administered by Cotillion Music Inc.

About the author

Coline Covington, PhD, BPC, received her BA in Political Philosophy from Princeton and then moved to the UK where she received her Diploma in Criminology from Cambridge and her PhD in Sociology from LSE. She worked for nearly ten years as a consultant with criminal justice agencies throughout England and set up the first UK mediation project between victims and juvenile offenders with the Metropolitan Police in London.

Coline is a Training Analyst of the Society of Analytical Psychology and the British Psychotherapy Foundation and former Chair of the British Psychoanalytic Council. She is a Fellow of International Dialogue Initiative (IDI), a think tank formed by Professor Vamık Volkan, Lord Alderdice, and Dr Robi Friedman to apply psychoanalytic concepts in understanding the effect of trauma on intransigent political conflict.

From 2011 to 2013, Coline was Visiting Research Fellow in International Politics and Development at the Open University and Senior Scholar at the Woodrow Wilson International Center for Scholars in Washington, DC.

Coline's publications include *Terrorism and War: Unconscious Dynamics of Political Violence* (Karnac, 2002), *Sabina Spielrein, Forgotten Pioneer of Psychoanalysis* (1st edition, Routledge, 2003), *Shrinking the News: Headline Stories on the Couch* (Karnac, 2014), *Sabina Spielrein: Forgotten Pioneer of Psychoanalysis* (2nd edition, Routledge, 2015), and *Everyday Evils: A Psychoanalytic View of Evil and Morality* (Routledge, 2017).

Coline is in private practice in London.

Preface

It was a clear, crisp spring morning in London as I walked through Grosvenor Square to the US Embassy. Nearly a year before I had made the decision, reluctantly, to revoke my US citizenship. I knew I wasn't going to return to live in the United States, my country of origin, and my decision was based on practical financial reasons. Although I had had dual citizenship with the UK for many years, I identified myself as American, not British. I had been warned by a friend to expect an interrogation as to my reasons for wanting to revoke my citizenship—along the lines that I was betraying my country. The very fact that there was a hefty exit fee to pay to revoke one's citizenship suggested that a penalty was due. As I walked up the steps to the Embassy, I nervously rehearsed my reasons, aware of my defensiveness. Inside the Embassy, at the administrative counter, I was asked to swear an oath on the Bible or by my word that no one had forced me to revoke my citizenship. As I gave my oath, to my complete surprise, I burst into tears. The woman looked at me sympathetically and said, "Lots of people find this very distressing."

This moment vividly brought home to me the deep importance of what the country of my birth and my childhood means to me, and how very painful it was to give up my entitlement to belong. Although I was rationally clear about why I had made this decision, emotionally it made no sense to me. I was grief stricken and angry that the draconian US tax laws for expatriates had led me to this. I also felt I was betraying an intrinsic part of my identity along with the values that I had held so dearly throughout my life. While many of us take our country of origin and what it means to us for granted, my act of effectively disowning my country made me powerfully aware that we all have some kind of national identity, whether we acknowledge it or not, and that this deeply affects not only our personal identity but how we see the rest of the world.

I continued to think about my reaction to this separation that I had instigated, and wondered if it had affected me so profoundly because I had also been estranged, by choice, from most of my immediate family for many years. Was I in tears about the loss of my own family? While this may have colored my reaction, I was aware that my feelings about my country were of a different order. Having come of age in the heady and turbulent time of Vietnam, Haight Ashbury, Nixon's impeachment, and Martin Luther King's fight for racial equality, I had absorbed the principles of the American Dream and held these passionately to heart. The liberal ideology of the time and place pervaded my youth and, most importantly, provided a structure for meaning—both for myself as an individual and for myself within a collective. Ironically, it was this democratic ethos that allowed me, in my last year in high school, to espouse the vision of communism, quoting from Mao's Little Red Book in my school assembly. Little did I realize then the luxury of freedom of thought.

While writing this book, the world has changed, in many ways unrecognizably. Liberal democracy has failed in its promises, and populism has erupted across the world. The prosperity of the nineties has primarily impacted international corporations and the small segment of the very rich who are getting even richer. The rest of us are becoming worried about our futures. As economic inequality begins to bite, "strongman" leaders are more and more appealing. They will make their countries great again! They will keep out immigrants! They will protect us from the rest of the world! There are few political ideals and many falsehoods. The only political subject that indisputably crosses borders is the weather and what we do, or don't do, about climate change. It feels like a particularly bleak time of "existential anxiety." It is also a time when we urgently need courage and imagination to shape a future that will enable us to go on living together and to honor what is best about being human.

Introduction

As individuals and as groups we ascribe our identity, often unconsciously, to the patriotic values we grow up with and that guide our behavior. From childhood, no matter what society we come from, we aspire to the ideals of our parents, our teachers, our leaders, and our country—to our culture; we also begin to form some sense of our own inner conscience, what feels "right" to us. This is a complex idea and is not always the same as what is seen to be "right" within our social group—but it plays a vital part in determining our actions and in understanding the compelling power of our political belief systems. Being able to stand up and act on what we believe requires bravery; it gives voice to our patriotic beliefs and it also forms our identity.

For Goodness Sake: Bravery, Patriotism and Identity examines how the concepts of bravery, patriotism, and identity are intrinsically inter-linked through the question, "What does it mean to be true to oneself?" Those who commit acts of bravery attribute their actions not to empathy but to following their conscience or adhering to the moral ideals they hold up as a mirror to themselves. Most of us understand the power and the appeal of a "higher authority" that inspires us to live according to certain principles or values. This is commonly experienced in our religious beliefs, but it is also deeply felt in our political beliefs.

In my previous book, *Everyday Evils: A Psychoanalytic View of Evil and Morality*, I tried to illustrate how susceptible we are to adapting and conforming to changes in our belief systems, even when they contradict our own sense of what is "right." Our adaptability to changing social norms is often at the root of what enables large groups to commit atrocities against others. We now see much more clearly, for example, how the societal ideals of Weimar Germany became transformed and perverted to serve the political aims of the Third Reich. Our social norms and beliefs, which we often imagine as set in stone, are in fact fluid and subject to social pressures that we are sometimes only marginally aware of. Hannah Arendt's description of the "banality of evil" is as relevant today as it was at the time of the Holocaust. The highest ideals within a group can be used as an inspiration to respect our fellow human beings, or they can be perverted to exploit and dehumanize them.

Bravery is of such value to us because it embodies Kant's imperative that man should not be treated as a means to an end but an end in himself. In this respect, bravery is the opposite of evil, and its greatest opponent. The individuals who dissent and go against the prevailing political forces are often those who stand against perverse ideologies and the atrocities committed in their name. Their acts of brave opposition come from their own personal and political beliefs. Members of the resistance during World War II, rescuers of victims, spies serving their countries—all risked their lives for the beliefs they held and in allegiance to some form of higher authority, whether in the form of patriotic ideals or individual conscience. These instances of bravery make us acutely aware of the moral and political nature of bravery and why it is such an important emblem in our world. Acts of bravery, perhaps more than any other action in our lives, assert what it means to be "true to oneself" and express the ideals we hold for ourselves of the person we want to be and how we want to live.

The question of what it means to be "true to oneself" is also at the core of my professional practice as a psychoanalyst; it is what marks psychoanalysis as a truly revolutionary process. Madness is not being able to be true to oneself or to have a tangible sense of self, that is, feelings and judgments derived from and consonant with our perceptions of reality. The work of analysis is to enable patients to discover that they have a self they can not only trust but be true to. This means being brave enough to acknowledge and separate from dysfunctional relationships and from the mad parts of the mind that rob us of reality. Using examples from my work with patients* of their own acts of bravery, I explore the themes of political identity, the influence of social ideals and ideology, the differences between betrayal and dissent, and our need to belong to and to identify with large, powerful groups that make us feel safe in the world. On a wider social level these themes are illustrated through the lens of current events. Although these events are necessarily dated, they depict the timeless dynamics of bravery in its different manifestations.

The book starts by laying the foundation for understanding some of the psychological processes that create our sense of belonging and enable us to risk our lives for the sake of our beliefs and principles. Our moral sense of what is right and wrong develops within a framework of personal experience and the cultural values we grow up with. Our conscience is guided by what Freud called our "superego," that part of our psyche that judges and guides our actions within the parameters of what is considered right and wrong. The "superego" also binds us to the norms of the groups we belong to, whether it is our family, our community, or our country. When these norms change, or when they are experienced to be at odds with our own individual beliefs, this creates psychic dissonance, and can lead to dissent or madness or both. Being true to oneself is a fundamental act of self-agency.

In Chapter Two we see how being true to oneself is at the core of bravery and is the common factor in each act of bravery. Within any atrocity or life-threatening situation, there is the silent presence of the brave individuals who act and stand apart from the crowd, who risk their own lives by rescuing others and, in other ways, by voicing their dissent. The actions of these exceptional individuals raise questions as to why they were able to do what they did and why other people don't. But if we look closer at the histories of these individuals, what we discover is that they may not be as exceptional as we think. Acts of bravery also take different forms in different contexts and often remain unrecognized and private. Clinical material of a young male patient, a war hero struggling to separate from his refugee parents, illustrates the role of the ego ideal, insofar as it is consonant with innate morality, as the primary factor

---

*Case studies have been disguised for the purpose of confidentiality.

motivating acts of bravery. The compulsion to act bravely is primarily attributed to conscious, in other words, being at one with oneself. Those who act bravely do not feel they have a choice because not to act is experienced as a betrayal of self. As such, bravery is a fundamental assertion not only of the self but also of a moral order necessary to sustain the self.

Acts of bravery are commonly recognized within group behavior and especially within the context of war or civic duty. The brave soldier is the archetypal example of the individual who risks his life for his country and protects the values of the group. Most societies have long traditions of heroic individuals who come to represent the "ideal citizen" for their group. What is striking is that this "ideal" rarely differs in its basic composition, regardless of the political and social structures within which it applies. Chapter Three points out that the concept of the "ideal citizen" who places the values and survival of the group above personal interests is, for example, as relevant in modern-day North Korea as it is in the USA. What is perhaps more revealing is to look at how bravery has also come to be associated with self-agency and dissent. Plato's writings about the life of Socrates highlight the juxtaposition between acts of civic and personal bravery. Socrates was renowned for his martial bravery in rescuing Alcibiades in the battle of Potidaea in 432 BC and for his civic courage in refusing the demand of the tyrannical junta in 404 BC to arrest an innocent man. At the end of his life, scapegoated for the coup of 411 BC and found guilty of opposing the democratic constitution of Athens, Socrates decided to accept the death sentence rather than challenge the laws of his city. However, he notably argued in his defense that rather than being punished, the state should reward him as being "a gadfly stinging the conscience of the city" (D'Angour, 2019, p. 135). This story exemplifies the complexity of what the image of the "ideal citizen" means within different contexts and what happens when personal values oppose political ones.

The question of identity and belonging arises when there is a break or dislocation in one's life. At these moments, we are faced with choices— not only between past and present, between membership in one group or another, between geographically staying and leaving—but a more fundamental choice that concerns our identity; who we see ourselves as being, what it is we believe in, and how we are perceived by others. The implicit defining relation between place, belief system, and identity is suddenly laid bare. This caesura creates a mental space within which we become acutely aware of how much our identity is linked to a complex network of loyalties, beliefs, and communities, and the traumatic impact of losing these ties, leaving us in a state of diaspora while opening up the possibility of re-defining our identity. This liminal state and its effect on identity are explored in Chapter Four.

The experience of being uprooted from one's country is illustrated by a patient who struggled to bridge his past with his present and to make sense of the rupture in his own identity and his family's history. This rupture is particularly difficult when there have been dramatic political and social changes within one's country of origin. Our primary attachment to our country has profound implications on how we understand our identity, especially in the context of globalization and the erosion of national borders. With the traditional structures that form identity under threat, making people feel insecure about who they are in the world, it is not surprising that there is a rise in nationalism and a wish to return to the past.

The concept of heroism is universally linked with the act of sacrificing one's life for one's country or the survival of one's group. In warfare, physical courage is praised and held up as both a manly and a patriotic virtue. The idea of dying for a cause, whether it is in the service of one's nation, one's religious beliefs, or ideological tenets, is seen as the acme of bravery—a hero's death. And yet we assign very different values to the soldier who dies while trying to save others, whether it is in Vietnam or Afghanistan, in the name of democracy and the terrorist suicide bomber who dies trying to save the souls of others in the name of Allah. In each case, the hero achieves immortality through his death. The causes may not in fact be so different in their visions of a righteous and moral society and the bravery that is required to realize these ideals. Similarly, our human need to find meaning in our lives, expressed in terms of trying to aspire to the ideals we have of ourselves derived from our social norms, may be just as consonant with fighting for democracy as it is with fighting for Allah.

Chapter Five focuses on the psychological roots of why we need to find meaning in our lives and the importance our belief systems have in relation to defining our identity. Our need for meaning is intrinsic to being human, but the way in which this is actualized may either be toward respect and recognition of the individual or it may negate the value of the individual in obeisance to a higher power. Kant's moral imperative to "treat others how you wish to be treated" is applied to bravery as a means of differentiating between the ersatz, or perverse, and the authentic act.

Bravery is often traumatic and can become addictive as a way of managing the trauma. This is the dark side of bravery, fueled by the guilt of rescuing some while others have perished. Chapter Six highlights the seductive aspect of heroism that can tip the rescuer into taking extreme risk to the point of recklessness and death. Although acts of bravery are normally described as "selfless," the glory of bravery can enhance the rescuer's narcissism. When this happens, the rescuer's judgment is likely to be impaired and this is a crucial step toward dangerous miscalculations. Then the act of bravery becomes more of a gambler's game producing its own adrenaline in a dance with death. This omnipotent state of mind is an emotional defense that is common with soldiers and journalists who have served on the front lines of war; it both heightens immediate sensate experience and it enables the actor to transcend a sense of self. But there is a high price to pay, as these scars remain painful for life. The chapter concludes with the reminder to heed our fear as it is what enables us to survive and ultimately to help others survive.

Being true to oneself is not only expressed through physical acts of bravery, it is also expressed in voicing one's beliefs, challenging what one feels is wrong, exposing corruption, and opposing destructive group behavior. Chapter Seven examines these vocal forms of dissent, the whistleblowers who risk their lives or their well-being to uphold their principles, the journalists who speak out against injustice, protestors challenging political decisions, and interest groups, such as the "Me Too" campaign, that fight discrimination and racism. Perhaps the most hidden and sometimes most powerful act of dissent takes place in the privacy of psychoanalysis. Within this personal sphere, patients need great courage to face their most profound fears, their shame and guilt, and their love and hate. For many patients this may mean changing their lives radically, eschewing old belief systems, embarking on relationships that are new and unfamiliar, and severing ties with dysfunctional relationships. Enabling patients to be "true to themselves" is at the heart of psychoanalysis; this is what creates true change.

The final chapter picks up on the theme of change and the loss that accompanies every change. Using the example of Odysseus' struggle to resist the nostalgic lure of the Sirens' song while sailing home from Troy, we see what a powerful force drives us to the illusory safety of the past as a way of not having to face loss and an uncharted future. The political wave of populism that is spreading across the world exemplifies this psychological regression in which the charismatic all-protective dictator is chosen in the wish for security and certainty. Recreating an imaginary, idealized past is preferable to the liberal democracies that are perceived to have failed with the rise of global economic inequality and new corporate nations. We are at a turning point in history and to weather the journey forward, like Odysseus, we need to be able to resist our fantasies of the past, to acknowledge what has been irretrievably lost, and to be able to discriminate between what is true and what is false and what we can control and what is beyond our control. Each wave as it approaches, whether it is globalization, totalitarianism, or climate emergency, will present a different complex of problems and challenges. How we broach these challenges will inevitably affect our belief systems and our political identity.

These chapters present different facets of bravery and I hope, cumulatively, they demonstrate that every brave act is not simply an assertion of individual self-agency but also a political act. Bravery expresses the values that are most important to us as humans in relation to each other. We cannot act in good conscience without acting on behalf of others. Although many acts of bravery may occur in private and are never witnessed, they do not occur in isolation; bravery by its very nature affirms our respect of the other and their significance to us. At this point in our history, when political power is so much in flux and global problems such as climate change are threatening our everyday lives and our expectations of the future, it is crucial to be brave for ourselves, for others, and for goodness' sake. This book is in homage to those who have been brave enough to risk their well-being and their lives in order to protect the future. We can only hope to follow their example.

Reference

D'Angour, A. (2019). *Socrates in Love: The Making of a Philosopher*. London: Bloomsbury.

CHAPTER ONE

Identity and what it means to be true to oneself

Indeed, it is not one of our actions which, by creating the man we want to be, does not at the same time, create an image of the man as we think he ought to be.

—Sartre, *Existentialism is a Humanism*

Introduction

In Sophocles' play *Philoctetes*, the wily Odysseus and his crew arrive on the deserted island of Lemnos where Philoctetes, the master archer, has been stranded with his magical bow by none other than Odysseus on a previous trip. The Trojan war is taking place and can only be won by returning the bow to Heracles' funeral pyre. Philoctetes continues to suffer badly from a snake bite on his foot incurred during the war. It was the stench from his injured foot and his unbearable pain that caused Odysseus to abandon Philoctetes on Lemnos in the first place. Understandably, Philoctetes hates Odysseus. On his return, Odysseus is careful to remain hidden, and persuades the young and honorable Neoptolemus, a member of his crew, that he must trick Philoctetes into

1

giving up his bow so that it can be returned to Troy. Odysseus argues this will fulfill the prophecy of the seer Helenus and allow the Greeks to win the war. Odysseus emphasizes that this deceit will save many lives and win glory for the Greeks—the end will justify the means. Neoptolemus takes some persuasion, but eventually agrees, and wins Philoctetes' trust by telling him a story that Odysseus is also his enemy as he stole his father's (Achilles') armor that rightfully belongs to him. Neoptolemus is embraced as Philoctetes' ally and, in a sudden seizure of pain, Philoctetes hands Neoptolemus his bow. Odysseus then appears and the game seems to be up until Neoptolemus, who has been equivocating about returning the bow to Philoctetes, decides to be honorable and does so. Dismayed by Neoptolemus' change of heart, Odysseus persuades Neoptolemus to strike up a deal with Philoctetes. Instead of taking the bow—and Philoctetes—by force and deceit, Neoptolemus agrees to take Philoctetes back to Greece on the condition that he accompany Odysseus and his crew to Troy, bow in hand. The conflict of trust is resolved at the end of the play when Heracles (as a god) appears and reassures Philoctetes that not only will Greece win the war if he goes to Troy, but his wounds will be cured.

The central conflict in the play is between individual conscience and what is "right," or of greatest benefit to the group, especially when being "true to oneself" might jeopardize the survival of the group. Heracles' appearance at the end, as a kind of *deus ex machina*, resolves the conflict by rewarding Philoctetes for putting aside his own personal grievances for a higher cause. This ending does not resolve the fact that Neoptolemus, despite recanting, has acted against himself in bad faith and, as he says in anguish, "I shall be seen to be a traitor; that is what has long been paining me" (Sophocles, 1994, p. 345). Ashamed of his betrayal, Neoptolemus states, "Everything is distasteful, when a man has abandoned his own nature and is doing what is unlike him!" (ibid.).

The idea of man's "own nature" and "doing what is unlike him" is strikingly modern—and suggests that it was understood in much the same way as we think of being true to oneself today. It is an idea that is not only understood but its meaning is relatively unquestioned. But what does it mean?

Being true to oneself

Like Neoptolemus, most of us at different times in our lives are confronted with a situation that requires us to make a choice between being true to ourselves, or not. Being true to ourselves, or not, is ultimately realized through our actions, but we also reveal or betray ourselves with our thoughts which, when they are expressed openly, have an impact on others and on the way we frame reality. Our decisions or actions may be life-changing, such as rescuing a drowning man, or they may be relatively minor, for example, sticking to one's principles when they are not shared by others. As sentient beings, we are aware that it is our actions that determine not only the shape of our lives but also how we see ourselves and how we perceive ourselves in relation to others. In other words, we cannot understand this question without first having some common understanding of what we mean by "self," "identity," "truth," and "reality."

In referring to these key concepts of "self," "identity," "truth," and "reality," I am aware that there are a number of pitfalls and objections to using these terms as if they are actual, consistent, identifiable, and consensually accepted ideas. It is also the case that if we pick each concept apart and examine it within different contexts, each begins to lose its meaning and becomes essentially unusable. These are fundamentally philosophical ideas that help us to describe our experience of ourselves, of others, and of our reality. We recognize that the idea of "truth" changes according to our knowledge of the world, after all, we no longer believe the world is flat or that the sun revolves around the earth. We also acknowledge that the ideas of "self" and "identity" are complex and may mean different things to different people and across different cultures. Even the concept of "I" is contingent on how it is perceived culturally. The concept of "reality" also becomes questionable at a certain level; we can agree when we see an object, such as a tree, in front of us, or when we see a man die, but what this means to us may not be shared or interpreted in the same way by everyone. These are all fluid concepts that may take on different meanings within different contexts and change over time. Nevertheless, in trying to understand our experience on an emotional and psychological level, we need to deploy a language that reflects our cultural perspective.

I will venture some broad definitions as a guide to how I am trying to understand what it means to be true to oneself. Starting with the concept of the "self," I refer to its colloquial meaning as "a person's essential being that distinguishes them from others, especially considered as the object of introspection or reflexive action" (OED). Strawson elaborates that the experience of self—of an entity or mental presence that can be imagined or thought about—is "fundamentally grounded, in all ordinary human beings, in the experience of embodiment" (Strawson, 2009, p. 8). The experience of embodiment is necessary to have a sense of existing over time, of having a past, present, and future that one has experienced and has an impact on. There is an essential timeline, based on our need to create narrative meaning in our lives, that enables a sense of self to exist and to develop and that gives us what Winnicott refers to as an experience of "going on being" (Winnicott, 1960). An aspect of one's sense of self is one's "identity," a concept that is less to do with one's existential being and rooted more in one's function and place in the world. "Identity" is socially determined and confers not only certain characteristics with which we can describe ourselves but establishes our relationship with others and with the communities we belong to. Because our identity is determined by our social relationships, it is necessarily fluid insofar as we need to be able to adapt to changes in our social relations in order to survive. The sense of self, on the other hand, may evolve and deepen over one's lifetime, but I will argue that its essence does not change, that it is embedded in our awareness that we as individuals are separate and distinct from others, no matter what value we place on "I."[1]

The primary element of a sense of self is our capacity to self-reflect and to employ judgment and not simply to react instinctively. In his review of Christine M. Korsgaard's book, *Fellow Creatures: Our Obligations to the Other Animals*, the philosopher Thomas Nagel writes:

> Humans, with their capacity for language, historical record-keeping, long-term memory, and planning for the future, have a strong consciousness of their lives, not just successions of momentary experiences; what happens to an animal at one time changes its point of view at later times, so that it acquires "an ongoing character that makes it a more unified self over time." It is a matter of degree, but the lives of most mammals and birds, at

least, have this kind of unity, so we can think of them as having good or bad lives, not just good and bad experiences.

The big difference between us and the other animals is that we are self-conscious in a way they are not. Korsgaard marks this as the distinction between instinctive and rational lives. Unlike the other animals, we act not just on the basis of our present perceptions, desires and inclinations. We can step back from the immediate appearances and withhold endorsement from them as grounds for belief or action if we judge that they do not provide adequate justifying reasons—as when we discount a visual impression as an optical illusion or a negative evaluation as the product of jealousy. This type of rational self-assessment has given rise to both science and morality. Animals, by contrast, as far as we know, do not evaluate their own beliefs and motives before acting on them.

(Nagel, p. 42)

Nagel makes the important point that rational self-assessment, what we might call the capacity for self-reflection, is what enables us to evaluate the world we live in and our actions in the world, that is, science and morality. It is our capacity for self-reflection that I will refer to subsequently as the observing ego, meaning that part of our psyche or consciousness that observes our feelings, thoughts, and actions and, in doing so, acknowledges our internal, psychic reality. While the observing ego can be overridden by impulse (the id) or by conforming to social pressures (the superego), it is the ultimate litmus test of what being oneself means to us.

Lastly, there is the question of what we mean by being "true" to ourselves; what does "truth" mean in this context? The concept of "truth" as applied to our experience of external phenomena generally entails the acceptance of certain basic laws that govern our biological existence along with shared perceptions of events that take place in time and space. This definition derives from the Greek concept of Aletheia, elaborated by Heidegger in his idea that truth must correspond to the external conditions of reality to be validated. While the emphasis in the concept of Aletheia is on disclosure or bringing to light what has been hidden, Heidegger focuses on the ontological meaning of our perceptions—how we make sense of the world that is revealed to us.

In thinking about "being true to oneself," the locus of what is "true" shifts to the intra-psychic experience of the self. Here our capacity to self-reflect (i.e. the observing ego) has the job of determining whether our thoughts or actions are congruent with our feelings. This is what constitutes being able to say, "I am being true to myself," or not. We can see this in Neoptolemus' conflict with Odysseus' desire for him to take Philoctetes' bow from him. Neoptolemus is aware from the start that Odysseus is asking him to do something immoral in deceiving Philoctetes to hand over his bow. Yet Neoptolemus wants to please his commander, Odysseus, he wants to assist his countrymen in winning the war against Troy, and he has been taught to obey his superiors, especially in warfare. Neoptolemus is persuaded—at least temporarily—that the ends justify the means, and that his "duty" to his country and his fellow warriors is more important than his own individual sense of what is right and wrong. However, when Philoctetes demonstrates his trust and asks Neoptolemus to guard his sword while he is having a painful fit, Neoptolemus is faced with the harm he is inflicting by his deceit and, with reflection, he has a change of heart. What is striking about Neoptolemus' change is that it does not seem to be motivated by guilt, although he is aware of the hurt he causes, so much as acting in bad faith against his sense of himself and the kind of person he sees himself as being. It is his self-harm, his betrayal of himself, that affects Neoptolemus most deeply. The self that Neoptolemus knows he is going against consists of a synthesis of his own moral values and how he sees himself as an actor in the world. Together these form an image for Neoptolemus of his ideal self (i.e. his ego ideal). This is an image we have within us from our early development that represents how we want to act in the world and how we want to be seen—it configures our best characteristics, those we admire in others and in ourselves. For Neoptolemus, what was fundamental to his sense of self and his self-esteem was being attuned to his feelings and acting in accordance with them, even if it meant defying authority and collective mores.

Within psychoanalysis, the question of what it means to be "true to oneself" is at the core of our professional practice and it *should* be at the core of our theoretical thinking; it is what marks psychoanalysis as a truly revolutionary process. Madness is not being able to be true to oneself or to have a tangible sense of self, in other words, feelings and judgments derived from and consonant with our perceptions of reality. The work of analysis is to enable patients to discover that, first of all, they have feelings that are valid, that don't just come out of nowhere but are a reaction to things that have happened to them or ways in which they have been treated in both the past and the present. Once patients can begin to acknowledge their feelings, rather than having to disavow or deny them, they become aware that they have certain choices about the ways in which they want to be treated as well as how they relate to others. Most importantly, being able to trust one's feelings enables us to reflect on and assess our reality; we have a "self" that we can relate to and that allows us to be responsible for our choices and for what happens to us. In the case of most patients, this means being brave enough to acknowledge and separate from dysfunctional relationships and from the mad parts of the mind that rob us of reality. Being able to recognize and exercise one's internal judgment makes us into moral and political beings, responsible to ourselves and to others for our actions. It confers self-agency.

The superego and the ego ideal: a clinical example

I am assuming that being true to oneself is a good thing because it affirms or establishes consonance between internal and external reality. This is how we know what we feel and, accordingly, how we perceive reality. With this information, we are then equipped to make a judgment and a choice about our actions. If we don't know how we feel or if we suppress what we feel because we think it is wrong, then we have no real information with which to base our judgment, and we simply follow the orders of our superego in terms of some prescribed formula of what we ought to think and do. A clinical example of this emerges in the middle of a session of a middle-aged mother who is worried about her delinquent son.

Sarah complains she has had a relapse of her migraines.

Sarah: I don't know what to do about them [her migraines]. I've been fine for the last five months, maybe more—since I went to the migraine clinic I think. I'm sticking to my diet and there's no reason why they should come back—but they have, and with a vengeance! ... Andrew [her sixteen-year-old son] has been so helpful recently. He's helped around the house, with the dishes, he's even cleaned his room, and just the other night he went to the pub with his father and this really is a first! They're like buddies now … Last night he did come home very late—early this morning it was—after his curfew. I can't go to sleep until he's come in. He did make a lot of noise … he crashed into the sideboard in the kitchen on his way upstairs and I'm pretty sure he was drunk, even though he assured me he had stopped. I need to keep my head and not panic about this, not get all worked up. I know that doesn't help him or me.

CC: Perhaps your migraines are a silent protest about not getting all worked up about this?

Sarah: You know how Ted [her husband] accuses me of being angry all the time, of making mountains out of molehills. He isn't worried about Andrew's drinking—and, of course, Andrew denies he is. Ted says it is just normal teenage behavior and that I interfere too much. Ted is always so level-headed about everything—and he never raises his voice. He's a lot like my mother was—calm, unflappable, and always so reasonable, and kind. I felt like a mess of emotions around her, like a messy child who was always getting something wrong or being too demanding or too angry. I've tried so hard to be reasonable.

CC: And remembering how you felt with your mother—and how you feel with Ted—is making you angry now.

Sarah: Yes, it makes me want to do something drastic.

CC: Mm?

Sarah: Like get drunk, lose it, and overturn the kitchen table—make a big mess. Instead, what do I do but act like a self-righteous cop and lay into my neighbor who puts litter from her doorway into the street. At the same time I feel so sorry for Andrew—maybe because I'm identifying with him. I can see he's also trying to be calm and reasonable and I think his drinking is his way of blowing off steam.

CC: Hard to know how to be with him when you're trying to be the perfect parent and yet it feels like going against the grain.

Sarah: Too nice, it's all just so nice. We're all so polite and reasonable. But it's not what I feel inside and most of the time I'm saying to myself I shouldn't have these feelings, there's something wrong with me, I'm a bad person.

CC: Enough to give anyone a migraine!

Sarah: Maybe so … You know it makes me remember something over the weekend. My daughter deliberately tipped some paint over the doormat. She knew I was watching her and she knew she was being naughty. Everything was crystal clear. I had no compunction about getting angry with her. I told her [to] stop it immediately and said I wasn't going to take her out for an ice cream later on. Then I told her to go to her room for the next half hour. The problem I have with Andrew is that I know he is still drinking but if I confront him about it and show how angry I feel, his father makes me feel I'm not loving enough with him and that's why he's drinking. If I don't confront Andrew I feel I'm letting him—and myself—down, but if I do confront him I feel I'm the one who is creating problems. With Jenny, I knew I was right to be angry and it wasn't a problem. With Andrew, I get completely lost and muddled and don't know what I'm feeling and then I have no idea what to do. I become paralyzed.

In this short vignette, we can see some of the unconscious dynamics that are provoking Sarah's migraines and her paralysis. She idealizes her calm, reasonable mother who never got angry with her and has internalized this ideal as something to aspire to, while she denigrates her messy feelings, and in particular her unreasonable anger. Her super-ego has clear instructions to follow in order to keep her "good" and to demonstrate her loyalty to the family ethos. On the other hand, as she admits later on in the session, despite her son's denial, she knows he is still drinking and this makes her both anxious and angry—angry primarily because he is lying to her and angry with her husband, Ted, who is turning a blind eye to his son's drinking, if not actively encouraging it. By pointing out that Sarah's memories of her mother and of her husband are making her angry, I am performing in the role of an observing ego—I am observing that she is feeling something, what she is feeling, and what this is linked to. My observation doesn't indicate that Sarah's feelings make her "bad"—I suggest instead that "anyone" might be angry in her position—enough to get a migraine. Sarah then seems to be able to recalibrate her feelings and her judgment and remembers a very different incident when she reprimands her daughter for being naughty and can be angry with her without losing control or feeling guilty. As Sarah described it, she felt "crystal clear." She was sure about her feelings and could act appropriately on them—she could be true to herself. When she doubted the legitimacy of her feelings, because of her anxiety that they would reveal she was a "bad" mother, she became mindless and paralyzed and lost her sense of herself. At the same time, she knew that she was in this state because she was torn between two masters—between an outmoded ideal of herself modeled on a distorted or idealized self, and an ideal of herself that was congruent with her feelings and with her perception of reality and, most significantly, an ideal that wasn't reliant on pleasing others. Sarah's struggle to disidentify herself with an idealized ego also affected a modification in her superego from supporting an old, idealized image of herself to adopting a more protective and enabling position in relation to her feelings and her experience of being true to herself.

Although Freud's concept of the ego ideal was eventually incorporated into his idea of the superego (Freud, 1923b), it remains an important construct in our understanding of the development of the ego, specifically in our object relations and the process of socialization within groups.[2] The ego ideal provides a model for who the child wants to be like in the future, and in this respect facilitates maturation. The superego is our internal judge that monitors how the ego is living up to its ideal, with praise or rebuke depending on how the ego is performing. What is crucial in this process is the nature and plasticity of the ideal that the ego has adopted; if the ideal is not in accord with reality its effect on the ego is to make it feel that it is continually disappointing and a persecutory superego develops, as we can see in Sarah's presentation.

As we mature and develop, our image and the constituent parts of our ego ideal change in accord with our stage of life. The ego ideal represents the best of who we want to be, it is an aspirational image that guides us in our behavior, our social role, and our morality. It is derived partially from conscious self-constructions and from unconscious identifications formed from our relationships with others. Most significantly, there is an inherent choice that has to be made by the ego in determining what kind of person one wants to be. This is not to say that this choice is entirely a conscious one but that the ego ideal is realized through action. Neoptolemus provides us with a good example of this. He is swayed, against his better judgment, by Odysseus' argument that deception may be justified if it is used for the greater good, that is, winning the Trojan war. If Neoptolemus had believed that obeying orders for the greater good was of paramount importance, he might well have decided to override his misgivings and to identify entirely with this ideal. In its extreme form, the anthropologist, George A. De Vos, describes this position as "role narcissism," as evident in the self-sacrifice of the Japanese kamikaze pilots (De Vos, 1973). "Role narcissism" takes place when the ego becomes completely identified with the ego ideal and is subsumed by it, with the promise of narcissistic glory transcending the limits of the ego and mortality itself. It is a dynamic that enhances the ego's narcissism at the cost of relationship and recognition of the other. For Neoptolemus, however, his behavior toward Philoctetes reflected his attitude toward himself. In deceiving Philoctetes, he was essentially deceiving himself and this realization was ultimately what mattered most.

Inner authority

While the ego ideal is an imago of the desirable self, versus the existent self, it can, of course, like any psychic function, be used to strengthen one's sense of self (and being true to oneself) or it can be used perversely against the self, for example, to foster the ego's illusion of omnipotence in its identification with an idealized ego. The way in which the ego ideal is conceptualized and acted upon is determined by the degree to which the individual is cognizant of his/her own inner authority and not simply following the tenets of external authority in whatever form that may take. In attempting to distinguish between the healthy versus the perverse use of the ego ideal, I turn to Kant's moral imperative of treating our fellow humans[3] and ourselves as *sui generis* ends in ourselves and not as means to an end. Once the other is treated as a tool to be used in the service of a higher ideal and in this respect, dispensable, this necessarily applies to the self as well (see Covington, 2017). Our recognition of the other as demanding the same respect we give ourselves establishes our sense of agency and confers responsibility on us. Sartre's concept of freedom is based on the premise that it is our acknowledgment of the other that gives us the ability to shape our lives and our sense of who we are. He writes:

> I cannot discover any truth whatsoever about myself except through the mediation of another. The other is essential to my existence, as well as to the knowledge I have of myself. Under these conditions, my intimate discovery of myself is at the same time a revelation of the other as a freedom that confronts my own and that cannot think or will without doing so for or against me. We are thus immediately thrust into a world that we may call "intersubjectivity." It is in this world that man decides what he is and what others are.
>
> (Sartre, 2007, p. 41)

Our acknowledgment of our separate, and inevitably isolated, existence confronts us with our responsibility toward ourselves and, by extension, toward others. In the reverberation of our actions we experience what Sartre describes as "anguish"; at the same time, "anguish" is the necessary companion of freedom (ibid., p. 27). While Sartre's existential equation makes sense on a rational level, it begs the question as to how we as individuals discover ourselves or come to some approximation of what it means to be true to oneself. We can only guess that for Sartre the realization of an "inner authority" comes from our relational exchanges with others, in other words, "intersubjectivity" and from questioning what may be seen as "external authority." In *The Age of Reason*, Sartre writes, "The individual's duty is to do what he wants to do, to think whatever he likes, to be accountable to no one but himself, to challenge every idea and every person" (Sartre, 2001, p. 138).

Sartre describes a rational process over which the ego appears to have control—a kind of absolute free will. He emphasizes the importance of "intersubjectivity" but does not elaborate on what this means and does not allow for "intrasubjectivity," or the possibility of an internal dialogue that might inform and be a necessary dynamic in knowing oneself. Our experience of separateness and the other informs and shapes our relationship with our self. This intrusion of our narcissism is not only necessary for psychic growth but it opens up an awareness within us of our unconscious, of that which is beyond our knowledge and control and yet which influences our lives in countless ways as a kind of hidden director operating silently off-stage. Our acknowledgment of the unknowable other within us is the beginning of reflexivity, of intrasubjectivity, and self-knowledge. André Green, in writing about narcissistic object-cathexis, describes how the ego internalizes the other in the service of both self-protectiveness and creativity. Green writes:

> Narcissism thus serves as a substitute internal object for the subject which watches over the ego just as the mother watches over her baby. It shields the subject and protects it. How are the object's vicissitudes to be coped with if one does not protect oneself narcissistically? It would seem to me that artistic creativity (even on a minor or minimal scale) has a role to play here.
>
> (Green, 2001, p. 21)

Green is essentially arguing that our narcissistic need to protect ourselves is at the root of internalizing our primary relationship with a nurturing environment, the mother who watches over her baby. I would argue that this is the source of what develops into an auxiliary or observing ego, that part of the psyche that "watches over" the self, that is both part of the self and an other. By providing protection to the nascent ego, this watchful third allows for the space between self and other to be tolerated and this in turn gives rise to "as-if" symbolic representation, that is, to creativity.

The analogy of an observing ego with a watchful mother implicitly conveys that this is not simply an impartial witness, as a camera that records events, but its protective role necessitates some form of judgment that is able to temper and inform other forces within the psyche. In this respect, we can see the observing ego as an inner voice or guide that comments on our thoughts and actions and mediates between the ego ideal, the id, and the superego, and is at the same time separate and transcends these functions. In theology, this function can be likened to the soul or that part of our being that is connected to and expressive of God. It can also be conceived of as that part of us that directs our fate and comes from a spiritual world that is both beyond and within us. The Nigerian writer, Chigozie Obioma, in his novel, An Orchestra of Minorities, speaks in the voice of the "chi," in Igbo culture meaning the personal spirit or guardian that guides and protects the self:

Ezeuwa, when my host sought an answer to something beyond his understanding, I often ventured to supply it. So before he slept that night, I impressed on his mind that he should return to the river in the morning; perhaps he would still be able to find the fowls. But he paid no heed to my counsel. He thought it an idea that originated from within his own mind, for man has no way to distinguish between what has been put into his thoughts by a spirit—even if it is his own chi—and what has been suggested to him by the voice in his head.

(Obioma, 2019, loc. 333)

How many of us have heard a voice in our minds urging us to consider something and dismissed it, not trusting its source and fearful of being led astray?

I am proposing here that "being true to oneself" requires a knowledge and capacity to listen to our own "chi," or spiritual voice, or observing ego, or whatever refers to that inner voice of authority that we experience in our daily lives but which may often go unnoticed or unattended. Furthermore, this inner voice is not value free; it expresses an innate morality that reflects our human condition and our need to survive both as individuals and as a species. Innate morality is distinct from cultural morality as it pertains to our survival instinct and is not determined by social context, which may require different responses and behaviors. In thinking of this inner voice as expressing our fundamental sense of morality, what Neoptolemus referred to as his "own nature," it signifies our capacity to reflect on ourselves and our actions and in doing so to form a judgment about what actions and thoughts are congruent with our sense of who we are and who we want to be. This process is not a conscious process of thought but derives from being able to listen to ourselves freely, without the censorship of our superego, and to allow unspoken aspects of ourselves to surface.

Being able to listen to oneself paradoxically challenges the idea that there is a unity of self as one discovers ideas and feelings that have never been disclosed before and which inevitably alter one's conception of who one is. This inner revelation is precisely what makes psychoanalysis revolutionary—and frightening. As Freud explains, "the patient becomes aware of a thought of his own being kept secret from his own self. It looks as though his own self were no longer the unity which he had always considered it to be, as though there were something else as well in him that could confront that self" (Freud, 1962b, p. 188).

Kohon elaborates:

> When the subjects in analysis are capable of accepting the exis-
> tence of a psychic reality alien to themselves, when they recognise
> that their self contains something secret or different or contradic-
> tory to their wishes and thoughts and that this something might
> be part of a conflict that is making them suffer, we say that they
> are psychologically minded (Coltart, 1987, 1988). The patients
> can then contemplate the idea that anything that takes place in
> that psychic scenario, even the most inexplicable psychological
> event, might have meaning and thus is worth thinking about.
>
> (Kohon, 2019, p. 55)

Freud's talking cure offers a protected space in which the patient's internal cognitive dissonance can be exposed and identified as the source of
suffering. In this respect, the analyst, at least initially, serves in the role
of the watchful mother who can think about the patient's psychic reality.
We deny or disavow our psychic reality in order to survive dysfunctional
environments. The suppression of psychic reality can lead to severe mental illness or to mild forms of depression, a feeling of not being "oneself."
In validating the patient's psychic reality, the analyst also brings to light
and confirms what is harmful or painful in external reality and enables
the patient to understand the dissonance in his/her life and to find ways
of managing or mitigating these conflicts.[4]

Returning to Ancient Greece, one of our earliest exemplars of being
true to oneself is Socrates, not only in the ultimate act of taking his own
life but as seen earlier in his life when faced with fateful decisions. It was
Socrates' daimon, or inner voice, that averted him from making mis-
takes. In the Symposium, Plato recounts Socrates' behavior as he faced
the decision about remaining or withdrawing from the battle of Potidea
(429 BC). Plato writes:

> One day, at dawn, Socrates was immersed in some problem and
> stood on the spot trying to work it out. He couldn't resolve it,

but he wouldn't give up. He simply stood there, trying. By midday, many soldiers had seen him, and in amazement said to one another 'Socrates has been standing there meditating since dawn!'

He was still there when evening came. After dinner some Ioanians brought out their mattresses and rugs to sleep in the cool—this took place in the summer—and they waited to see if Socrates was going to stay out there all night.

He stood on the spot until dawn came and the sun rose, then made his prayers to the Sun and left.

(quoted from D'Angour, 2019, pp. 38–39)

D'Angour points out that Socrates was considered by his fellow soldiers as "atopos, 'eccentric' or 'unconventional' (literally 'out of place')" (ibid., p. 40). At the same time, Socrates' "main biographers, devoted as they were to Socrates' memory, are inclined to view his behaviour with great respect, and they treat his episodes of apparent silent contemplation as an indication of his extreme (and probably, to their minds, divinely inspired) devotion to the life of the mind" (ibid., p. 40). We don't have an account from Socrates about how he understood his process of contemplation, but it seems to have been a way of communing with himself in order to find a way through conflicts he was facing. It does not appear to be a rational process but one that would take as long as it took to discover, and trust, an inner voice.

Conscience and betrayal

Sartre, in *Existentialism is a Humanism*, describes a young man's moral dilemma in which he had the choice of going to England to join the Free French Forces—which would mean abandoning his mother—or remaining by her side to help her go on with her life. He realized that his mother lived only for him and that his absence—perhaps his death—would plunge her into utter despair. He also realized that, ultimately, any action he might take on her behalf would provide the concrete benefit of helping her to live, while any action he might take to leave and fight would be of uncertain outcome and could disappear pointlessly like water in sand.

(Sartre, 2007, p. 30)

The moral dilemma is framed by the conflict between potentially saving one life or many and the risks contingent with each decision. The flaw in Sartre's example is that the mother's life does not actually depend on her son staying by her side. The son may have found it painful to abandon his mother and have felt guilty about this, but leaving her would not necessarily result in her death. I think the story highlights the difference between the nature of guilt and the nature of bad conscience; a distinction that is tied to what it means to be true to oneself and the limits of our responsibility.

In Sartre's example, the son is under emotional pressure not to leave his mother on the basis that she needs him to keep her alive. In this equation, the mother is making her son responsible for her life and has abnegated responsibility for her own life. He is aware of the pain his departure will cause her and for this he feels guilty—but this is a different order to accepting responsibility for keeping her alive. His decision to join those fighting for French liberation, on the other hand, is related to a profound belief in upholding the principles that represent the kind of world he wants to live in and the kind of person he wants to be. If he were to decide not to fight for these principles, he would be betraying himself and his conscience. If the young man's dilemma was purely about the choice between saving the life of someone he loves and saving the lives of people he has no relation to, he would have to consider the circumstances, chances of survival, and so on. For example, a woman soldier, fighting on the Russian front during World War II, decides to kill her crying baby rather than put her comrades at risk of being detected and killed by the enemy (Alexievich, 2017).[5] In this case, we could say that the mother was following what she felt she had to do in these circumstances and in this sense, being true to herself, while at the cost of the life of her child. Her guilt about killing her child was overridden by her conscience. From an evolutionary psychology point of view, it is also possible to understand the mother's choice as one that pragmatically aimed to secure the survival of the group. Babies can be reproduced and cannot survive on their own, whereas adults need to survive in order to ensure the survival of the species.

The factor that is most important in determining what it means to be true to oneself—and in assessing the morality of one's actions—is the level of harm an action will or will not do to oneself. This can be phrased as, "Am I acting to please myself, in accordance with what I feel is right for me, i.e. using my own agency, or am I acting out of my own narcissistic need to be loved, even when this goes against what I feel is right for me?" While we all need to be loved, as we develop into adults and our sense of ourselves becomes more defined and less dependent on the approval and love of others, we also develop a clearer idea of what we value in ourselves that may not always be congruent with the values of others around us. In the story of Philoctetes, Neoptolemus decides he would rather be true to himself, and risk losing Odysseus' patronage, than betray himself. Neoptolemus is also in anguish at the thought that he would be seen as a "traitor" by others, untrustworthy to himself and ultimately to the world. This fundamental betrayal can only result in isolation and alienation from oneself and others. It is not surprising that in many countries across the world, treason is an offense punishable by death.

Conclusion

What it means to be true to oneself is inevitably determined by a mixture of personal experience, such as the ego ideals derived from and shaped by our families and the authority figures in our lives, and our primary experience of what Green describes as the internalization of the watchful mother that fosters an inner voice or what I have called an observing ego. These experiences combine with our basic perceptions of physical pain and pleasure, the basis for our morality, to create a sense of oneself as a moral agent (Covington, 2017, Chapter Two). As we all exist within some form of political structure or ideology, along with national boundaries, identities, and value systems, these also play a part in our largely unconscious attachments to the groups within which we live and identify with. The ego ideals we form and aspire to are inevitably colored by the political belief systems we live within and how such ideas as social justice, freedom, and self-agency are interpreted and take on meaning within these systems. In other words, the self does not exist apart from the social world. In trying to understand what it means to be true to oneself on a psychological level, it is therefore necessary to address not only our relationship to ourselves but our relationship to the groups we belong to and to examine the various ways in which our political culture affects our very identity.

It is our relationship with our inner voice that gives us the possibility of judgment and choice, the qualities that constitute free will and that allow us to be the best we can be. When our inner voice is lost or when there is what Obioma calls an "irreconcilable difference between a man and his chi" (Obioma, 2019, loc. 5466), we lose our connection with our self and with the world around us; we lose our identity and our sanity.

Notes

1. Strawson argues that self-experience is universal; it is not something that differs between cultures but is expressed differently in accord with cultural differences. He writes: "Mbiti considers the replacement, in [traditional African societies], of the Cartesian 'I think, therefore I am' with 'I am because we are, and since we are, therefore I am' (1969; p. 106). Senghor suggests replacing or complementing 'I think, therefore I am' with 'I think, I dance the other; I am'" (Strawson, 2009, pp. 8–9).

2. Charles Hanly differentiates the terms "ideal ego" and "ego ideal," explaining "that the former connotes a state of being whereas the latter connotes a state of becoming ... The ideal ego is the ego in so far as it believes itself to have been vouchsafed a state of perfection—it refers to a positive state even if this state, in reality, is an illusion. In fact, the ideal ego is a self-image that is distorted by idealization but it may be experienced as more real than the ego itself. The ego ideal refers to a perfection to be achieved; it refers to an unrealized potential; it is the idea of a perfection towards which the ego ought to strive. The ego ideal establishes purposes, goals and aims for ego activity, and particularly for maturation" (Hanly, p. 252). In Hanly's distinction, the "ideal ego" pertains to a narcissistic state that in its most extreme form protects the ego of infancy from a lack of relatedness at the cost of reality and development. As Janine Chasseguet-Smirgel has eloquently elaborated, the "ideal ego" is manifest in perversions and totalitarian political structures; these are situations in which the individual ego or, in the case of groups, the group identity is threatened and defends itself by promoting an illusion of an idealized image of itself, whether it is in the form of an ideal ego or an omnipotent, ideal leader (Chasseguet-Smirgel, 1985).

3. There is a growing argument in moral philosophy that Kant's imperative must also be applicable to our treatment of animals. See Peter Singer (2017), *Ethics in the Real World*, Princeton: Princeton University Press, and

Christine Korsgaard (2018), *Fellow Creatures: Our Obligations to the Other Animals*, Oxford: Oxford University Press.

4. It is important to note here that cognitive dissonance is a binary defense against a set of realities that appear to be in conflict. A psychologist, working with an adolescent boy dying of cancer, recounted that a week or so before the boy's death, the boy told him that he knew he was going to die in the next few days. The boy paused and then told the psychologist the news that he had just signed up as an apprentice engineer. In recognizing that both of the boy's thoughts were true, the psychologist enabled the boy to imagine life and death concurrently (personal communication).

5. See Chapter Two for a fuller discussion of bravery and being true to oneself, and p. 26 for the full account of the mother soldier's actions.

References

Alexievich, S. (2017). *The Unwomanly Face of War*. London: Penguin.

Chasseguet-Smirgel, J. (1985). *The Ego Ideal: A Psychoanalytic Essay on the Malady of the Ideal*. London: Free Association Books.

Covington, C. (2017). *Everyday Evils: A Psychoanalytic View of Evil and Morality*. London: Routledge.

D'Angour, A. (2019). *Socrates in Love: The Making of a Philosopher*. London: Bloomsbury.

DeVos, G. (1973). *Socialization for Achievement: Essays on the Cultural Psychology of the Japanese*. Berkeley: University of California Press.

Freud, S. (1923b). *The Ego and the Id. S.E. XIX*. London: Vintage.

Green, A. (2001). *Life Narcissism, Death Narcissism*. London: Free Association Books.

Hanly, C. (1984). Ego Ideal and Ideal Ego. *International Journal of Psychoanalysis*, 65:253–261.

Kohon, G. (2019). *Concerning the Nature of Psychoanalysis*. London: Routledge.

Nagel, T. (2019). What We Owe a Rabbit. *The New York Review of Books*. 21 March.

Obioma, C. (2019). *An Orchestra of Minorities*. London: Little, Brown.

Sartre, J.-P. (2001). *The Age of Reason*. London: Penguin.

Sartre, J.-P. (2007). *Existentialism is a Humanism*. London: Yale University Press.

Sophocles (1994). *Philoctetes*. Edited and translated by H. Lloyd-Jones. London: Harvard University Press.

Strawson, G. (2009). *Selves: An Essay in Revisionary Metaphysics*. Oxford: Oxford University Press.

Winnicott, D. W. (1960). The Theory of Parent-Infant Relationship. *The International Journal of Psychoanalysis, 41*: 585–595.

CHAPTER TWO

No choice but to act: the role of self-agency in bravery

Mankind's common instinct for reality has always held the world to be essentially a theatre for heroism.

—William James, *The Varieties of Religious Experience*

Introduction

On the night of 1 October 2017, a gunman opened fire on a large crowd of concertgoers at the Route 91 Harvest music festival on the Las Vegas Strip, killing fifty-eight people and injuring 489. It was the deadliest mass shooting committed by an individual in the history of the United States.

Bailey Thompson, aged seventeen, had bought a ticket to the concert at the last minute. Forty-five minutes after the concert had begun, the shooting started, and mayhem erupted. Drawing on his army medical training, Thompson saved over two dozen lives.

In an interview with Jon Snow on Channel 4 News (5 October 2017), Thompson describes what happened:

> I looked to my left, looked to my right and I'd see people covering their loved ones—men on top of their girlfriends shielding them, mums on top of children shielding them and at that point it was

a fighting instinct. I don't know what kicked in but something did. There was a lady laying on the floor covered in blood. I put direct pressure on the wound, take shoelaces, belts, or whatever you can, tie it two to three inches above the wound and tie it tight. And I moved on to the next person and the next person and the next person. I knew I could make it to my truck under cover. I brought the truck around and I was just loading as many people as I could on the back of my truck. As soon as I felt the truck was full and there was nobody else I could fit in, I left for the hospital and I let that group of people out and without hesitation I went back for another. I got a hold of my Mom and she just broke down crying. You know it's a mom's worst nightmare. At an early age my parents kinda made it a point where they didn't want to shelter me from the world because the longer you shelter people the less they're going to know. To the families of the victims I couldn't get to at the time, I want to send my sincerest apologies. Because that's the biggest thing with me is the whole hero thing and everybody calling me a hero. I'm not a hero—heroes save everybody—I couldn't get to everybody no matter how much I wanted to. No matter how much I wanted to.

Without hesitation, Thompson reacted spontaneously to the crisis and, using his medic's training, attended to those who were wounded and planned a safety route to his truck and then to hospital, returning to the festival to continue rescuing others. Thompson attributes his actions to a "fighting instinct." He also refers to his parents' positive decision not to shelter him from the world when he was a child. While we don't know what this actually meant in practice, Thompson suggests that he grew up being aware of the dark side of reality. Thompson emphasizes that he was not a hero. As he explains, "heroes save everybody." The greatest distress Thompson conveys in the interview is when he states, "I couldn't get to everybody no matter how much I wanted to." At this point, he turns his face away from the camera, holding back his tears.

In interviews with rescuers in the Holocaust, the common strands expressed by the rescuers were that (1) they never considered that they had a choice *not* to act; (2) they had been raised by parents who had strong religious or moral beliefs; and (3) they did not feel they had been "heroes" but felt instead guilty they had not been able to do more, to rescue more people. The rescuer is not so much traumatized by the violence he has witnessed as by being haunted by a sense of failure (Monroe, 2004).

In the midst of atrocities, whether it is the Las Vegas massacre, or the Holocaust, or genocides across the world, we find a silent presence hidden in the shadows of these horrific events. These are the brave individuals who act and stand apart from the crowd, who risk their own lives by rescuing others and, in other ways, by voicing their dissent. The actions of these exceptional individuals raise questions as to why they were able to do what they did and why other people don't. But if we look closer at the histories of these individuals, what we discover is that they may not be as exceptional as we think, and that bravery takes different forms in different contexts.

I am using the term "bravery" to refer specifically to actions that stand out above the norm and in some way risk the well-being or life of the actor in favor of protecting or saving the lives of others. I am not referring to tests of mental or physical endurance, such as braving the elements, or of individual survival. Bravery describes a mental process or dynamic that is rooted in an innate moral code that is intrinsic to developing a sense of self.[1] Bravery is manifest in the risk of life to uphold certain moral or ideological beliefs—to uphold what is perceived by the actor to be his conscience, or what we may think of as psychic reality, in the face of illusion and denial.

One distinguishing feature of bravery is commonly considered to be the ability to act according to one's principles and to overcome fear of the consequences. However, the conquest of fear is often more in the eye of the observer than it is in the brave actor who may not be aware of feeling fear at all. Overcoming fear implies that there is a choice to be made, whereas for those who commit acts we would consider to be brave, there is no choice. This does not mean that there is nothing to fear but that the actor's own reality creates a necessary set of actions for survival. For the hero or rescuer, fear takes hold when it is *not* possible to act, when he is helpless (see Barrett and Martin, 2016, p. 18).

Svetlana Alexievich, in her recently published collection of interviews of Russian women serving on the front lines in World War II, describes numerous accounts of extraordinary bravery of the women soldiers, adjutants, and military staff fighting alongside men. One woman disclosed a particularly harrowing account of individual and collective bravery:

> We hid in the wild thickets, we were saved by the swamps where the punitive forces didn't go. A quagmire. It sucked in equipment and people for good. For days, for weeks, we stood up to our necks in water. Our radio operator was a woman who had recently given birth. The baby was hungry … It had to be nursed … But the mother herself was hungry and had no milk. The baby cried. The punitive forces were close … With dogs … If the dogs heard it, we'd all be killed. The whole group—thirty of us … You understand?
>
> The commander makes a decision …
>
> Nobody can bring himself to give the mother his order, but she figures it out herself. She lowers the swaddled baby into the water and holds it there for a long time … The baby doesn't cry anymore … Not a sound … And we can't raise our eyes. Neither to the mother nor to each other …
>
> (Alexievich, 2017, p. xxxii)

Thompson in Las Vegas and the young mother at the front were certainly aware of making a choice but it was a choice they knew they *had* to make—any other choice would have been unthinkable because it would have meant putting others' lives at risk. They also knew they had the means to avert further death and it was up to them, individually, to take action.

This absolute and instantaneous judgment is vividly recounted by John, a Dutch rescuer during World War II, brought up in Switzerland by a father who was a Seventh-Day Adventist pastor, who taught the family the importance of living by their conscience. John remembered:

> A group of Jewish people was arrested and deported. One of the ladies had a baby in her hands, and the baby started to cry. It made a lot of noise at the railway station. The officer told the lady to make the baby stop crying. She did not succeed. The officer

took that baby out of her hands, crashed the baby on the ground, and crushed the head of the baby with his boots. At that time, if I had a gun, I would have shot. But I could not do it. Had I, I would have been arrested and then I could not help.

(Monroe, 2004, p. 109)

John refrained from acting not out of cowardice but out of calculation. He knew that if he had had a gun he would have shot the soldier but he also knew this would have been an impulsive reaction that would not have served any purpose—a dissent and retaliation that would have been entirely wasted and would have prevented him from saving others. Even if the act of bravery appears to be instantaneous, there is always an element of calculation involved with respect to whether the act *can* be done. The man who sees someone drowning in the sea does not jump in to rescue him unless he knows how to swim. If he did, this would be an example of recklessness, not bravery.

In each of these examples, acting or not acting were not simply impulsive, visceral reactions to extreme threat or violence, they were considered responses within particular contexts fueled by the urgency of survival—but it is not only the actual survival of the individual or the group that is at stake, it is also the survival of a belief system, a moral order, that is perceived by the rescuer as fundamental to ensuring the continuation of his world and his self within that world, what we often associate with the meaning of identity.

The act of bravery itself always follows or is triggered by a rupture in what is perceived to be the moral or social order. This happens at extreme moments when an individual or group's belief system is threatened or overturned, most obviously in situations of atrocity and more commonly in our everyday abuses of power. They also occur in disasters, for example, the Grenfell Tower fire, earthquakes, or tsunamis, that destroy our sense of security and predictability in the world we live in. Our common reaction is, "This is not right! This should not be happening!" At these times, an individual's sense of self, contingent upon his/her belief system, is directly threatened, and dissent becomes a vital way of protecting and restoring the self in the face of an alternative and opposing belief system. We can see this in the actions taken by Bailey Thompson, who defied the slaughter taking place around him and counterbalanced this with the normative behavior of rescuing the wounded. In his actions, Thompson was attempting to re-establish a moral order that had been broken. Similarly, the young Russian mother upholds her belief in the "Motherland," her bond with her comrades, and her hopes for the future, paradoxically, by killing her baby. John also overcomes his personal reactions to the murder of an infant by placing primacy on his life in the service of protecting the lives of others and, underlying this, ensuring the survival of a higher cause.

A surprising act of bravery and a vivid example of an attempt to restore a moral order is recounted by Edith Eger when she and her sister, Magda, were held prisoners in Auschwitz. Magda was herded into a different selection line; it was unclear which line was for work and which for death but staying together, regardless of the outcome, was of paramount importance and gave each sister a reason to live. In a split second, Edith makes her choice:

> I don't have a plan. Time is slow and time is fast. Magda and I share a glance. I see her blue eyes. And then I am in motion. I am doing cartwheels, hands to earth, feet to sky, around and around. A guard stares at me. He's right side up. He's upside down. I expect a bullet any second. And I don't want to die, but I can't keep myself from turning around again and again. He doesn't raise his gun. Is he too surprised to shoot me? Am I too dizzy to see? He winks at me. I swear I see him wink. Okay, he seems to say, this time, you win.
>
> In the few seconds that I hold his complete attention, Magda runs across the yard into my line to join me. We melt back into the crowd of girls waiting for whatever will happen next.
>
> (Eger, 2017, p. 63)

Edith's cartwheels are not only an act of defiance in the face of the inhuman horror of the selection lines but in performing a "normal" act at odds with the situation, she was turning reality on its head and highlighting the absurdity and dissociation of the camp's norms and belief system. In this respect, normative acts serve as important forms of dissent and reminders of another reality. It is also possible that Edith's act went unpunished because it created a rupture in the camp's culture by reverting to "normal" behavior.

This example also highlights the fact that Edith was able to sustain enough mental functioning that she was able to act and was not paralyzed by fear. In his book *War Memoirs: 1917–1919*, Bion observes, "In war the enemy's object is to terrify you that you cannot think clearly, while your object is to continue to think clearly no matter how adverse or frightening the situation" (Bion, 1997, p. 322). Within the concentration camps and in the midst of atrocities, the perversion of social norms is so extreme that it is literally unthinkable, unimaginable. While Edith did not consciously think about what she was going to do and acted spontaneously, she was able to contain her anxiety sufficiently to be able to act— and to dissent. What makes this possible within the mind of the rescuer is the question I address in this chapter.

Clinical example

Although the examples I have given so far of bravery are acts that take place in the outside world, largely witnessed by others, there are also less visible acts of bravery that take place within our own internal worlds which are driven by a similar need to act on behalf of one's moral principles in order to survive psychically. As analysts, we are very aware of the bravery our patients show in wanting to know about their own psychic reality as they face the hard facts of their external reality and their pasts. The process of uncovering reality, and discarding defense systems that have for many years guarded the ego against what may have been experienced as an unbearable reality, is also an act of bravery, in which for many patients there is simply no choice. Despite the risks of changing, once patients become aware that their old defense systems no longer function adequately or function at a cost to themselves, and regardless of how long it may take, they have already begun to act by acknowledging their internal resistance to their own psychic reality.

The following clinical vignette illustrates one patient's bravery, both externally on the battlefield, and internally within his psychic reality.

It was Aaron's ninth month in four-times weekly analysis. He nodded to me as he entered my consulting room, lay on the couch, and, after a moment of silence, announced, "I want to die for my country."

I knew that Aaron had some years before gone back to his country of origin and had fought in a special branch of the army for eighteen months.

I replied, "It's getting worse?"

"I have no choice after what has happened there recently—it's terrible. Now my uncle is in prison and some of his family have been killed. I need to honor my father. And I need to do what I choose to do, not what he is telling me to do. I need to have my own honor."

Aaron was a lanky thirty-two-year-old, son of a refugee family who had fled their war-torn country of origin when Aaron was six years old, leaving relatives and friends behind, many of whom were subsequently killed by insurgent groups as violence intensified. Aaron, along with his parents and a younger sister, fled to England where the family settled in a quiet suburb outside London. While the family had considerable money that had been invested abroad to support them, Aaron's father continued to be driven by his need to accumulate more, and had built up a highly successful global business. His father's credo was that only money could provide security and warned Aaron about seeking security in anything else, especially relationships with others. As a result, apart from relatives, the family remained isolated, with virtually no social relationships. Aaron's father was a generous employer, known for his concern about his employees' welfare, and in addition had set up several charities to provide aid to family groups in his home country. He was clearly the patriarch, whom others depended on not only for their economic well-being, but also for his advice about all decisions in their lives.

Aaron's announcement that he wanted to die for his country and his explanation that he needed to do what he chose to do, not what his father told him to do, pointed to complex layers of loyalty, belief, and rebellion in relation to his father, his family, and his country.

Aaron continued,

> I have a choice to start working for my father, which is what he wants me to do, to take over the business at some point, or to find out what I want to do … When I was in the army I felt alive, I knew what I was doing was important and it meant something to other people. Here I feel I'm living in a corrupt world, part of it. Most businesses, including my father's, are

part of the multinational, global exploitation. I saw it when I worked in the bank and no one cared what the money was used for, what the consequences were, who was hurt.

I commented, "I think you're also talking about your feelings about the corruption in your family. A father who wants to use you to fulfil his dream of even more money and a mother who pushed you to succeed in school as a kind of surrogate for herself, who has wanted to live through you. But everything came at a price. With the army there is a common cause that is against corruption."

Andrew responded,

> Maybe you're right. In the army, you know where you stand, everyone has to act together or else you will risk lives. At home, everything is motivated by money—although my father always gave me plenty of money, this is how he controls everyone. He has given me all these assets and an allowance and then he complains that everyone wants something from him. I have never, in fact, asked him for anything because I don't want him to see me as greedy. But my sister is always asking him for more—and our relatives. It is how he buys loyalty, but I also see how unhappy this makes him. When he is not working, he becomes depressed and he even looks ill. He's old now and I want to help him, but the only thing I can do is not to rely on him. Then he feels like I'm rejecting him. I feel guilty either way.

Aaron was not only in a double bind with his father with the threat of being hurtful if he attempted to become independent, but he also felt this with his mother. While she encouraged him in his studies and desire to find out what he wanted to do, she called him several times a day to ask how he was doing and was always at hand to listen to him whenever he had a problem. Aaron described her as neutral and non-judgmental and always available to listen, seemingly the perfect analyst-mother. At the same time, whenever there was the slightest conflict between them or when he didn't respond to her calls, she would either withdraw into a depressed silence, or threaten to leave the family. The result was that Aaron felt highly dependent on his mother's calm listening but increasingly trapped in their co-dependency. With both parents, Aaron's increasing wish for independence was bound with guilt along with fear of overwhelming loss—his own and that of his parents.

In the following session, Aaron complained that he had been depressed after the last session and felt there was no way out for him. He explained,

> It is the first time in my life when I started having thoughts about killing myself. When I was very little and my mother was depressed after the birth of my sister, I remember feeling really anxious about her. I thought she might die and now I wonder if I was in fact worried that she might kill herself. When I thought this it made me feel even worse, that I'm just like her and I can't get anything right. Both of them have lost their homes and their families—they no longer have their land—and they can't go back, they're not accepted here. I can't stay here and make my own life, I don't belong here, but I can't go back either. The only thing I can do is to have my own land that will support me.

I commented,

> When you talked about your parents' depression, and their rage, at their own losses yesterday, it makes you feel there's nothing you can do for them and you become filled with despair. Nothing you can do will make it right for them and you become just as helpless as they feel they are. They could not rescue their families and you cannot rescue them without in some way killing your own desires. The only way out is to be self-sufficient—to have your own piece of land and not to be attached to anyone or anything you might lose yourself.

"Yes," Aaron replied, "everything is always taken away in life, that's how it is, it's better not to expect anything different."

Aaron became silent for a long time and then recounted a dream he had had the night before.

> I was standing on the shore of a long strip of beach. There was no one else around. In the distance I saw a little boat going out to sea and I suddenly realized my parents and my sister were in it. There was no sail or oars and they were drifting away. I knew they were in danger and yet I

was paralyzed. I thought they might be close enough for me to swim out to them, but I also knew I wasn't strong enough to pull the boat back to shore. Then everything went black and I felt a breeze at the back of my head.

Aaron put his hands to his face and for the first time in his sessions showed his distress. Then he said in a hushed voice, "I can't go on with this."

It was the end of the session and I remained silent but thought that Aaron was telling me that not only could he no longer go on feeling so responsible for his family but, simultaneously, he could no longer go on with his analysis as it was making him aware of the painful losses of his family and his own prospective loss.

The next week Aaron arrived and announced that he had volunteered for another period of service in the army that would mean leaving his analysis for a few months. I felt a visceral attack, as if I had been kicked in the stomach, and at the same time realized that I had partially expected this sudden flight from his analysis.

Aaron said, "Look, I have to do some army service and it makes sense to do this now. I can always come back. But I realized over the weekend that this is really what I need to do—I need to get away from my parents for a while and I need to be active. I never told you what happened a couple of years ago when I was hurt."

Aaron continued,

I was with three other soldiers in the mountains and we were under fire. We couldn't locate exactly where the attack was coming from—I thought we were surrounded. We kept firing back and then it became silent—it was very spooky. Suddenly one of the enemy soldiers, wrapped in a headscarf, came towards us waving a bit of cloth. I had this sixth sense that there was something wrong—perhaps it was the way he zigzagged towards here—something wasn't right. I heard Ben next to me open the catch on his gun to fire and, without thinking, I leaped forward to throw Ben down so he would miss the soldier. The gun backfired into my shoulder and I didn't even realize I was covered in blood and had been hurt until later. I then walked to the soldier, and as I got closer I realized he was crying. I knew in an instant that he was frightened and had been sent out as a decoy with a detonator attached to him. I started talking gently to him, he let me get close to him, and I managed to get the belt off him, throwing it behind us where it exploded. One of our soldiers was hit by a bit of shrapnel and lost an eye. I still feel awful about this. But I knew I had saved the enemy guy's life and I had probably saved our own lives at the same time. I got a medal for exceptional bravery. But it wasn't brave—it was something I simply had to do. I had no fear and no hesitation. I can't go on staying here when this is still going on at home.

I was struck by Aaron's use of the word "home" and suggested that there might be a link to his family in the pressure he felt to return to their rescue. Aaron conceded this was the case but added,

It's different from my family. In the army, it's usually pretty clear what you need to do. You know this is really happening, it's in front of you, and you just react, you know what you need to do, and you do it. Of course, there's everything that my family has been through and somewhere inside of me I know this too—and I'm sure this makes a difference—but because the reality is so clear, I can act with complete intention. It's a bit like swimming, when your body and the water and swimming all become one. With my family, it is not clear—not the reality or what I need to do. There is only the sense that I might make everything worse— for them and for myself.

Aaron's decision to return to the army at this point revealed a complex of different motivations. I felt, in relation to his analysis, that it was a defensive escape from his increasing sense of feeling attached to me and to his sessions so as to avoid the inevitable loss of ending. At the same time Aaron began to express his negative transference to me as the mother who calmly listened to him but wanted to keep him in analysis interminably for my own needs. Alongside these fears, Aaron's plaint that he could not go on also expressed his fear of separating from his parents and the consequences of this. As he explained about the difference with the army, the dynamics within his family were not so clear to him. Like most patients, I think Aaron was aware that once the reality of his family relations could no longer be doubted, he would have no choice but to act, as he had felt no choice but to throw himself on his fellow soldier to divert his firing. The anxiety of leaving his parents was not simply about their welfare, it was bound to deeper fears that his aggression toward them would destroy their relationship, if not actually kill his parents. In contrast, in the context of the army Aaron's aggression was rewarded—as long as it was directed against the enemy, his internal conflict with his aggression toward his objects could be deflected.

Although I interpreted Aaron's flight as his resistance to feeling attached to me and his fear of loss, I also thought his return to the army was perhaps a way of building up courage to face his internal conflicts with his parents. In this sense, I wondered if it was an enactment that might serve a healthy purpose—of reinforcing Aaron's conviction of what was "right" for him and helping him to differentiate situations in which his choice to rescue was as congruent as his choice not to rescue. I was careful not to interpret his actions as primarily an attack on his analysis as I felt I would then be in the role of his parents who had each made him feel that his anger with them and his need to separate from them could only be damaging. In any case, Aaron insisted that this was of paramount importance to him and I agreed to see him on his return should he wish to continue with his analysis.

Over three months later Aaron contacted me to say he was ready to resume his analysis. He arrived tanned and healthy-looking after his time away, and told me it was good to be back. He quickly lay on the couch and started to tell me about the welcome he had received in the army from soldiers he had fought with before, the worsening conditions, and also the fervor of fighting for their land together—a land that would never be the same but belonged to them nevertheless. Aaron stressed, "We cannot abandon our families' pasts, we have to vindicate ourselves."

I suggested, "All is not lost?"

Aaron said,

> It's to retrieve a future. My father's future has always been about money—but it was also to protect himself from his past. And to escape. But going back was exciting. It was like the first time. I felt alive. Everything mattered and there was a feeling that we really worked well together—like a smooth-running machine. It was exhilarating. It also made me think that my family never felt like this—nothing ran smoothly, everything was problematic and there was always something disjointed in our relationships. It made me wonder whether this was why I wanted to go back to the army—it felt so different from life at home. But I also wondered whether it was a kind of glorified family for me where I could in fact

rescue them and make things all right. Where I could do something that mattered, even if I could not save everyone.

Although Aaron had returned on a high from his recent experience, he had become more acutely aware of the toxicity within his family and how much of his childhood and adult life he had spent in trying to "save" his parents from their own traumatic damage. Aaron had grown up in an environment typical of many refugee families, in which the injustices of the past held an important, if not silent, role within the family. Honor and vindication of wrongs were emphasized as ideals holding the family together and crucially sustaining a moral order that linked them with a larger group identity that had been violently severed. However, both of Aaron's parents' reactions to their losses were to withdraw into the family and to try to protect themselves and their children by keeping them dependent on them, as if frozen in time. The relentless pressure to produce more and more wealth was also an attempt to shore up the coffers against loss, while leaving the emptiness of grief within the family untouched.

After Aaron's return from serving in the army for the second time, his animosity toward both his parents shifted noticeably. His absence from his analysis, along with discontinuing his intense, daily contact with his mother, mitigated his negative transference and enabled him to differentiate between a mother who could not separate from him and encouraged his dependency on her and a mother who wanted him to establish his own life. He told me, "When I was talking to her I could see for the first time how needy she is and that what I used to think was her sympathy and her impartiality did not make me feel stronger but more inadequate. It was like stepping in quicksand. Since I've been back, I'm not turning to her in the old way. I ask her about herself and she mumbles something and is silent. It makes me incredibly sad and angry."

A couple of months after his return, Aaron had a long talk with his father about taking over the family business, in which Aaron for the first time made it clear that he wanted to do other things in his life. He described his father's deflation, "His body slumped, and he looked away as if he couldn't bear to look at me. I knew he was on the verge of tears. After all these years of feeling controlled and angry with him—and guilty—I just felt this sadness inside." At this point Aaron went silent trying to hold back his own tears. "I can't give him his life back. And I can see that I never could have done this; in that moment my choice was utterly clear. I love him but this is what is right for me and I suppose it is thanks to him that I know this too."

Aaron continued,

> I remembered my dream of seeing my family drifting out to sea and not being able to do anything. They are all adrift—my father, my mother, my sister. And then there was this blackness—this terrible sadness and depression—and then a breeze from behind me. I thought of the breeze when I was away, and remembered a nanny I had had as a child who would soothe me when I was upset about something by blowing against the back of my neck. I loved this nanny, she wasn't sad, and she was the only one who played with me. My nanny was a refugee too and had lost all her family, her only child and her husband, but she was full of life. I felt accepted and safe with her. I thought the dream was about leaving my family and being able to do this because I had you behind me. I think I can be brave now in a way I never could before because I don't have to fight against myself anymore.

Aaron's internal conflict had been not only about separating from his parents but also separating from the ideal he had felt his parents wanted him to be. This was a process, as with many of our patients, of being able to acknowledge the damage in his parents, and Aaron's damaged internal object relations, without taking responsibility for their damage. This enabled Aaron to free himself from having to be a "hero" and rescue the world, i.e. his family, and to take responsibility for his own choices. He no longer had to conform to an ego ideal that he felt had been imposed on him that had essentially functioned to shore up his parents' fragmented sense of self. Paradoxically, when Aaron no longer had to be the "hero," he could exercise the bravery required to be himself and to have his own identity.

Bravery, reality, and the auxiliary ego

A Polish woman who survived World War II through great hardships, and harbored a Jewish family, arranging for their escape to safety, said: "I did not ask myself, should I do this? But, how will I do this? Every step of my childhood had brought me to this crossroads. I must take the right path, or I would no longer be myself" (Monroe, 2004, p. 139).

The act of bravery here is clearly attributed to and aligned with identity and with the family principles that formed individual identity. As Monroe writes with regard to rescuers,

> no single factor can be said to have caused their rescue behaviour. Duty, socialization, religion, an innate moral sense, even the explicit mention of Kant's categorical imperative—all these factors were mentioned by one rescuer or another … [W]e are struck by the remarkable extent to which none of the rescuers agonized over what to do … [I]nstead of moral dilemmas and agonist choices, we find identity … Identity played such a crucial role in shaping their treatment of others that their extraordinary actions seemed matter-of-fact, unremarkable, and unnoteworthy to the rescuers themselves. Moreover, this influence from identity appeared to operate through a cognitive process that consistently drew particular parts of rescuers' complex identities to the fore.
>
> (ibid., pp. 187–188)

Monroe concludes,

> For the rescuers, certain moral values had become so intricately integrated into their basic sense of who they were that their commitment to these values—human life and well-being—shaped the core of their identity. It thus became unthinkable for rescuers to intentionally engage in behaviour that would contradict the essence of their identity.
>
> (ibid., p. 261)

To act differently from their moral principles would be to betray themselves at a profound level.

Monroe's emphasis on one's sense of identity as the most important determining factor underlying acts of bravery begs the question as to what we mean by "identity" or a sense of oneself. Freud's idea of the ego ideal is relevant here, particularly as it is embedded in family values and aspirations and is formed at a very early age (Freud, 1914c). The child initially develops an image of who he wants to be in the future, based on what he admires in his parents and on the valued behavior/roles his parents convey to him. As the child grows up, this ideal may be tempered by other role models and by the child's own strengths and what is valued within his social milieu. The ego emulates and strives to become the ego ideal with the help of the superego that keeps the ego on target. In this structural view, identity can be broken down into the interaction between these three basic psychodynamic functions.

There is also the factor of dissonance between ideas of what should be happening in reality, informed by a sense of morality and social norms, versus what is actually happening in reality. While rescuers are clear that they had no choice but to act and that not acting would be a betrayal of their sense of themselves, it is also clear that rescuers are able to assess the reality of what is happening in the moment. Aaron, for example, like other rescuers, was able to quickly ascertain that there was something strange about the way the enemy soldier was walking toward them on the front line and that to open fire, as they had been taught to do, would be a mistake. Aaron sensed at that moment that there was a discrepancy between the actual behavior of the enemy soldier and how he and his fellow soldiers had been taught to perceive similar situations in which surrender was an enemy ruse. While this situation was also a ruse, what Aaron picked up was the fact that the surrendering soldier was being used as a kind of Trojan horse to detonate Aaron's men. Aaron described a kind of "sixth sense" he was aware of, which often occurs when there is a disjuncture or rupture in an anticipated reality. There is some element within the picture that does not fit, whether it is in the subtle cue of a zigzag walk or whether it is suddenly evident in the automatic firing of bullets into a crowd of people enjoying themselves.

Alongside the ego ideal that provides a template of "good" behavior that is congruent within the reality of certain situations, there is also within us an observing or auxiliary ego that is able at any time to perceive the facets of external reality based on a spectrum of pain and pleasure. This immediate form of perception that originates in bodily responses alerts the ego to danger or equally to something that is desirable in the environment. If, for example, someone is having a cavity in a tooth filled, he can feel the pain and continue to submit to it because he knows it is a means to save the tooth. In this example, over-riding the experience of pain is consistent with the belief system of the dentist helping the patient and is reinforced by experience. Many of our patients come to us because they are used to over-riding their own judgments and dismissing their own alarm bells. The idea of "being true to oneself" is a complex process of acknowledging feeling (e.g. one's gut reaction), being able to assess whether external reality makes sense, that it matches with what is felt/ perceived, or whether there is a rupture in external reality that requires a particular response in order to survive. "Being 'at one' with ourselves implies that there is a consistency between our internal perceptions and affects and our external actions" (Covington, 2017, p. 71). Our experience of relying on our affects to validate our perceptions constitutes the foundation for developing an innate sense of morality and conscience.

In the case of Aaron, we can see that his response to the surrendering soldier was an action that he considered to be "true to himself." This was strikingly not the case in his attitude and behavior toward his parents. At the start of his analysis, Aaron felt he had "no choice" but to fulfil his parents' wishes for him and that in doing so this would be his way of not only making them happy but rescuing them from their past and enabling them to have a different future. Whenever Aaron felt that he was going against his parents' wishes, he was overwhelmed with crippling guilt to the point of feeling trapped. He could not fulfil his internalized ego ideal of the dutiful son he thought he needed to be in order to be loved and consequently was doomed to be a failure. At the same time, he also knew that there was something wrong with his parents and that this "gut" awareness could not be ignored—he had to think about it. As Aaron's perception of his parents' damage was validated in the course of his analysis, he reached a point when he had no choice but to act, to do otherwise would have meant living, as he put it, "in bad faith." But acting in this instance paradoxically meant *not* acting. Being true to himself meant withdrawing responsibility for others who could not bear their own reality. Through this act of separation, Aaron was also free to feel empathy for his parents in a way he had not felt before when his neurotic sense of obligation had plagued him with hatred and guilt.

Fear obliterates the ability to think and to observe reality clearly. In Aaron's case he was anxious that if he did not fulfil his parents' expectations it would not only damage them irreparably but he would also be responsible for destroying their love for him. This is a common conflict in patients who have experienced insecure attachments. Therapy provided a reflective space in which his fears could be expressed and thought about—and mitigated. Aaron's awareness of what he needed for his own development and what it meant to him to be "true to himself" could then emerge along with a growing confidence in his identity; that is, how he saw himself and what gave meaning to his life. At the heart of being able to act bravely is a conviction in one's belief system and that this belief system or moral code is congruent with being loved. This congruence between the ego ideal, the superego, and the ego is essential for the capacity for thought, for what Bion describes as alpha functioning. This is what Aaron achieved through his work in therapy and this is what seems to be evident in the case of many rescuers whose strong belief in moral principles plays such a crucial role in protecting the ego from being overwhelmed by fear. This may be why so many people who have acted bravely claim they have not been frightened.[2]

Empathy and aggression

There is a common assumption that an intrinsic element of bravery is empathy. If we cannot put ourselves in others' shoes, why would we risk our safety or our lives for them? While on the surface this may seem like a reasonable proposition, there is in fact scant evidence of it. Monroe asks one woman rescuer whether she had acted out of empathy? The woman asked what this meant, and Monroe explained, "Feeling that this could be me." The woman answered, "No, never even thought of it" (Monroe, 2004, p. 49). Her compulsion to act was because all the moral values she had grown up with meant that she felt there was no choice.

Monroe makes the salient point that bystanders can feel empathy but this does not necessarily lead them to act (ibid., p. 249). Conversely, the torturer uses his empathy to induce pain in his victim. Empathy, in so far as it refers to our capacity for human feeling, is not necessarily used for positive ends and does not appear to be a driving force in bravery. The rescuer, as we've seen above, may be less concerned about the other than about following an internal moral imperative. Monroe elaborates:

> For the rescuers, the cognitive aspect of empathy appeared to enter through the structure of knowledge that formed an expectation

of a coherent sequence of acts and events in a given situation. These sequences appeared to have been stored in the rescuers' memories, often subconsciously, both in the form of scripts about how one treated those in need or in the form of schemas about how one viewed one's self. These important self schema, the existence of such scripts and schematic frameworks, explained the rescuers' habitual, spontaneous, and nonconscious or reflexive altruism. The behavioural consequences of such scripts and schemas were the rescuers' automatic help for the weak and their continuing habits of caring.

(ibid.)

The constant factor in Monroe's rescuers' perception is their recognition of the humanity of the other. This means that the plight of the victim is perceived to be of "direct concern" or relevance to the rescuer (ibid, p. 248). The victim cannot be dehumanized or put into the category of an "other," outside the world of the rescuer. This acknowledgment of the relevance of the "other" is at the core of the impetus to help. Identification with the "other" is clearly an important aspect of bravery but this is different from feeling empathy for the "other." Identification affirms our connection with our fellow human beings and establishes our collective functioning. In so far as the rescuer is compelled to act, the act is primarily driven by selfish needs, such as the need to act according to one's conscience. However, as the need to act is rooted in individual conscience it also serves to ensure collective survival.

Empathy is in fact not always helpful in situations that call for acts of bravery, and can impair mental functioning. The Russian mother who drowned her infant had to suppress her empathy for her child in order to be brave. Soldiers sent to the front line become inured to the brutalities around them and need to learn to kill in order to survive. Combat training intentionally desensitizes the soldier to the act of killing by dehumanizing the "other." By suppressing empathy, the anxiety and resistance to killing is lessened so that mental functioning is protected; the soldier can go on thinking without succumbing to panic.[3] In warfare, especially, antipathy to the enemy is cultivated as an encouragement to be brave. At its extreme, this may result in the ideal of the hero-warrior who is not vulnerable to his feelings toward others. Under the Third

Reich in Germany, the word *Haarte*, meaning tough and hard, became a military virtue to be emulated. Stargardt writes:

> During the final, difficult weeks of the retreat from Moscow, the 4th Panzer Division's chief doctor noted with approval how the men had learned to be "hard on themselves." The word was now acquiring something of the meaning Hitler gave it in closed briefing sessions, when he used "hard" as a metaphor for genocidal measures. Hinting at the process of self-brutalisation, "hard" and "harsh" increasingly complemented the sacralising language of heroic self-sacrifice in both official and private accounts.
>
> (Stargardt, 2016, p. 209)

This kind of distortion of an ego ideal is a common feature of authoritarian regimes that need to maintain group solidarity and rely on the demonization of others to support the regime.

Although empathy may not be the driving force that motivates someone to act bravely, most, if not all of the rescuers I am writing about describe themselves as being aware of the violence and harm we are capable of doing to one another. Thompson stresses that his parents did not shelter him from life as he was growing up with the belief that this would not help him cope with the vicissitudes of life. My patient, Aaron, as a refugee, was all too conversant with the extreme violence and suffering his family had gone through. Those who act bravely during war have invariably been exposed to brutality, either directly or as witnesses. These background accounts suggest that not only were the rescuers not naïve but there is also some indication that they were not afraid of their own aggression. John makes it clear that if he had had a gun, despite his religious upbringing that prohibited murder, he would have shot the soldier who had thrown the crying child to the ground. Aaron's desire to serve in his country's army stemmed from his desire to protect his family and his country but it was also his anger at having had to emigrate that fueled his need to fight. At the same time, when he rescued the surrendering soldier, he told me, "I knew I had to do stop him from being killed but I also knew I was sick of all the killing—this also had to stop. I was angry." For John and Aaron, it was perhaps their awareness of their own anger and hatred that enabled them to use their aggression to act. For people who are frightened of their aggression, this may in itself prevent them from being able to act or to intervene, particularly if they are anxious to obey external authority.

Dissent and common cause

Bravery is an act of self-agency, and in this respect it is an act of dissent; it defies human passivity in the face of life-threatening events. Every act of bravery upholds a moral order both in terms of social norms and our innate sense of morality, although the two do not always coincide. While what constitutes a moral order and how it is perceived is complex, its existence necessarily establishes a profound connection between the individual and the group. Even Aaron's separation from his parents and refusal to continue to be subjugated by them was an act that not only upheld his own welfare in opposition to theirs but, in reinforcing his own internal values, it also made him more acutely aware of his own belief system and the import of his actions on others. At the end of his analysis, Aaron expressed this in saying, "I feel much freer now that I feel that I'm the one who is in charge of my life, and it can be lonely too, but it also somehow makes me feel that in standing up for myself and what I believe, I am connected to everyone else at a fundamental level."

Aaron's remark recalls the writings of Camus. Camus makes the point that rebellion is not only an outcry against the infringement of rights but also for the rebel it is "a complete and spontaneous loyalty to certain aspects of himself" (Camus, 1951, p. 19). Following on from this, Camus observes that

> rebellion, contrary to present opinion and despite the fact that it springs from everything that is most strictly individualistic in man, undermines the very conception of the individual. If an individual actually consents to die, and, when the occasion arises, accepts death as a consequence of his rebellion, he demonstrates that he is willing to sacrifice himself for the sake of a common good which he considers more important than he is. He acts, therefore, in the name of certain values which are still indeterminate but which he feels are common to himself and to all men. We see that the affirmation implicit in each act of revolt

is extended to something which transcends the individual in so far as it removes him from his supposed solitude and supplies him with reason to act ... An analysis of rebellion leads us to the suspicion that ... a human nature does exist ... Why rebel if there is nothing worth preserving in oneself? The slave asserts himself for the sake of everyone in the world when he comes to the conclusion that a command has infringed on something inside him that does not belong to him alone, but which he has in common with other men—even with the man who insults and oppresses him.

(ibid., pp. 21–22)

Camus' emphasis on the importance of common cause is essential in understanding acts of bravery and echoes Monroe's point about the "relevance" of the "other." As he asks, why rebel against individual harm or injustice if the act has no meaning beyond the individual? If, however, we view the act of rebellion as an assertion of individual humanity, whether it pertains to the self or other, then it necessarily has a vital role to play in defending our sense of what it means to be human. This differs significantly from fighting for a common cause, such as in the case of warfare, in which it is the group's identity that is at stake. The distinctive characteristic of rebellion for Camus lies in its assertion of humanity, derived from our identification with our fellow human beings, "even with the man who insults and oppresses him" (ibid.).

Camus' notion of common cause becomes evident at the moment of dissent. Bravery in dissent requires the actor to oppose the subverted norms of the group and to restore what has been ruptured. It is not an act of reparation but an act that highlights what has been destroyed and what needs to be set right in order to restore the possibility of creativity and our capacity to bear conflict and loss—to restore the meaning of being human. Although dissenting may threaten one's actual individual survival, it ensures an internal consonance, "being true to oneself," that opposes fragmentation and, ultimately, psychosis. The malignant or perverse system that denies reality in its dehumanization of others requires the individual to ignore, if not attempt to obliterate, an observing ego that registers our experience of reality. Dissent can be seen as an attempt to restore our relation to reality in terms of privileging our internal experience and, through this privileging, recognizing the humanity of the other.

Conclusion

I have tried to show that the act of bravery is a complex process that directly affects and is an expression of one's sense of identity, however this is defined. While it may appear in many cases to be a visceral reaction to extreme danger or violence, the act is propelled by an internal psychic construction, or what Monroe refers to as a "nonconscious script." This script is created from the kind of ego ideal we have internalized in our development and experience of the world along with the conviction that our actions—or failures to act—matter and have an impact on others. Camus' conception of dissent is based on this conviction as is Monroe's emphasis on the "relevance" of the other. It is not simply the act of bravery that matters but it is an implicit assertion that the other exists through one's actions—that our identification with one another gives us collective meaning and a sense of self. This is most vividly apparent when we hear the explanations of those who have failed to be brave; explanations such as, "I didn't want to get involved because it wasn't anything to do with me," or "I could have done something, but it wouldn't have made any difference in the long run and it would have been risky for me in any case," or "They're not like us, so why should we risk our lives for them?" We can see in these explanations the psychological defense of denial, disavowal, and splitting. These are the defenses that alienate us from ourselves and from our connection to others and allow injustice and dehumanization to occur.

Acts of bravery stand out in our minds because they signify a common belief system that we, individually and collectively, matter. This is the foundation of our moral being, it is what gives meaning to the idea of "being true to oneself." In this sense, acts of bravery bring us face to face with our reality, a reality that cannot be distorted through our defense mechanisms but must be borne with all its consequences. For Aaron and the other heroes I describe, their capacity to act bravely was directly contingent on recognizing the incontrovertibility of the reality in their lives. At the moment when we become acutely aware that we have no choice over our reality, we have no choice but to act accordingly.

Notes

1. Although the terms bravery and courage are often used interchangeably, I view the term courage as more of a characteristic describing someone's personality.
2. It is striking that so many of the rescuers and dissidents during World War II were Jehovah's Witnesses whose strong belief system was fundamental to their behavior and their survival. In the concentration camps during the Third Reich, Jehovah's Witnesses were renowned for their efforts to share their rations equally and support one another. "The 'simple and satisfactory belief' in their own salvation and life after the impending Armageddon, provided they kept to the tenets of their faith, 'lent them strength and made them able to stand the long years of concentration-camp life and all the indignities and humiliations and still retain their human dignity.'" Their strong faith similarly shielded them from the fear of death and enabled them to contain their anxieties and preserve their mental functioning for survival (Fulbrook, M. (2018). *Reckonings: Legacies of Nazi Persecution and the Quest for Justice*. Oxford: Oxford University Press, p. 160).
3. See the work of the sociologist Randall Collins who argues that humans have a natural antipathy to violence and murder, even when it is sanctioned by the group (Collins, R. (2008). *Violence: A Micro-sociological Theory*. Princeton: Princeton University Press).

References

Alexievich, S. (2017). *The Unwomanly Face of War*. London: Penguin.

Barrett, E. & Martin, P. (2016). *Extreme: Why Some People Thrive at the Limits*. Oxford: Oxford University Press.

Bion, W. R. (1997). *War Memoirs: 1917–1919*. London: Karnac.

Camus, A. (1951). *The Rebel*. London: Penguin, 1971.

Covington, C. (2017). *Everyday Evils: A Psychoanalytic View of Evil and Morality*. London: Routledge.

Eger, E. (2017). *The Choice*. London: Ryder.

Freud, S. (1914c). On Narcissism: An Introduction. *S.E. XI*. London: Vintage.

Monroe, K. R. (2004). *The Hand of Compassion*. Princeton: Princeton University Press.

Stargardt, N. (2016). *The German War: A Nation Under Arms, 1939–45*. London: Vintage.

CHAPTER THREE

The good citizen: traditions of bravery and dissent from Plato to the present

It is not always the same thing to be a good man and a good citizen.
—Aristotle, *Nicomachean Ethics*

The ideal citizen

On the evening of Saturday 26 May 2018, Mamoudou Gassama, a twenty-two-year-old undocumented migrant from Mali, was walking along a street in the 18th arrondissement of Paris when he heard a crowd of people shouting and car horns sounding at the sight of a four-year-old-boy dangling from the balcony of a fourth-floor flat.

"I didn't think twice, I just climbed up," Gassama, who had never climbed before, explained. In the video, which quickly went viral, we see Gassama scaling the balconies of the apartment building until he lifted the crying child to safety. The child had been left alone in a flat in the building and had already dropped one floor before Gassama came to the rescue. In the safety of the flat's living room, Gassama broke down. "I felt afraid when I saved the child ... I started to shake, I could hardly stand up, I had to sit down." Nicknaming Gassama "Spider-Man of the 18th," Anne Hidalgo, the mayor of Paris, praised him for his "act of bravery" (*Guardian*, 28 May 2018).

49

Gassama not only risked his life to save the child, but, as an illegal migrant, he also risked deportation. Far from being deported, Gassama was honored by President Macron with French citizenship. In a meeting at the Élysée Palace, Macron rewarded Gassama for his "bravery and devotion," giving him, along with his brother, French residency and ensuring they would be fast-tracked to receive French citizenship.[1] Gassama was also offered a position as trainee in the fire brigade. The official decree announced, "This act of great bravery exemplifies the values which help unite our national community, such as courage, selflessness, altruism and taking care of the most vulnerable" (BBC News, 13 Sept 2018).

Gassama's heroic deed soon became a shining example of what it means in France to be a good citizen, as stated in the decree. By publicly conferring the honor of citizenship to an undocumented migrant, Macron was also projecting a more complex message. Citizenship embraces the individual within the group, legally and socially, while it cements the social pact of the group—the state provides employment (Gassama's trainee position with the fire brigade) and other welfare benefits (in Gassama's case, housing) in exchange for further public service (the fire brigade is a public service). As an illegal immigrant, Gassama had none of these privileges and protections, nor did he have these obligations. Macron was not only promoting the concept of citizenship as an ideal in itself, he was using the honor as an attempt to unify a fragmenting population and to curry political favor at a time when his popularity was waning and nationalist values were being re-formulated. The civil servant who processed Gassama's citizenship request noted, "[Gassama] helped someone in danger, which is not such a common thing in our society." This comment suggests that Gassama's act served as a significant reminder of the traditional ideal of the "good citizen," an ideal which may have lost its allure over time. While Gassama qualified to be a citizen because of his "good action," the status of being a citizen does not require one to be "good" despite the ideals that it stands for. Granting citizenship as an honor also brought into focus what some critics described as France's repressive policy in relation to migrants. The French documentary maker Raphael Glucksmann commented on Facebook: "Like everyone else, I admire the bravery of Mamoudou Gassama. But I dream of a country where it won't be necessary to put one's own life at risk scaling a building to save the life of a child in order to be treated like a human being when one is a migrant."

Gassama's award of citizenship underscores the common idea that the "good citizen" is someone who altruistically puts the community and the lives of those within the community above and beyond his or her own personal interests. The individual is secondary to the collective and upholds the collective set of values. Within this context, civic acts of bravery, particularly as they defend the collective, stand out as the epitome of the "ideal citizen." The brave soldier is the archetypal example of the individual who risks his life for his country, ensuring the survival of the group, and above all the group's political ideology and set of beliefs. Although the specific characteristics of being a "good citizen" may differ across cultures, it is nevertheless a common social meme, passed down from one generation to the next, forming a collective ego ideal for the group.

The origins of citizenship

Most of our ideas in the West about what it means to be a citizen stem from the Ancient Greek foundation of city-states in which the bond between the individual and the state was formalized, ensuring protection of the city-state against its enemies and, internally, a sharing of power and responsibilities. The status of being a citizen, conferred through ancestral bloodlines, importantly signified the differentiation between slavery and freedom; slaves had no legal status and hence no power or civic responsibility. Barbarians, women, and children shared the plight of slaves as they too were considered outside the bounds of citizenship. The parallel today, as in the case of Gassama, is clear with the unprotected status of the illegal immigrant who is as vulnerable as a slave. In Ancient Greece, the growth of slavery and the threat of becoming a slave, either through penury or warfare, was a very real anxiety. Citizenship was not only a means of defending the supremacy of the city-state but it granted certain freedoms that were not available to all. Citizenship and the notion of freedom became inextricably and fundamentally linked. In classifying who was included and who was excluded within the governing of the polis, citizenship also became an important feature of individual and collective identity. Citizens had a vested interest in defending their freedom, as this was an integral part of their identity.

Individual affinity with the polis created a strong link between personal destiny and political association. The small-scale communities of the polis further established ideas about social norms and appropriate civic conduct that formed the basis of what evolved into participatory democracy and was essential in maintaining local sovereignty and military effectiveness. The historian Geoffrey Hosking writes about the origins of democratic obligation that subsequently became embedded in ideas of patriotism:

> If you've got a lot of soldiers of rather modest means, and you want them to enthusiastically participate in war, then you've got to have a political and economic system which doesn't allow too many of them to fall into debt, because debt ultimately means slavery, and slaves cannot fight in the army. And it needs a political system which gives them a say on matters that concern their lives.
>
> (Hosking, 2005, pp. 1–2)

In her 2018 Reith Lectures, the historian Margaret Macmillan makes the salient point that having a say in government means that its citizens want to defend it. Along with obligations and loyalty, citizenship brings with it an expectation that young men will fight for their country (Macmillan, 2018).

In Ancient Greece the obligations of being a citizen included obeying the law, participating in political life, and serving in the army and, in this capacity, risking one's life for the state. Rights covered owning land, voting and standing for public office, and receiving the protection of the state in war. Together, rights and obligations constituted the backbone of citizenship and created a common interest within the elite (i.e. free) members of the state and a common identity. Citizenship was also conceived of as a peculiarly human social function. Aristotle stressed that being truly human required the individual to be an active citizen of the community, arguing that, "to take no part in the running of the community's affairs is to be either a beast or a god!" In his funeral oration at the end of the first year of the Peloponnesian War (431 BC), Pericles praises the democracy of Athens, the importance of self-rule, and the obligation on all citizens to contribute to political life. He notably asserts, "We are unique in considering the man who takes no part in public affairs not to be apolitical, but useless." The "private citizen," that is, the citizen who did not participate in civic duties, was described by the Greek word, "idiotes," signifying someone who was isolated and ignorant of public affairs. For Aristotle, the idea of citizenship was important not just in conferring the freedom to take part in political discussions and the wielding of political power, but citizenship itself symbolized freedom and the higher value of the political world of the polis as compared with the domestic, personal life of the oikos (the family).

The link between citizenship and freedom is equally powerful in our world today, whether it is perceived as an essential democratic principle or as a tenet of the totalitarian state. Membership ensures a set of obligations, duties, and protections that allow the individual a political identity aligned with the group and the relative security needed to establish at least a simulacrum of freedom and certain clearly established rights. In her book, *The Origins of Totalitarianism*, Hannah Arendt emphasizes that having "the right to have rights" is a concept that only exists within the bounds of citizenship as recognized by the state (Arendt, 1966, p. 296). While actual political structures vary along with conceptions of the systems by which the power of the state is legitimized, "freedom" seems to serve as a universal goal albeit in different guises. Within more traditionally democratic systems, freedom is associated with individual choice and equality in the opportunity to govern. Within autocratic regimes, the state itself becomes the symbol for freedom from various oppressors, whether economic, religious, or racial. Citizenship in this context serves an ideological loyalty and adherence that promotes freedom of the group first and foremost and then of the individual as a member of the group.

For the Ancient Greeks, the concept of freedom directly referred to the ability of a man to govern himself, as opposed to being a slave, and for each citizen to have an equal opportunity to participate in political life. The emphasis was very much on the individual citizen as a participant and creator of the state with a specific focus on the higher communal good. However, recognizing the voice of the individual in relation to the group and its governance immediately introduces a tension between the individual and others within the group. The idea of "what the people want" is, as we know from current politics, fraught and open to interpretation. This is similarly the case when we are confronted with the contradictions of supporting democratic principles that bind us to majority rule and what we as individuals believe to be in our collective best interests.

Socrates, the dissenting citizen

Given that there is an inevitable, built-in tension in the Greek concept of citizenship, it is not surprising that this conflict was played out most markedly in the life of Socrates. Plato highlights the juxtaposition between Socrates' acts of civic and personal bravery and we see the emergence of a new concept of citizenship that incorporates the voice of dissension. Socrates had proved himself an outstanding, if not ideal, citizen in his youth on the field of battle. He was renowned for his martial bravery in rescuing his friend, Alcibiades, in the battle of Potidaea in 432 BC. In Plato's *Symposium*, Alcibiades praises Socrates' indomitable strength, writing,

> He took the hardships of campaign much better than I did, much better in fact than any of the troops. When we were cut off from our supplies, as often happens on campaign, no one else endured hunger as well as he did.
>
> In addition, he had an extraordinary ability to withstand the cold, though winter in that region was awful … Socrates went out in that weather wearing nothing but his old light cloak, and even in bare feet he walked more steadily through the ice than other soldiers did in their boots …
>
> (D'Angour, 2019, pp. 44–45)

Alcibiades then recounts his rescue by Socrates:

> If you want to know what Socrates was like in battle, let me praise him as he truly deserves.
>
> You know that I was decorated for bravery during that campaign. Well, during that battle Socrates rescued me single-handed, and without doubt his action saved my life. I was wounded, and Socrates not only refused to leave me behind, he retrieved my armour as well.
>
> At the time, Socrates, I said that it was you, not I, who should be decorated for valour …
>
> (ibid., p. 45)

Here we have a picture of Socrates as the archetypal brave soldier, performing his martial duty while risking his own life. In his acts of heroic selflessness, Socrates conforms to the image of the ideal citizen who acts in common cause with Athens and its citizens, putting the interests of the polis and of his comrade, Alcibiades, above his own.

Socrates' acts of loyalty, are however, seemingly turned on their head in his later life when he refused to obey the demand of the ruling junta in 404 BC to arrest an innocent man. This marked Socrates' first public challenge of the rule of the state and in particular the Athenian hegemony that some believed had arisen as a perverse result of democratic practices. Socrates continued to object to the Athenian oligarchy until he was brought to trial in 399 BC, scapegoated for the coup of 411 BC and accused of corrupting the minds of young Athenians, for "not believing in the gods of the state," and introducing new gods (Plato, 2017, 24–27). The religious charges leveled at Socrates are likely to have masked the political grievance that he was associated, rightly or wrongly, with the aristocratic subverters of democracy (personal communication from D'Angour). Rather than being punished, Socrates argued,

> I am the gadfly of the Athenian people, given to them by God, and they will never have another, if they kill me. And now, Athenians, I am not going to argue for my own sake, as you may think, but for yours, that you may not sin against the God by condemning me, who am his gift to you. For if you kill me you will not easily find a successor to me, who, if I may use such a ludicrous figure of speech, am a sort of gadfly, given to the state by God; and the state is a great and noble steed who is tardy in his motions owing to his very size, and requires to be stirred into life. I am that gadfly which God has attached to the state, and all day long and in all places am always fastening upon, arousing and persuading and reproaching you. You will not easily find another like me, and therefore I would advise you to spare me.
>
> (Plato, 2017)

In his refusal to accept he had done anything wrong, Socrates claimed to be stinging the conscience of the Athenian citizenry and to be upholding the democracy of the state.[2] Plato wants to persuade us that Socrates is innocent and depicts his death as his submission to the jury's decision to execute him and to what we would now describe as due process. In willingly assisting his execution, Socrates was not voicing his dissent against the state but was instead acting as a "good" citizen of Athens who had, as a fellow citizen, enjoyed its democratic freedoms.[3] At the same time, by executing himself (i.e. drinking poison), Socrates superseded the authority of the state in assuming the role of the executioner. This extreme act of obedience to the state held an implicit criticism, by example, of those who did not adhere to the principles Socrates espoused. The gadfly had been transformed into the exemplary citizen in a sleight of hand. Socrates' final act of self-agency highlights the complexity of what it means to be a "good citizen" and to what extent being a "good citizen" can be consonant with dissent.

Citizenship today and education

At the center of our identifications with the different groups we belong to—our family, our school, our religious community, our local community, our town or city, and our country—we accept and aspire to the group's values and ideals. Our acceptance and internalization of these values is the glue that binds groups together and provides a sense of group identity and individual membership. Within our psyches, these values constitute what Freud described as the ego ideal, that is, the image we have within our minds of the kind of person we would like to be, the best of ourselves. Our relationship to authority and to being governed by group norms and structures is founded on adherence to the values of the group that in turn strengthens group identity and acts to ensure protection if the group is threatened. This process of identification hinges on early socialization, beginning in the family setting but most importantly elaborated and reinforced through the education of children.

It is commonly acknowledged that across the world, regardless of political regime, the education system of any given geographical area provides the first template for the concept of what it means to be a "good citizen," more often than not as it reflects the type of government that is in power. In the world today, whether we grow up in the UK, the United

States, or North Korea, we are imbued as children with the importance of government, what values it represents, our relation to government as individual citizens and the different ways of showing respect and loyalty to the ideals government represents. One important aspect of the "good citizen" is to demonstrate loyalty and allegiance to one's country— the country that confers citizenship. Children in schools across the US pledge their allegiance to the flag as part of the school ritual. In Hong Kong, draft legislature is pending that will require children in international schools, attended by high-ranking Chinese students and diplomats, to sing the Chinese national anthem and attend classes on China's anthem, covering such topics as "the history and the spirit" behind "The March of the Volunteers" and the "etiquette for playing and singing the national anthem." Citizens, including students, who insult the Chinese anthem will become liable to criminal proceedings and a jail sentence of up to three years if they are found guilty (Liu and Boyde, 2019). This seems to be an extension of the criminal prohibitions imposed on desecration of the flag not only in China but in other countries such as Turkey, South Korea, Saudi Arabia, New Zealand, France, Portugal, and Austria to name only a few.

Alongside conforming to public displays of national allegiance, the civic virtues enumerated by Macron in the case of Gassama of "courage, selflessness, altruism, and taking care of the most vulnerable" can be seen as universal ideals that within most education systems form the basis for promoting the concept of the "good citizen," regardless of political ideology. These qualities are exemplified in a British school report card, praising a sixteen-year-old female student:

> She has shown citizenship by representing the school on a netball trip, in a maths competition and by donating to a variety of good causes, as well as helping the charity Mary's Meals as part of the Duke of Edinburgh's Award Scheme ...
>
> (Personal communication, 2018)

What is notably missing in this list of noble qualities is the lesson Socrates gave us of thinking for oneself, questioning what is just, participating in public debate and, ultimately, dissension as a form of civic obligation.

The mission statement of a private girls' school in New York City similarly emphasizes the importance of bravery, compassion, and service to others. These traits are singled out as qualities needed for leadership and citizenship. The mission statement elaborates:

> The School is dedicated to empowering a diverse, ambitious and resolute community of young women to thrive and lead in their world … By advancing and deepening each student's agency, confidence and resilience within an affirming and joyful learning environment, [the school] strives to ensure that each student is emboldened to pursue distinction as a leader and contributing citizen.
>
> (Personal communication, 2019)

The central aim is to produce ambitious leaders. While agency, confidence, and resilience are listed as essential tools in creating good leaders, thinking for oneself—with the possibility of dissenting—is not amongst these.

In writing about civil war and peace-building, Jeremy Cunningham, an education consultant, points to the central role of education in being able to reconcile and repair divisions within communities and to instill concepts of self-agency and mutual respect through the curriculum, the idea of self-governance within schools, and accessibility to education. Cunningham writes:

> Conflict transformation after civil war means accepting that the interests of individuals and groups will inevitably differ, but that conflicts of interest can be transformed into productive energies instead of destructive violence. Schools have a part to play in conflict transformation, because of their widespread access to young people who will influence society in future. These include those who have been involved in armed conflict or suffered from it directly and indirectly, and those further removed. Schooling can play a part in conflict transformation through access—the process of enrolling, attending, and finishing—but also at a deeper level through the curriculum, which I define below as the overall

experience of the learner in school. The curriculum can contribute to conflict transformation through:

- truth-seeking—the effort to give meaning to the range of experience of those who participated and suffered in the war rather than the search for one uncontested story;
- reconciliation—the readiness to forgo revenge and the ending of a cycle of hatred and fear;
- inclusive citizenship—the collective effort of previously warring groups towards the elimination of social injustice and structural violence.

(Cunningham, 2018, pp. 2–3)

Cunningham makes a clear argument for the importance of education in shaping the citizens of the future and in combating violent political conflict.[4] Unfortunately, a liberal education that encourages independent thinking may not necessarily translate into the political sphere, especially during times of crisis or economic inequality when group behavior may be driven more by the need for security. We are also aware that just as education (i.e. the curriculum) may foster self-agency and "independent" thinking, it may equally inculcate unthinking obedience to authority, as in the case of totalitarian regimes. In either situation, what is evident is the fundamental promotion of an ego ideal albeit one that differs significantly in its intrinsic qualities.

The power of the collective ideal

Perhaps nowhere in modern history is the power of the collective ideal more apparent than in the sweeping mass movements that spurred individuals and groups to commit genocide. In the last century we have witnessed the rise of Nazi Germany and the dawning of the Final Solution, Rwanda's bloodbath of the Tutsis and moderate Hutus in the wake of previous genocides, Cambodia's Khmer Rouge Killing Fields, the racial slaughter of the Bosnian war, and more recently the expulsion and extermination of Rohingya Muslims and other religious groups in Myanmar, along with genocides in other countries. The pervading incitement that has caused people to kill can be found in two tell-tale indicators, the first being the demonization and dehumanization of another racial group and the second, accompanying indicator, being a gradual shift in the collective ideal of what it means to be a "good citizen." I will give two brief examples of how the collective ideal can be manipulated and perverted in the service of political violence in Germany during the Reich and in Rwanda's genocide.

In her detailed analysis of German diaries and correspondence during and after the Third Reich, the historian Mary Fulbrook provides numerous illustrations of the incipient shift in values and norms that many of the population adopted at the beginning of the Reich, some consciously and others as a kind of unconscious reflex or response to their changing political and social environment. The habit of signing off letters with "Heil Hitler" is a case in point. Fulbrook comments on the correspondence of a committed Nazi, whom she calls Herr Lorenz, as revealing an increasing need to "grasp what we have to do or not to do" in the changing political climate and, most urgently, in the changing demands of being a good party member. In a letter of 22 September, 1935, he signs off with "Heil Hitler" using quotation marks.[5] This habit continues until two years later, on September 12, 1937, for the first time Lorenz drops the quotation marks. Fulbrook comments:

> Herr Lorenz, for example, was not only donning the new language of "Heil Hitler" in signing off his letters. He had quite clearly fully internalized the goals and vision of the national community ... in his letters of the 1930s there is a sense of real excitement ... [Referring to the successes of a charity in which his son had been active], Lorenz ... exclaimed, "Everywhere there is life and activity."
>
> (Fulbrook, 2018, pp. 36–37)

Another example is Elisabeth B. who, despite coming from an anti-Nazi family,

> recalled how even she had on a couple of occasions unexpectedly experienced the potential attractions of belonging to a national community that was awash with enthusiasm ... [At a Wannsee festival] she was given the opportunity to meet Goebbels personally.

> She records how, "quite mechanically, just like the others, I spoke
> with Dr. Goebbels, laughed with him, and shook his hand." Writ-
> ing from the United States, at a critical distance from Germany,
> she went on: "It is still a mystery to me today as to how I could
> bring myself to do this."
>
> (ibid., p. 38)

She later saw herself at this time as having "'stopped thinking' for herself or seeing herself as an individual, but just as part of a 'mass'" (ibid.,
pp. 38–39).

Fulbrook portrays the overwhelming excitement of being part of a
new vision of the future and belonging to a new "national community,"
a new belonging that often meant betrayal of their families, their friends,
and their own minds.

Both Herr Lorenz and Elisabeth B., who were of opposing political
views, illustrate the infectious exhilaration of being part of a political
movement that was promising a golden future.[6] The powerful appeal of
belonging was strengthened by a set of ideals that united the group and
made each individual strive to be worthy of its membership. As one pro-
Nazi woman reflected in the aftermath of the regime's fall, "from our
youth onwards these people had been set before us as ideals and role
models, in whom we had faith and whom we worshipped, so that it is
now impossible for me to think badly of them, let alone say anything
bad about them" (ibid., p. 218). Growing up with such role models who
represented a revitalized set of ideals was difficult to resist and quickly
became normative, establishing collective ideals to conform to.

Within the context of the Rwanda genocide, a similar process of public propaganda, emphasis on group belonging, a new political vision of
the future, and the manipulation of collective ideals were also evident.
My book examining the roots of evil, with regard to the Rwanda genocide, deals with this (see Covington, 2017a, p. 115). In a talk connected
with the book I made this comment:

> The Hutus used different rationales and justifications to nor-
> malize their task of killing. They were encouraged to think of
> themselves as employed by the state to do a good job and in this
> way they could become a valued member of the community.

They also saw themselves as part of a militia fighting to defend their community. They were protecting the environment from pollution—using the image of the garden, they were killing off the weeds (i.e. the Tutsis) that were overrunning and destroying their land. The Hutus who killed the most Tutsis were also rewarded the most highly. In short, the new set of norms, borrowing from traditional roles that were respected and valued, had taken over, perverting the old norms and promoting adherence to a new set of beliefs. Killing the "other" is not only justified, it confers status and recognition within the group … [T]he ideal of killing as many Tutsis as possible became a recognized feature within the Hutu population.

(Covington, 2017b, p. 12)

What is so striking about both of these snapshots is that the traditional ego ideals of the group, such as being strong and courageous, putting the group or the country before themselves, fighting to protect their country, and so on, have been maintained if not amplified; what has changed is the identification of an enemy who becomes the scapegoat and repository for social ills and who, as a consequence, needs to be conquered and ultimately eradicated. The psychic structure of the group remains in place, the collective ego ideal upholds the promise of goodness and purity in the future, while a distorted, paranoid perception of reality has changed the dramatic *mise en scène*. The superego is needed to ensure that the ego conforms to the new reality—determining "what we have to do or not to do"—and can only really function in accord with the principle that the means justify the ends.

Conclusion

The danger in ideals is that they can be used for good purposes or for bad; they can lead us to act as heroes or as cowards, as defenders of the truth or as deceivers. This is the conflict that Socrates exposed and that lies at the heart of what it means to be a "good citizen." We have the examples of Socrates who embodied the "good citizen" as one who is true to himself, of Gassama who unwittingly became a "good citizen" because of his act of bravery, and of the German and Hutu citizens who were motivated to behave as "good citizens" for a variety of interrelated reasons to do with group belonging, status, and identity, as well as needing to conform to an ideal that was in some way familiar or traditional and, because of this, helped to provide a sense of continuity with a past that was in many respects radically different. The "good citizen" is the one who risks his life for his country or fellow citizens[7] and at the same time he is the one who risks his life in opposition to the state in order to protect the ideals on which it is founded. Many are put to these extreme tests every day, but for those of us who are not put to these tests, unless we are refugees, we are citizens of one country or another and a fundamental part of our identity inevitably rests on our background assumptions about what it means to be a citizen and how the collective ideals of our culture directly affect our lives and our judgment of ourselves and others. As citizens we are given certain protections and privileges, but these come with obligations that may be visible and legal, such as taxation, and in some countries military enlistment and voting, or less visible in terms of our moral and actual participation in public debate and the life of the polis. It is through our citizenship that we exercise our self-agency and protect ourselves from falling into a state of slavery in which we lose our voice, our rights, and our judgment—the qualities that make us human.

Camus, in his postwar novel La Peste (The Plague) of 1947, dramatically illustrates the conflict of being a member of a community—a citizen—that is suddenly beset by the plague and the ensuing moral and philosophical questions that confront its population. The narrator, Dr. Rieux, converses with his friend, Jean Tarrou, who as an outsider has been quarantined within the community and in his belief that everyone is responsible for the plague acts to fight against it. Rieux asks:

> "Come now, Tarrou," he said. "What makes you want to get involved in all this?"
> "I don't know. My sense of morality, perhaps?"
> "What morality?"
> "Understanding."
> Tarrou turned towards the house and Rieux did not see his face again until they were in the old asthmatic's flat.
> Tarrou started work the very next day and mustered a first team that was to be followed by many others.

However, it is not the narrator's intention to attribute more significance to these health groups than they actually had. It is true that nowadays many of our fellow-citizens would, in his place, succumb to the temptation to believe that by giving too much importance to fine actions one may end by paying an indirect but powerful tribute to evil, because in so doing one implies that such fine actions are only valuable because they are rare, and that malice or indifference are far more common motives in the actions of men. The narrator does not share this view. The evil in the world comes almost always from ignorance, and goodwill can cause as much damage as ill-will if it is not enlightened. People are more often good than bad, though in fact that is not the question ...

(Camus, 1947, p. 101)

Here we see Rieux, much like Macron's critic, Raphael Glucksmann, questioning the ideal of "fine actions" as if these represent a true good. Instead, Tarrou presents the dichotomy between ignorance and understanding, equating understanding with morality.

Rieux continues his thoughts,

[T]here always comes a time in history when the person who dares to say that two and two make four is punished by death. The schoolmaster knows this quite well. And the question is not what reward or punishment awaits the demonstration; it is knowing whether or not two and two do make four. For those of the townspeople who risked their lives, they had to decide whether or not they were in a state of plague and whether or not they should try to overcome it.

(ibid., pp. 101–102)

Rieux is in some agreement with Tarrou in that it is one's understanding of reality and how one chooses to respond to this that forms the basis for morality and, most importantly, gives us the capacity to act. He concludes:

Yes, if men really do have to offer themselves as models and examples whom they call heroes, and if there really has to be one in this story, the narrator would like to offer this insignificant and self-effacing hero who had nothing to recommend him but a little goodness in his heart and an apparently ridiculous ideal.

(ibid., p. 105)

Rieux concludes with the assertion that the "hero" is the one who carries on fighting against the plague with the "apparently ridiculous ideal" of being able to overcome it. Perhaps this is also the key to being a "good citizen"—freely choosing to participate in the polis in the knowledge that plagues may appear to subside and die out but they recur time and time again despite our efforts to combat them.

Notes

1. Gassama joins a small number of undocumented migrants who have been granted residency in France in recognition for acts of public service or "exceptional talent" (*Guardian*, 28 May 2018).
2. I. F. Stone argues that it was in fact reasonable to view Socrates as a danger to democracy (see Stone, I. F. (1989). *The Trial of Socrates*. New York: Anchor Books).
3. Socrates' friends urged him to allow them to bribe the prison guards so he could escape to freedom, albeit to live in exile. However, Socrates decided that even if the judgment of his fellow-citizens had been flawed he had a duty to abide by their decision. The classicist Mary Klefkowitz points out that Socrates was also aware that "a heroic death would bring him immortality: no Greek could forget the names or deeds of Patroclus, Hector and Achilles … It was only by allowing himself to be executed that Socrates was able to remain in control of his own biography" (see Klefkowitz, M. R. (2008). Review of Emily Wilson, *The Death of Socrates* (Cambridge, MA: Harvard University Press, 2007). *Reason Papers* 30: 107–112).
4. It is by no means clear that creating an education culture that promotes thinking for oneself and questioning authority leads to a lessening of political violence. There is, for example, a tradition within the Israeli school system of questioning what happened in the Holocaust as an illustration of the dangers of a citizenry that does not challenge authority (personal communication from Liana Amunts). And yet in 2019 Israeli political policies and behavior are increasingly belligerent and racist.

5. Effective 13 July 1933, it was mandatory for government officials to use this salutation. In September 1933, prisoners were forbidden to use it, as were Jews in 1937.
6. Trump's promise to "Make America Great Again" chillingly echoes the allure of Hitler's vision for Germany.
7. In the US and Western Europe, there is increasing questioning about risking one's life for one's country in war. Although every war has its dissenters and deserters, there is mounting cynicism about the political rationale for war, particularly in the case of protecting the democratic status of foreign countries, such as Vietnam, Afghanistan, and Iraq. With the erosion of political authority in the wake of unprincipled warfare what is considered a just cause for war and dying for one's country can no longer be taken for granted. When government loses its authority in this way the ties of citizenship are accordingly weakened.

References

Arendt, H. (1966). *The Origins of Totalitarianism*. New York: Harcourt.

Camus, A. (1947). *The Plague*. London: Penguin, 2001.

Covington, C. (2017a). *Everyday Evils: A Psychoanalytic View of Evil and Morality*. London: Routledge.

Covington, C. (2017b). Public talk given at Festival of Debate in Lewes, UK (unpublished).

Cunningham, J. (2018). *Conflict Transformation Through School: A Curriculum for Sustainable Peace*. London: Institute of Education Press.

D'Angour, A. (2019). *Socrates in Love: The Making of a Philosopher*. London: Bloomsbury.

Fulbrook, M. (2018). *Reckonings: Legacies of Nazi Persecution and the Quest for Justice*. Oxford: Oxford University Press.

Hosking, G. (2005). *Epochs of European Civilization: Antiquity to Renaissance*. Lecture 3: Ancient Greece. United Kingdom: The Modern Scholar via Recorded Books.

Liu, N. and Boyde, E. (2019). Hong Kong international schools to be forced to sing China anthem. *Financial Times*. 9 January.

Macmillan, M. (2018). *Managing the Unmanageable*. Lecture 2: Reith Lecture Series, BBC Radio 4. 21 July.

Plato. (2017 [380 BC]). Apology. In Plato, *The Dialogues of Plato*. London: Oxford University Press. Translated by B. Jowett.

CHAPTER FOUR

My country, my self: separation, identity, and dissonance

> *It is the symbolic codes of our first language and culture which provide the first scaffolding for the self, and our first existential maps—ways of perceiving and organizing human and social experience through which, or within which, we can feel and think.*
>
> —Eva Hoffman, from the Hubert Butler
> Annual Lecture, 2017, Kilkenny, Ireland

Masha Gessen, a Russian journalist now living in the US, writing about her parents' decision to leave Moscow for America when she was thirteen, describes the "syncope of emigration" as "the difference between discovering who I was … and discovering who I could be … It was a moment of choice and, thanks to the 'break in my destiny', I was aware of it" (Gessen, 2018). Only when there is a break in one's life does the question of identity and belonging arise. At these moments, we are faced with choice—not only between past and present, between membership in one group or another, between geographically staying and leaving—but a more fundamental choice that concerns our identity; who we see ourselves as being, what is it we believe in, and how we are perceived by others. The implicit defining relation between place, belief system, and identity is suddenly laid bare. This caesura creates a mental space within which we become acutely aware of how much our identity is linked to a complex network of loyalties, beliefs, and communities, and the traumatic impact of losing these ties, leaving us in a state of diaspora while opening up the possibility of re-defining our identity.

In this chapter I will draw on the experience of several patients who have been uprooted from their countries for different reasons and what this means to them and their families as well as the experience of rupture and dissonance when there have been dramatic political and social changes within one's country of origin. In conclusion I question the importance of individual national identity in the context of globalization and view the renewed rise of nationalism as an attempt to restore traditional forms of identity.

Rupture and restoration

Sophie had retired from being a secondary school teacher and in the ensuing months had suffered depression and insomnia. She came to see me a year later and at the start of her first session when I asked her to tell me about herself, she replied:

> I'm German, my father was Jewish and escaped to England at the beginning of the war, my mother was English. She was Church of England. My grandparents and aunt and uncle stayed in Berlin and died in the camps. I was born here in London. I've spent my life teaching children English and raising my own children. I've tried to be kind and considerate of others. I have lots of loving friends. I love my husband although he can be very dictatorial at times—his nickname at home is Hitler but he is also a kind man. I thought everything was fine in my life but since I've retired I feel like I don't know whether I'm coming or going. I don't know where I belong. I feel locked up and I don't know how to get out of this state. I don't feel myself and I'm not sure what that even means.

From Sophie's initial description of herself, it was clear she felt confused about her divided past, her German Jewish father and English Christian mother, coming from two countries at war with each other. After escaping to England, her father had met her mother, married after only a month of knowing each other, and joined the British army to fight against Hitler. During battle his left arm was injured and amputated and he lost the sight of his left eye. Sophie's childhood had been focused on behaving well, thinking of others, not making a "fuss" and strong Christian principles of "turning the other cheek" and "forgiveness." Life at home for Sophie and her little brother, Eric, was quiet and orderly, only punctuated by her father's sudden violent outbursts of anger when he exploded over relatively minor infringements and mishaps committed by the children, or at night when Sophie remembers hearing him screaming with anger and fear. Sophie's mother explained that her father was still suffering from losing his arm and his eyesight in one eye. As an adult, Sophie thought her father had probably been suffering from PTSD, but as a child, his night horrors had terrified the whole family. Sophie said that the best way to be in the family was to keep one's head down and to be as quiet and unobtrusive as possible. No arguments or expressions of anger were allowed, neither was there much laughter or spontaneity. Sophie recognized that she had managed to recreate and perpetuate this controlled environment not only in her marriage to a man who, like her father, had a fierce and volatile temper, but also in her workplace, which was a school run on highly principled Christian ideals. Her retirement had suddenly left her adrift without the security of a repressive container.

Little by little, Sophie's anger with her parents, especially with her mother, emerged. At the age of thirteen, Sophie was diagnosed with curvature of the spine and had to wear a back brace throughout her teens. As a child, Sophie had been praised for her golden hair and angelic appearance with the expectation that she would grow up to be a great beauty. This discovery of her deformity came as a severe blow and, knowing it was a genetic inheritance from her father's family, she felt betrayed by her Jewish heritage. Her Jewishness was nothing but a blight on her life. At the same time, she was angry with her mother for never standing up to her father's treatment of her and her brother and for making her feel that she had all the opportunities in the world at her feet only to have these swept away when it was evident her back was deformed. Her mother kept insisting that she would be all right and that she should be grateful for the relatively privileged life she had. Sophie had no chance to be angry or sad or fearful.

At a later session, Sophie was talking about an injury her oldest son had incurred to his knee during a football game. The doctor had warned them that a muscle had been torn badly and that his knee might never heal properly. Sophie had tried to reassure her son that it really wasn't so bad because he could do other things in his life and he still had his friends. I pointed out the similarity with her mother's response to her about her back, minimizing what a loss this had been for her, warning her not to make a "fuss" about it. Sophie then remembered an earlier moment in her life when she had been reprimanded by her father and mother for making a "fuss." She was three years old and her mother had suddenly disappeared for several days. When she asked her father where her mother was, he simply said she had gone to collect a new baby for the family. Sophie was mystified and outraged by this news. She was the baby and what did it mean to have another baby? When her mother returned from hospital with baby Eric, and urged Sophie to kiss him and make him feel welcome, she was overcome with hurt and anger. She ran to the loo and recalled locking herself in for what seemed like hours. She thought it must have been the only place where she felt it was safe to let her feelings out. Sophie was then able to compare this to the locked-in state of mind she had complained about in her first session, a no man's land where she could be hurt and angry but where she was also trapped.

As Sophie's rebelliousness against her own internal dictator strengthened, she began to be able to stand up to her husband's hegemony in the family and to discover that getting angry with other people who had hurt or bullied her could have a positive effect. She became increasingly aware of how identified she had been with her compliant, all-suffering mother as well as with her harsh, all-suffering father who had persecuted the family by taking on the role of the victim. It was at this time that the news was full of accounts of Germany's offer to reinstate German citizenship to all those who had fled due to persecution before and during World War II.[1] The offer was not only to those who had fled but extended to their offspring. Moving accounts of German immigrants applying for new passports along with their children were published in the press. For Sophie it was an opportunity to clear her family of the shame of expulsion and to reclaim what she felt was an inheritance that had been taken away from her. Through her father, Sophie had grown up with a strong sense of a highly principled and culturally rich Germany—a Germany that she associated with self-expression and freedom of thought. The country's offer to restore citizenship to those who had been persecuted became significant in Sophie's mind insofar as she saw it as a return to a set of values and beliefs that had become destroyed and perverted with the coming of the Reich. While we could both see the parallel with Sophie's own wish to return to an earlier imagined "state of grace" when she was the only baby at her mother's breast, this was not simply a nostalgic fantasy of the past. As Sophie said, "This is not just about saying we'll make everything as it was before, it's about admitting there was an injustice done to a whole group of people. I abhorred Germany before and, although it was always a silent presence in my family, I felt ashamed to be half German. I also felt ashamed to be Jewish! Now, with this door open, Germany is a country I can feel proud of."[2]

Sophie, along with her three children, acquired German passports and Sophie decided to take a trip to her "new country." She had been to Berlin before with her husband to see the areas where her father's family had lived but had felt alien, dissociated from her feelings. She had described it as looking at a kind of display case that she knew she had something to do with but at the same time had nothing to do with. It was a closed world in which she had lost any part to play. She was curious to discover what she might feel now that she had a legitimate place there.

Sophie spent two weeks traveling around Germany with one of her sons and returned eager to share her experiences with me. She said it had felt very strange to have another passport and to be traveling on a German passport. She had expected to be stopped at the German border and questioned—what right did she have to be in this country and to be holding a German passport? To her surprise, when she showed her passport to the immigration officer, he said, "Danke," and she breezed through. She felt euphoric, saying, "I was allowed back!" She then remembered that she had left her British passport at home in London and suddenly panicked. She thought that if people needed to find her, they would find her British passport and assume she was still in England and that something had happened to her. At worst she would have disappeared. Sophie remarked on this in the session as feeling it was unimaginable that she could be in two places at once. By acquiring a German identity, would her British identity disappear? Or was one identity real and the other merely a doppelgänger? Which one was real and which one a copy?

For Sophie, this entry into a "new country" which was nevertheless a country she had been connected to from birth, created a rupture in which she became aware of the importance of belonging to a specific country and what this meant to her image of herself, to her identity. As Gessen expressed, it opened up a new possibility: "This is who I could be." At the same time, it opened up the loss of "This is who I might have been." This awareness gave her a heightened sense of belonging—to both countries—and a detachment that brought home the importance of choice in aligning herself with a set of values and beliefs. While in therapy Sophie was differentiating herself from both her parents and finding her own mind, with the acquisition of her German nationality she was also discovering what it meant to see herself as German, and what it meant to be seen by others to be German. In writing about his German Jewish grandparents' assimilation into British culture, Ian Buruma observes that "identity is not only a question of how one sees oneself, but also of how one is perceived by others" (Buruma, 2016). Sophie was to find out that describing herself as German or as British produced very different responses depending on who she told.

In the aftermath of Sophie's visit, she talked about the importance of being "accepted" by Germany; she had convinced herself that taking up a German passport and entering the country as a citizen was an act of forgiveness on her part. Sophie's Christian upbringing came to my mind and I questioned whether this was in fact an act of "forgiveness" on her part or something else, asking her what she was "forgiving" them for? Sophie replied:

> Well, I suppose I see it as some admission of wrongdoing on Germany's part—and, if this is the case, it is important. But what it feels like is being recognized, that something that has been taken away from me and my family has been returned. I don't think it heals anything, but it acknowledges the theft—it was a kind of theft of our identity itself. The idea of "forgiving" the Germans now sounds a bit pompous to me—who am I to forgive them for a past I was never part of? But being given my citizenship back feels like I am no longer alien, I count as human and being German is an affirmation of this.

Sophie continued to describe her trip, particularly her impressions of Münster and Cologne. She said,

> Both cities had been severely bombed and in Münster everything had been immaculately restored as if it had never been bombed. But in every church there were before and after photos to remind people of the damage that had been done and its restoration.

She continued,

> It made me think about our work together, the repairs I've needed—but this is different from seamlessly restoring things as they once were, as if nothing has happened, as if there has been no irreparable damage. When I first came to you and felt so adrift, I had some idea that you could just put me back together again and all would be as it was before, even though "before" had its own problems. Now I can see how much my identity rested on being a victim, a victim of my parents' strict repressive regime, a victim of my bent back, a victim because I was half Jewish, and at times I have thought of myself as a victim in my marriage. I thought it could all be erased, like invisible mending. What was strange about Münster was that there were no scars and so it seemed like a replica of itself, in denial of the destruction that had been wrought. Maybe this is what it means to identify with the victim? Instead, in the cities, like Cologne, where the remnants of the bombings had become memorialized, it was a reminder of the past and this is what made it feel hopeful too.

Sophie's early loss of being the only golden baby in the family came to my mind. I commented that perhaps being allowed to enter Germany felt like trying to retrieve her special place in her mother's mind and that her reflections on Münster and Cologne signified the huge difference between wanting to eradicate her little brother's birth as if it had never happened and at the same time wanting her parents to recognize how traumatic this had been for her. I added that it was also important to see that Germany could recover from the war, just as she was discovering that her anger did not destroy her relationships with others close to her but actually strengthened them and, most importantly, that she did not have to continue to be a victim. Sophie welled up in tears and asked me, "How do you know so much about Germany?" I replied that I thought she wanted to know whether I could understand what it felt like to have something so important taken away from her and what it meant to recover from this loss and humiliation. Sophie said that she knew I understood this but her question was more how to live with this understanding, how to live with the different worlds within her, to belong to both and to be a stranger to both, and how to find her own country inside herself.

Although Sophie's father had been an immigrant, he had taken pride in his assimilation within British culture. Perhaps as a reaction to his exile from Germany, he considered his adoptive country as his real country, the country that had saved his life. For Sophie, however, this was not the case; she had grown up with the ghost of having lost her German national identity and, when she was able to recover it, it was both confusing and challenging because she was able to choose between countries freely and to hold dual citizenship. Although Sophie had been aware of the different characteristics and values of each culture, in taking up German citizenship she also became aware of how much her image of herself and her ego ideal had been shaped by her British upbringing and in particular her father's experience of assimilation. In her essay, "Heimat," Natasha Walter describes her grandparents' experience of emigrating to Britain from Germany at the start of World War II. She writes:

> Did they ever feel British? I never asked them. I doubt they would have said yes. Jews who arrived in the UK during the war were given a leaflet by the British Board of Jewish Deputies admonishing them to abide by British customs and never to speak loudly in public. They always knew that their too-German voices could disturb the British.
>
> (Walter, 2017, p. 12)

Assimilation meant repressing one's native culture and behavior, and conforming to local customs so as to "get by" without being noticed as different. In the case of Sophie's father, she felt that while he was grateful and proud to be British, it also meant that he felt he had to hide his German background and his sense of shame in having to seek refuge from a country that had rejected him because of his race. The effect this had on the family was profound and most evident in the emphasis placed on not standing out, being quiet, dutiful, not questioning authority, and apologetic if anything was out of place or at the slightest mistake. Being a good citizen meant above all being considerate of others and not putting oneself first. Sophie described her first trip to Germany as a German citizen as a strange liberation.

> I entered the country, no questions asked and no mention of my imperfect German, and thought to myself, "Now I can be another person, not a person who cannot be a certain way, who is restricted, but a person who can be proud of myself and assertive." It's not that being German means being better, but it suddenly felt as if some of the expected behavior I grew up with was redundant and I was allowed to be loud and to say what I thought without endlessly qualifying it. It wasn't just that I could see myself differently, I was also seen differently by others. And being seen to be German made me feel different speaking the language; we did not speak German at home but when I was in Germany it felt like slipping into another skin. I no longer felt alien. During my time there I became different in myself.[3]

Sophie likened her experience of being re-connected to her father's family and her German roots as that of a frozen limb that is gradually coming back to life, painful at first and then a relief that she has recovered its feeling and use. This was also a metaphor for Sophie's experience in analysis as her repressed feelings surfaced and she became less censorious of herself.

Renunciation

While Sophie's experience of rupture was one that entailed a recovery of the past and its meaning and a restoration in some way of what had been lost, this is a very different experience from people who have had to renounce or flee their country of origin. For those in exile, the rupture with the past can be an overwhelming loss from which there can only be a partial recovery at best. Economic refugees, fleeing their country in order to survive and to create a better life, retain the possibility of future return or reunion, notwithstanding the reality. Political refugees, however, face permanent exile; they can never return to their country unless there is radical regime change.

This was the case for another patient of mine, Aaron, who featured in Chapter Two. Aaron's family had fled to the UK from what was effectively a genocidal civil war in their country of origin. Although Aaron had returned to serve in the army, the escalation in violence against his family's ethnic group made any further return impossible. Both his parents' families had been robbed of their land in a redistribution of property that effectively negated their tribe's histories and rights. Aaron's childhood had been overshadowed by his parents' dislocation, their depression, and his desperate attempts to make up for what his parents had lost. His father had become a very successful businessman, amassing a fortune and trying to convince his children that this was the only form of security in a precarious world. Aaron, trying to please his father, had pursued different jobs in the financial world with some success but then, aware of the extent to which investments rely on corrupt governments or work practices, he felt he could not ethically continue to operate in this world.

Aaron felt that his family had been blighted by racism and corruption. There was widespread, open corruption in his country of origin but there was also the corrosive effect of assimilation on his family's sense of self and identity. Aaron's father presented two personas to his family; his public persona of self-denigration as a means of "keeping his head down" within a racist, xenophobic society, similar to what Sophie had witnessed in her father, and a private persona of being proud of his national identity and origins. Aaron experienced his father's self-denigration as unbearably shameful and vowed to himself to not only try to restore what had been taken away from his family but to create a new life for himself in which he did not need to depend on others and compromise his values and his identity.

Trying to resolve the conflicts of his family and their losses, as well as his own fragmented identity, Aaron turned to the dream of becoming a self-sufficient farmer. In possessing his own land, he wanted to compensate for the land his family had been robbed of and to create a new self-sustaining country for his family to regain a sense of themselves as connected to a place that belonged to them. Just as Aaron's father had become obsessed with accumulating money as a way of ensuring security, Aaron viewed the ownership of land as the only way to ensure a secure identity. Land symbolized for Aaron the primary attachment that he and his family had been severed from; in his mind, no other attachment could be formed until he could feel that he had realized this vision. It was a doubly powerful vision in its purity from corruption, from the shame of debasement that was associated with dependency and loss of agency; a paradise lost. As Aaron described his fantasy of his new life as a farmer, living off the produce of his land, tilled by his hand, and becoming the provider for his extended family, I had a foreboding that the reality might be far more painful, as Aaron could not overturn the present, much less the past.[4]

In his analysis, Aaron was able to understand over time how his vow of not allowing himself to be attached to anyone or anything until he was able to establish his own belonging to an actual place had served as a defense against further loss and a barrier to developing. At the same time, I felt Aaron was right in his insistence that he needed to claim a place as his own, not only metaphorically but physically. Without this, would he ever be able to feel that he had the possibility of choice in his life and an end to exile? Writing on migration, Jenny Erpenbeck questions, "When you've arrived, can you still be said to be fleeing? And when you're fleeing, can you ever arrive?" (Erpenbeck, 2011, p. 102). Erpenbeck highlights the fluid, in-between state of being in exile, and the tenuous sense of belonging and not belonging that dislocates and ruptures identity.

Language

One of the most acute experiences of dislocation is language itself, whether it is an entirely different language or a loss or censorship of language. Our mother tongue is a fundamental aspect of our identity that shapes the way we perceive the world, our culture, our relationships, and our conception of ourselves. The Somalian writer, Nurrudin Farah, stresses,

> Here [in Somalia], mother tongue is important, very important.
> Not what one looks like. The Somali are a homogenous people;
> they are homogenous culturally speaking and speak the same

language wherever they may be found ... The Somali in the Ogaden [under Ethiopian rule], the Somali in Kenya ... lack what makes the self strong and whole, are *unpersons*.

(Farah, 1986, pp. 174–175)

Languages reflect and create different structures of experience and thought. Farah is pointing out that estrangement from one's mother tongue is equivalent to alienation from one's primary identity.

One's mother tongue is also a reminder of the country that has been lost and the ambivalence associated with what is left behind. In Ocean Vuong's novel, *On Earth We're Briefly Gorgeous*, the narrator, the son of a Vietnamese refugee, writes of his mother and his truncated heritage:

As a girl, you watched, from a banana grove, your schoolhouse collapse after an American napalm raid. At five, you never stepped into a classroom again. Our mother tongue, then, is no mother at all—but an orphan. Our Vietnamese a time capsule, a mark of where your education ended, ashed. Ma, to speak in our mother tongue is to speak only partially in Vietnamese, but entirely in war.

(Vuong, pp. 31–32)

Language carries its own personal and collective history. Language and accent place us, signifying whether someone is an outsider or a native, a member of an ethnic group, or from a certain economic and cultural class. Sophie became particularly aware of these nuances when she went to Germany as a newly reinstated citizen, speaking the language of her father and his family, and the consequent internal shift that took place in her perception of herself as a long-lost relative, both alien and belonging.

The Croatian writer, Dasa Drndic, powerfully describes the profound alienation that is transmitted through the use, and in this case political censorship, of language. A Serbian narrates her experience shopping for a scarf in Croatia:

[T]here are a lot of elegantly dressed people here, because, they say, elegance is a tradition here, ingrained, it goes back to Austro-Hungarian days. So I go from shop to shop and ask, *Do you have escarpe?*

The salesgirls look at me blankly, and out of spite I'm not going to describe what it is. Some salesgirls are obliging, some are not exactly, obliging, although on the whole people here are civil, they keep their distance … One salesgirl purses her lips into an "o" and through her pursed lips she says *Ooo, you must be Ortho-dox*. I say, *???!!!* with raised eyebrows, I can't see the connection between *echarpe/esarpa* and Orthodoxy, which is a euphemism for Serbianness here. The salesgirl then says that in their language my *echarpe/esarpa* is called a *padela* and that I'm in the wrong shop, to which I say that I'm not in the wrong shop but in the wrong town and possibly the wrong country. In the Dalmatian dialect *padela* means cooking pot or pan, from the Italian *padella*, which in Serbian is *serpa*, not *esarpa*, so the salesgirl was in the wrong shop, not I.

(Drndic, 2015, loc. 1444–1457)

National and cultural supremacy are established in this instance by denigrating and debasing the other's language; the insinuation is that the Serbian woman is not only in the wrong shop but that her very identity is out of place.

While being foreign, the outsider, signified most immediately by language and gesture, as in Drndic's illustration, can make someone feel alienated and rejected, it can also have a liberating effect. Ian Buruma describes the experience of an American friend who had lived for many years in Japan:

He, Donald, felt entirely at ease as an outsider. The great thing about Japan, he said, was that one was left alone. To be Japanese in Japan was to be caught in an almost intolerable web of rules and obligations. But the gaijin (foreigner) was exempt from all that. He could observe life with serene detachment, not being bound to anything or anyone. In Japan, Donald felt utterly, radically free.

(Buruma, 2018, p. 36)

The double estrangement from one's native country and not belonging within another country, made especially pronounced by a different language, not only allows for self-invention but more importantly for Buruma it is a means of being aware of one's inner self. He writes:

> Mimicking Japanese figures of speech, or even adopting the physical mannerisms that go with a language—the bobbing of the head in half bows when speaking on the phone, smiling all the while—sometimes made me feel like an actor in real life. One would like to think that operating in a different culture is enriching. And so it is. But there are moments when the performer in a foreign language feels that he is leaving something of himself behind, or, to put it differently, that the foreign language is just a mask, concealing something more real, whatever that something may be. I would sometimes resort to odd defense mechanisms. One method was to deliberately exaggerate the Japanese mannerisms, turning them into a kind of parody. This performance could very well come across as a form of mockery. But it had a distancing effect. It gave me the illusion, at least, that I was holding on to an essential part of myself.
>
> (ibid., p. 170)

Here imitation reveals the essence of both what is being re-created and its creator, the imitator. The rupture of culture and otherness is elided through the playfulness of the performance. This is in marked contrast to the rejection of the "other," when rupture or difference is perceived as threatening and destroys our capacity for symbolic exchange and the conception of different realities.

Dissonance

We do not have to be geographically displaced to experience a rupture in our social identity; ruptures of this kind can also take place "at home." What many of us can relate to and what is perhaps more commonly experienced and more mundane, and therefore less visible, is the experience of political dissonance when one's country's ideology or ideals—the ideals one has identified with as self-defining and signify national identity—become overtaken and denigrated by a new set of ideals. This happens at moments of political and social upheaval when there is an emergence of radical change in the culture, a rupture with the past and its norms and expectations, whether conservative or liberal, regressive or progressive. Modern-day examples of this can be seen in the rise of the Third Reich, the collapse of the Soviet Union, along with the thawing of the Cold War and the fall of communism in East Germany in 1989, the recent wave of populism and isolationism in the US, the rise of fascism in different parts of Europe, and the move toward the nation-state in reaction to globalization.

Although these political ruptures do not affect the geographical location or dislocation of where people live, they can profoundly affect their sense of belonging and their actual identity. The loss or attack on a set of beliefs that has formed the basis for people's ideals and behavior provokes depression, alienation, and ultimately anomie within the group that has lost power. As one American psychologist writes, protesting against the US detention and separation of children from their illegal immigrant parents, "Today, I no longer recognize the country we live in" (Beren, 2018). This sentiment is widely expressed by the so-called liberal elite in the US against Trump's authoritarian leadership and the overturning of American principles of justice and equality for all, freedom of speech, and the separation of powers. As populist and nationalist movements gain strength not only in the US but in the UK and across Europe, large segments of the population of these countries have become estranged, experiencing a kind of existential shock at the radical change occurring in belief systems and the denigration of democratic principles. Ironically, the backlash against the ruling "liberal elites" was fueled by a similar sense of alienation amongst the population who felt that their America had been taken over and altered by interlopers. Trump's battle cry, "Let's Make America Great Again," voiced precisely this estrangement from an idealized image of America that many felt had been lost.

This disaffection with changing social and political values is hardly a new phenomenon; indeed, social dissatisfaction can be understood generally as an indicator of dissonance within societies. In his memoir, *The World of Yesterday*, published in 1942, Stefan Zweig mourns the loss of a world he can no longer identify with that has changed beyond recognition. He writes:

> I must acknowledge with dismay that for a long time past I
> have not belonged to the people of my country any more than
> I belong to the English or the Americans. To the former I am
> no longer organically bound; to the latter I have never become

wholly linked. My feeling is that the world in which I grew up, and the world of today, and the world between the two, are entirely separate worlds.

(Zweig, Preface, p. xix)

Shortly after finishing his memoir, Zweig committed suicide.

The initial, often seemingly trivial, shifts that are the forerunners of more fundamental ruptures are described in Sebastian Haffner's haunting memoir of Nazi Germany, *Defying Hitler*. Haffner writes:

> I felt, intensely, the choking nauseous character of it all, but I was unable to grasp its constituent parts and place them in an overall order. Each attempt was frustrated and veiled by those endless, useless, vain discussions in which we attempted again and again to fit the events into an obsolete, unsuitable scheme of political ideas … Strangely enough, it was just this automatic continuation of ordinary life that hindered any lively, forceful reaction against the horror.
>
> (Haffner, 2003, pp. 113–114)

Haffner captures the paralyzing effect of living within an ever increasing state of dissonance, the "vain discussions" trying to make sense of what is happening to his world and the "continuation of ordinary life" that normalizes what would otherwise be out of the ordinary and unthinkable.

Rather than the often cited assumption that many Germans during the Reich had no idea of the atrocities that were occurring as the war progressed, there is increasing evidence that this was not the case.[5] But this does not, of course, mean that open dissent was possible. Friedrich Kellner, in his diary, entitled posthumously *My Opposition: A German Against the Third Reich*, produces a wealth of evidence that he, his friends and acquaintances, and others from his area knew a great deal about what was going on. Kellner asserts that "among like-minded acquaintances I pull out all the stops. I criticize every action of these Nazi subhumans with the strongest persuasive power I can muster" (Kellner, 2018, p. 67). Kellner is careful, however, to share his views only "among like-minded acquaintances," referring to attempts "to rein me in" (ibid., p. 67).

Knowing that "the truth may not be said," it is possible that Kellner was able to manage the dissonance between his own world and the external world in which he was living by being able to write his thoughts freely within his diary, a diary no one was to see until after his death. It may also have helped him to maintain his identity, and his sanity, while appearing to comply with what was required of citizens of the Reich.

Conformity, at least in behavior, is not only a means of survival but is a way of adapting to a changed belief system and in doing so creating an illusion of normality and continuity in the face of rupture. In her two-volume history, *Dissonant Lives: Generations and Violence Through the German Dictatorships*, Mary Fulbrook recounts an interview with a woman born in the GDR in the 1950s. The woman, Renate B., describes her working life, starting with learning how to be a sales assistant "in a perfectly normal way." She worked in a "normal sales outlet" and proceeded to be promoted "in a perfectly normal way" until finally she reached the highest stage, "that is as a normal colleague." Fulbrook comments:

> In this "perfectly normal" pattern, Renate B. did all the expected and usual things by way of training and work … through what she portrays as very little of her own agency … While it can be argued that the emphasis on "normality" was a post-unification defensive strategy, neither in Renate B.'s interview, nor in many others on similar lines is there any attempt to downplay what they saw as the "bad sides" of life. The use of "normal" references rather expected patterns, aspirations and achievements in a relatively predictable social world.
>
> (Fulbrook, 2011, pp. 122–123)

While those living within the GDR had to conform to the new communist system, Fulbrook points out that "this did not necessarily mean that memories were suppressed, and that legacies of the past did not linger on" (ibid., p. 124).

The need to "normalize" our experience in the wake of social and political rupture is paramount for our survival; adapting to new norms provides continuity, predictability, and some sense of security that we all need in order to maintain a sense of self and belonging to a group or community—even when these new norms may be antithetical to the beliefs and values of the old order. Freud recognized our instinctual need to be part of a group, both in terms of our physical and our emotional survival. Erich Fromm, in *Escape from Freedom*, echoes the importance of belonging, as he writes, "The kind of relatedness to the world may be noble or trivial, but even being related to the basest kind of pattern is immensely preferable to being alone" (Fromm, 1941, p. 34). Fromm quotes from Balzac's *The Inventor's Suffering*, "man has a horror for aloneness. And of all kinds of aloneness, moral aloneness is the most terrible" (ibid., p. 35).

While the adoption of new norms is necessary for our survival, this is under conditions of force when there is no choice except to conform; the alternative is to be expelled, to be criminalized, or to be killed.[6] However, ruptures also occur when there is a shift from a totalitarian system toward a more liberal, democratic one. These ruptures may be just as difficult to manage as repressive ones. The shift from a totalitarian regime toward one in which the individual is held to be responsible for taking care of himself signifies a profound loss and often creates an estrangement and disorientation of its own.

This is dramatically portrayed in the film *Cold War* by the Polish filmmaker, Pawel Pawlikowski (2018), set in Poland in the 1950s. A musical director is auditioning young singers and dancers who will perform traditional Polish folk songs as a tribute to the Polish communist state. He selects a promising and beguiling young blonde woman and they quickly becoming entangled in a passionate, illicit romance that must be kept secret at all costs. As the troupe becomes increasingly successful inside and outside Poland, state control over the content of the songs and the politicization of the performances tightens commensurately. Following a scene of intense love-making, the musician indicates that he wants to defect to the West and asks his lover if she will come with him. She discloses that she is being used as an informant against him, and in doing so asserts both her power over him and her ambivalence toward the state. She nevertheless agrees to defect with him but, at the assigned moment, fails to join him. The director forms a new life for himself in Paris but it is a transient half-life as he yearns for his Polish lover who, at the same time, represents for him the country he has left behind, a country that has tried to control him but from which he cannot entirely separate.

After years of contrived meetings when the lover's troupe is performing abroad, the lover eventually joins him in Paris. He introduces her
to a fashionable, influential and rich circle, encourages her to adapt her
Polish folk songs into American jazz, creates a hit record of her songs
and turns her into a success overnight. It is a trajectory of success that
is emblematic of what the West appears to offer—a pathway to individual recognition and self-expression. Despite, or perhaps because of, her
success, the singer is restless in her new surroundings and melancholic.
Following the glamorous debut of her new album, as she is carried home
in a drunken state in the arms of the musician, the singer turns to him,
saying, "In Poland you were a man. You're different here ... Maybe I just
imagined things ... But everything is wonderful. We are in Paris. I love
you with all my heart." The next day, she disappears back to Poland.
Although "everything is wonderful," it is different, the director is not
a man in Paris, nothing is quite real or to be trusted. It seems that she
cannot cross the boundary into her new life, the rupture is too much,
and she returns home, to the state that she knows and that is both her
existence and her exile.

When the musician discovers that his lover has disappeared, he goes
to the Polish Embassy to try to obtain re-entry. He is interviewed by an
administrator who says to him,

> "Honestly, I don't know how to help you. You're not French and you're
> not a Pole either. As far as we're concerned, you don't exist. But between
> you and me ... why on earth would you want to leave this place?"
>
> "I'm Polish."
>
> "Please, stop it."
>
> "I am."
>
> "You ran away. You betrayed us. You let down young people who
> trusted you. You don't love Poland."
>
> "I do."
>
> "No you don't ... But there is a solution. If you truly regret your deeds.
> You have a certain position in artistic circles here. You know all kinds of
> émigré."

We are transported back to the bleak, cold landscape of Poland as we
watch the singer traveling to the prison where the musician has been

interned. They meet in a bare room sitting at either end of a long table. She is dressed in black like a peasant in mourning. He is in a prison uniform, his head shaved, and we see that his fingers have been crushed and destroyed. The singer hands the guard some money to leave them alone. The musician looks at her lovingly, saying,

> "You look terrible."
>> "How many years?"
>> "Fifteen … Apparently I'm lucky. Illegal border crossings in both directions and it turns out I spied for the British."

She crosses the room, touches his cheek with her fingertips, and they are reunited in a world in which they are both imprisoned and in which the only release is suicide, the ultimate attack against the betrayals and the punishments that have bound them together and bound them to their homeland.

The love story is not simply one of ill-fated lovers caught in a sado-masochistic tug of war of rejection and longing; it portrays the powerful conflict of leaving a tyrannical country that nevertheless had formed the couples' identity. As the singer recognized, they could not be "themselves" outside of this culture—the musician was "different" in Paris—but, ironically, they could not be free to be "themselves" in Poland either.

The difficulty of leaving what we perceive as controlling, totalitarian regimes is often attributed to the difficulty of living within a system in which total care (or something approaching that) is provided in exchange for complete, unquestioning loyalty and adherence to higher authority. This seemingly alleviates the need to be responsible for one's own life or thoughts. The Polish journalist, Witold Szabłowski, writing about the fall of communism, compares peoples' experience of their new-found freedom to the enforced release of the dancing bears of the Bulgarian Gypsies that also occurred at this time. He writes:

> I learned that for every retired dancing bear, the moment comes when freedom starts to cause it pain. What does it do then? It gets up on its hind legs and starts to dance. It repeats the very thing the park employees are trying their best to get it to unlearn: the behaviour of the captive. As if it would prefer its keeper to come

back and take responsibility for its life again. "Let him beat me, let him treat me badly, but let him relieve me of this goddamned need to deal with my own life," the bear seems to be saying.

(Szabłowski, 2014, Introduction, p. xvi)

Freedom is interpreted as overwhelming and frightening with the mantle of individual responsibility too much to bear. Is this, however, a convincing argument for the bear's reversion to old behavior patterns, or the nostalgia experienced by people whose life under communism has ended? Is the rupture of an original attachment, whether it is to the Gypsy bear keeper or the state regime, not more to the point as a complex loss that is very hard to mourn and separate from? It is perhaps comparable to the extreme separation anxiety and guilt that is apparent with patients who have had ambivalent early attachments. If the original love object is wholly cruel and frightening, there is relatively little problem in rejecting it. However, even in extremely abusive relationships, there is more often than not some element of attachment that is experienced as life-giving and therefore necessary. In this context, rejecting the relationship can be experienced as not only life-threatening but, perhaps just as powerfully, as threatening one's identity, an identity that has been founded on this particular kind of relationship. Any rupture in this relationship is therefore a rupture in how one sees and defines oneself, as well as how we imagine we are seen by others. This is not the same level of discourse as what it means to be free; it cannot be reduced to an experience of responsibility over oneself because "freedom" in this context requires the loss of a system of beliefs which have shaped and guided our sense of ourselves within the group we belong to.

The Russian journalist, Svetlana Alexievich, in her numerous interviews of Russian citizens witnessing the collapse of the USSR, depicts the terrible loss of meaning and consequent angst experienced by so many people whose dreams of the future and vision of life had been so inextricably tied to the powerful ideologies of Leninist and Stalinist Russia (Alexievich, 2016).

One woman reminisces:

Those were Soviet times … Communist. We were raised on Lenin, fiery revolutionaries, so fiery, we didn't consider the Revolution an error and a crime. Although we weren't into that Marxist-Leninist stuff either. The Revolution was something abstract to us … Most of all, I remember the holidays and the anticipation leading up to them. I remember it all very vividly … overall, everybody seemed happy. There was music everywhere. My mother was young and beautiful. Everyone was together … I remember all this as happiness … Those smells, those sounds … The bang of the typewriter keys, the morning cries of the milkmaids … String bags full of raw chickens hung from the window frames. People decorated their windows, filling the space between two window-panes with glittery cotton and green apples. The stray cat smell wafting up from the basements … And how about the inimitable bleach and rag smell of Soviet cafeterias? These things may seem unrelated, but for me, they have all merged into a single sensation. A unified feeling. Freedom has different smells … different images … Everything about it is different. One of my friends, after her first trip abroad—this was already when Gorbachev was in power … she returned with the words, "Freedom smells like a good sauce." … The outside world would be revealed to us later. Back then, we only dreamed of it … About the things we didn't have, the things we wanted … It felt nice to dream of a world we knew nothing about … We had no doubt that our generation would go on living that way … Then something happened … [following Gorbachev's resignation in 1991] … We came down to earth. The happiness and euphoria suddenly broke. Into a million different pieces. I quickly realized that the new world wasn't mine, it wasn't for me. It required another breed of person.

(Alexievich, 2016, pp. 237–242)

This woman's testimony encompasses the complex mixture of cultural experiences that form our memory and, inevitably, our sense of who we are and how we locate ourselves. For this woman and many of her generation, revolutionary change brought about a new world that was suddenly devoid of meaning, alien, and required "another breed of person." Significantly, the new world described by the narrator is driven by material acquisition and success. She remembered:

The first thing to go was friendship ... Suddenly, everyone was too busy, they had to go make money. Before, it had seemed like we didn't need money at all ... that it had no bearing on us. Suddenly, everyone saw the beauty of green bills ... We turned out to be ill-suited for the new world we'd been waiting for. We were expecting something else, not this.

(ibid., p. 243)

The new world vision had changed radically; there was no sense of an overarching ideology aimed at building a collective future, the present was what mattered and actual wealth was what conferred status, power, and value.[7] The sense of identity that had been aligned so deeply with political ideology was suddenly set adrift.

The complaints of meaninglessness voiced by Alexievich's witnesses are strikingly similar to the interviews recorded by Fulbrook of those who had lived under the German Democratic Republic after the fall of communism. On the eve of the demise of the GDR, one woman writes:

If only one did not have to feel so afraid, today I would hang the DDR-flag out of my window with a wreath ... Today is for me just a farewell party ... The bad thing about it is that one can now do absolutely nothing any more, that one can't prevent it ... We are heading into life in a state that is totally foreign to us ...

(Fulbrook, 2011, p. 211)

Another woman, writing in her diary, describes this painful turning point:

Now only a few hours separate us from the historical event of the unification of the two German states. It is painful, as though someone were trying to tear apart my body and my soul. From tomorrow I will no longer have a Fatherland, I will first have to feel my way around the new one. That will take a while. One can't simply step out of one's body and look for a new one.

(ibid., pp. 211–212)

Another woman suffers a deep depression, writing:

> No one asks me for my advice any more, my experiences, my
> learning and my knowledge count also—as with so many—for
> nothing any more! ... I stand by my identity, I won't and can't
> deny my past (like so many are doing today!) ... I can't battle on
> any more, and ask myself: Have I perhaps lived, worked and been
> involved in vain?
>
> (ibid., p. 213)

Fulbrook comments that for the East Germans, unification not only
meant adjusting to a new culture and a new narrative of their own past,
but it

> had deep implications for people's personal identities, their very
> sense of self. It was, then not just a matter of anomie and not
> being able effectively to play the new "rules of the game"; nor a
> matter of inadequate depiction and understanding; but also of a
> far more fundamental challenge to identities that had been con-
> structed over decades in a set of social relations that were now
> being dismantled.
>
> (ibid., p. 212)

Whether the causes for these political and social ruptures are seen to
lead to a more or less beneficial state is secondary to the impact of loss
that is experienced regardless of the outcome. As Fulbrook points out,
it is not simply the loss of a political ideology along with its contingent
social structures, it is a loss of identity itself. We find meaning in the
ideals and values we hold in our lives—our *Weltanschauung* orientates
us in the world, providing a framework both for allegiance and dissent.
When this is eroded, attacked, and replaced by a different system of
beliefs, it is hardly surprising that it creates a breach of identity.

Statelessness and exile

I have looked at different aspects of political rupture and its effect on
our sense of identity. However, in the examples I have given, the people
caught in the rupture are in a state of transition and, no matter how

painful this may be and no matter how difficult it may be to adapt, there is nevertheless a new world to which they will belong. The mental in-between state of alienation or exile rests on the knowledge or belief that there is a place of arrival and a harbor of relative safety. In other words, there is still the assurance of having a home, even if it is not a familiar one. This is not the case for the displaced who have left their country of origin and remain stateless, those in refugee camps, trapped at borders, or denied citizenship. Once people become stateless, although they retain their cultural identity inevitably, they lose their entitlement to national identity and along with this the protections ensured by being a citizen, whether it is in a totalitarian or a democratic society. A Kashmiri man vividly describes the threat to Muslims of being expelled from their homeland:

> "The fear is now of losing our dignity, our honor, our respect, and basically becoming aliens in our own land because anybody can come and just grab our land and have it. And losing our identity is the greatest fear we have now ... In practical terms, we could literally be reduced to a place like Gaza where people come, they take your land away and you're just pushed to a corner where you've absolutely no rights."
>
> (Channel 4 News, 12 August 2019)

Recognition of territorial rights to land and place is vital to the identity of a group, not only culturally, but because the possession of land confers rights of belonging and protection within the group.

Hannah Arendt, in *The Origins of Totalitarianism*, stresses the vital importance to our identity and actual existence of belonging within a state. During the Third Reich, the establishment of concentration camps came to demarcate zones of people who had effectively been uprooted (Jews, homosexuals, criminals, prisoners of war, and so on) and made stateless. In the world of the camps, prisoners had no rights and were stripped of their identity. Arendt notes that for the prisoners in the camps, "being nothing but human was their greatest danger. Because of it they were regarded as savages and, afraid that they might end by being considered beasts, they insisted on their nationality, the last sign of their former citizenship, as their only remaining and recognized tie with humanity" (Arendt, 1951, p. 392). Without the protection of a state, the conditions and norms that we associate with being human unravel. Commenting on the aftermath of World War I with large migrant groups who were neither welcome nor could be assimilated into other countries, Arendt observes:

> Once they had left their homeland they remained homeless, once they had left their state they became stateless; once they had been deprived of their human rights they were rightless, the scum of the earth. Nothing which was being done, no matter how stupid, no matter how many people knew and foretold the consequences, could be undone or prevented. Every event had the finality of a last judgment, a judgment that was passed neither by God nor by the devil, but looked rather like the expression of some unredeemably stupid fatality.
>
> (ibid., p. 349)

Arendt's observations are relevant today as Europe reacts against the threat of immigration. She describes the predicament of the stateless:

> The stateless person, without right to residence and without the right to work, had of course constantly to transgress the law. He was liable to jail sentences without ever committing a crime. More than that, the entire hierarchy of values which pertain in civilized countries was reversed in his case. Since he was the anomaly for whom the general law did not provide, it was better for him to become an anomaly for which it did provide, that of the criminal.
>
> (ibid., p. 374)

Arendt's point that the stateless person is an anomaly within society is an important one. Not only does this leave the person without legal rights and protections but, as an "outsider," the stateless person becomes a social threat because he cannot be categorized within the group and as such presents the group with a physical reminder of expulsion from the group and what this means. The contrast of the anomaly both challenges and crystallizes group identity and group norms. Arendt suggests that one form of assimilation that can be imposed by the group is to re-define the stateless person as a "criminal." Paradoxically, this label brings the stateless person within the remit of the state, neutralizing his anomalous state, while it normalizes the stateless person as a "criminal." A vivid example of this process of labeling is Trump's election campaign description of Mexican illegal "aliens" as "drug dealers, murderers and rapists," deliberately sent across the border by the Mexican government. Trump declared that as a result of this "caravan" of illegal immigrants, "Women are raped at levels that have never been seen before" (Jacobs, 2018).

The effect of this sleight of hand in demonizing the immigrant, stateless group is to create a homogenous narrative that characterizes the group as a whole and, ultimately, dehumanizes them. As we saw in the Nazi drive for ethnic cleansing, the "outsider" is perceived as a mortal threat to survival of the group, as vermin threatening to pollute and destroy the group.

Our need to belong to a group is not just a necessary determinant of our identity, personal and social; it is necessary for our actual survival. The "outsider" who has been expelled or has fled from his country of origin confronts us with one of our most profound fears, not belonging. Without the signifiers of belonging, what is left of identity? Nurrudin Farah's narrator, a young boy called Askar, himself a refugee, comes across a young girl who is also a lone refugee. He holds his hand out to her and she shies away from being touched, explaining, "Because I am standing in a skin I've borrowed." Askar asks what else she has borrowed and she replies, "The tongue I'm speaking with isn't mine either ... all I own, the only thing that I can hold on to for as long as I want, the one and only thing no one has come for so far, is, would you believe it, a shadow?" (Farah, 1986, p. 136).

Amor Towles, in his novel about an aristocrat exiled by the Bolsheviks to a hotel in Moscow for the rest of his life, emphasizes the importance of holding on to the accoutrements of a past identity that has been in effect obliterated.

> From primitive tribes to the most advanced societies, someone has occasionally been told by his fellow men to pack his bags, cross the border, and never set foot on his native soil again. But perhaps this was to be expected. After all, exile was the punishment that God meted out to Adam in the very first chapter of the human comedy; and that He meted out to Cain a few pages later.

> Yes, exile was as old as mankind. But the Russians were the first
> people to master the notion of sending a man into exile at home.
>
> (Towles, 2017, p. 163)

The Count in Towles' story adapts to the world of the hotel, which becomes a metaphor for a new country, a country of transience with hotel guests from across the world coming and going, and in contrast a place of imprisonment for the Count. What enables the Count to assimilate within his new surroundings is, ironically, his identity as an aristocrat, that is, the "good manners" and respect for others that are a prerequisite to a position of privilege. The Count is also able to save certain family heirlooms and artifacts from his past life that provide a sense of history and belonging for him. In the end, however, he cannot continue living in this timeless world that is both sanctuary and prison, and escapes to return to his birthplace where, despite the fact that the traces of his past have been eradicated, he is nevertheless "at home."

No-man's-land

A young man came to see me suffering from what he described as an "identity crisis." He felt lost and didn't know who he was or what he wanted. His family had fled from their country of origin during a time of war and could no longer return without the threat of imprisonment or death. The country continued to be a dangerous place for foreigners or former citizens to return to. The young man had been born in the UK and had never set foot in the country where his family came from. He described the strange feeling he had when he was asked where he was from and could only answer that he was from the country of his family but had never been there. At the age of five, when his British teacher asked where he was born, he replied, "In a British Airways airplane." This aptly portrayed his state of dislocation, of being neither here nor there, but truly in a no-man's-land. As Pico Iyer, writing about the meaning of home, comments, "it is hard to get your bearings in mid-air" (Iyer, 2013).

Iyer explores what home means in the context of increasing globalization and the erosion of boundaries defining nation-states and our identification with our countries of origin. Born in the UK, of Indian origin, living in the US, and spending time in Japan, Iyer's experience of multinational and cultural identifications is shared by an increasing number of people. But what is markedly different about Iyer and others like him to the stateless refugee or those whose country has undergone fundamental political change is that the multinationals like Iyer have by and large chosen their locations; they have not been forced to move. Although this does not mean that their identifications are unproblematic, the fact that they have made such choices gives them a sense of agency that is experienced differently by the person who has been uprooted by force. The multinational is both an insider and an outsider at the same time, not fully belonging and therefore always exotic, but also belonging by right of being legally recognized and given a place within a new country. Environmental attitudes can either facilitate acceptance and the possibility of assimilation (whatever this may mean or however it is desired) or, if they are adverse, can deepen alienation and rejection.

While I am making a somewhat arbitrary distinction between these two groups, their national identities and experiences of dislocation are also deeply influenced by their family backgrounds. For someone who is fleeing from an abusive family and moves country to do so, he may feel as alienated as a stateless refugee because the meaning of home internally is a place of violence. Seeking a new, benign home may be desired but the attachment to belonging to one's old home remains very powerful, as we can see in the film *Cold War*. For the person who has come from a more benign and stable family background, separations can be managed without so much anxiety. In this case, there is also a stronger sense of family identity that enables adaptation to different cultures and circumstances to be more pliable as a sense of self can be maintained in the face of change.

Conclusion

We all have multiple experiences of belonging to various groups at different levels. Our first awareness of belonging is as a child in relation to a parent and then as a member of a family, however that is comprised. We also belong to local communities, towns, cities, and a nation, as well as having ethnic and religious affiliations. Someone may consider himself Muslim and American at the same time and this may only become problematic or even come into consciousness when there is a conflict between belonging to these two large groups, as, for example, evident in the rise of racism in the US. But the reason why these conflicts are so disturbing and disorienting is that they touch the core of our identity; they split us not only externally but create an internal psychic split and reveal to us how important these affiliations are to our sense of ourselves and who we are. The split is not only between affiliations that come into conflict; it is more importantly between the value systems and sets of beliefs that inform the individual's ego ideal. When these are at odds, an internal splitting occurs that is hard to reconcile and threatens to place the ego into exile.

The concept of national identity[8] may be thought of as a relatively recent historical phenomenon linked to the rise of nationalism and the idea of the nation-state, originating in the seventeenth century with the Peace of Westphalia. From this point onwards, the nation-state brought together the political and cultural entities of large groups and established national sovereignty. We can think of the developing differentiation between political and cultural territories as a reflection of, or coinciding with, the growing social importance attributed to the individual, along with citizen's rights and duties. Whereas prior to this a part of one's individual identity may have been located in smaller groups or tribes, with the idea of one's country as being more fluid and diverse, the concept of nationalism brought with it a more distinctive large-group identity that melded with pre-existing cultural values. This combination of cultural values tied to governance has shaped much of our current-day political thinking and behavior, and it has also formed the basis for our large-group identities to the extent that it ranks as a "primary identity."[9] In describing national identity as "primary," I am not saying that it has supremacy over other group identifications but that it is one of the principal ways in which we define ourselves and our relation to others. Our individual identity with our country stems from our primary experience within our families as part of a large group. For many of us who have grown up within the embrace of the nation-state, this provides the largest and perhaps most significant overarching group that shapes and determines our lives.

"My country" is indeed an integral part of who I am. If we accept this, is this a fundamental reason why the erosion of the nation-state that we are witnessing with globalization is so threatening, not only to large-group identities, but to our own individual identity? The reversion to nationalism that is sweeping across the world may be seen as a kind of global identity crisis, taking us back to the safety of borders that differentiate us from others and sustain large-group identities of the past. Are we in fact experiencing a new kind of dissonance in which the nation-state is being superseded by international corporations and our large-group identities are in flux, or as with my patient, born in mid-air?

Notes

1. Restoration of German citizenship is provided under Article 116 par. 2 of the Basic Law (*Grundgesetz*). This stipulates: "Former German citizens who between January 30, 1933 and May 8, 1945 were deprived of their citizenship on political, racial, or religious grounds, and their descendants, shall on application have their citizenship restored. They shall be deemed never to have been deprived of their citizenship if they have established their domicile in Germany after May 8, 1945 and have not expressed a contrary intention."

   The result of the Brexit referendum in the UK on 23 June 2016 prompted many UK citizens from German backgrounds, unhappy at the thought of leaving Europe, to apply for German citizenship. By October 2016, the German Embassy in London reported a twentyfold increase in the number of applications.

2. Not all emigrants share this feeling or want to take up German citizenship. Harry Heber, aged eighty-five, fled from Innsbruck, Austria, to Britain at the age of seven. When asked about whether he would apply for an Austrian passport, he replied, "I think people who are doing that need their brains examined … The proposition of seeking sanctuary in the very place that murdered my relatives absolutely appals me, and not least because for the last 78 years, my loyalties have been to Britain" (Connolly, Kate, "Descendants of Jewish refugees seek German citizenship after Brexit vote." *Guardian*, 30 October 2016).

3. Ian Buruma, writing about his German Jewish grandparents' assimilation into British society, notes, "For identity is not only a question of how one sees oneself, but also of how one is perceived by others. That is why it came

as such a shock to patriotic German Jews, who had fought for their country in the Great War ... when they were suddenly persecuted as hated aliens after Hitler came to power" (Buruma, I. "More British than the British: cultural assimilation today").

4. Primo Levi describes the exile's retreat to fantasy as a way of defending against the loss of place and what this means to identity. "This is the most immediate fruit of exile, of uprooting: the prevalence of the unreal over the real. Everyone dreamed past and future dreams, of slavery and redemption, of improbably paradises, of equally mythical and improbably enemies; cosmic enemies, perverse and subtle, who pervade everything like the air" (Levi, P. *If This is a Man*, 1991).

5. See Fulbrook, Kellner, Wolf, Edmund Bush, Horowitz.

6. I have written in detail about individual adaptability with regard to psychic survival in Chapter 3, "Invisible handcuffs: The masochistic pact in capture-bonding and the struggle to be free," in *Everyday Evils*.

7. See Timothy Snyder's book, *The Road to Unfreedom*, in which he outlines Putin's "politics of eternity," as adopted from the Russian fascist philosopher, Ivan Ilyin.

8. I am using the term "national identity" to mean an aspect of individual identity that is founded on being a member of a "national state," in other words, a recognized large group occupying geographical territory and with its own system of governance and imbued with the cultural values and traditions of the country it encompasses.

9. See, for example, Volkan, V. D. (2003). Large-group identity: Border psychology and related societal processes. *Mind and Human Interaction*, 13: 49–76.

References

Alexievich, S. (2016). *Second-Hand Time*. London: Fitzcarraldo Editions.

Arendt, H. (1951). *The Origins of Totalitarianism*. London: Penguin.

Beren, P. (2018). Children on the Border. Article presented to US House of Representatives 115th Congress, 2nd Session.

Buruma, I. (2016). More British than the British: cultural assimilation today. *Financial Times*. 15 January.

Buruma, I. (2018). *A Tokyo Romance*. New York: Penguin.

Drndic, D. (2015). *Leica Format*. London: Quercus, Maclehose Press.

Erpenbeck, J. (2011). *Visitation*. London: Portobello Books Ltd.

Farah, N. (1986). *Maps*. New York: Arcade Publishing.

Fromm, E. (1941). *Escape From Freedom*. New York: Avon Books.

Fulbrook, M. (2011). *Dissonant Lives: Generations and Violence Through the German Dictatorships. Volume Two: Nazism Through Communism*. Oxford: Oxford University Press.

Gessen, M. (2018). To be or not to be. *New York Review of Books*. 8 February.

Haffner, S. (2003). *Defying Hitler: A Memoir*. London: Phoenix.

Hoffman, E. (2017). The Hubert Butler Annual Lecture. Kilkenny, Ireland.

Iyer, P. (2013). What do you call home? *TED Talk*. 11 October.

Jacobs, B. (2018). Trump defends Mexican rapists claim during conspiracy-laden speech. *Guardian*. 5 April.

Kellner, R. S. (ed.) (2018). *My Opposition: The Diary of Friedrich Kellner, A German Against the Third Reich*. Cambridge: Cambridge University Press.

Levi, P. (1991). *If This is a Man*. London: Abacus.

Pawlikowski, P. (2018). *Cold War*. Film.

Szabłowski, W. (2014). *Dancing Bears: True Stories of People Nostalgic for Life under Tyranny*. London: Penguin.

Towles, A. (2017). *A Gentleman in Moscow*. London: Windmill Books.

Volkan, V. D. (2003). Large-group identity: Border psychology and related societal processes. *Mind and Human Interaction, 13*: 49–76.

Vuong, O. (2019). *On Earth We're Briefly Gorgeous*. London: Jonathan Cape.

Walter, N. (2017). Heimat. *New York Review of Books*. 23 November.

Zweig, S. (2011). *The World of Yesterday: Memoirs of a European*. London: Pushkin Press.

CHAPTER FIVE

Patriotism: living and dying for one's country

Well, I've had enough of people who die for ideas. I don't believe in heroism. I know that it's easy and I've found out that it's deadly. What interests me, is living or dying for what one loves.

—Camus, *The Plague*, p. 124

Introduction

The concept of heroism is universally linked with the act of sacrificing one's life for one's country or the survival of one's group. In warfare, physical courage is praised and held up as both a manly and a patriotic virtue. The idea of dying for a cause, whether it is in the service of one's nation, one's religious beliefs, or ideological tenets, is seen as the acme of bravery—a hero's death. The soldier who dies in the name of democracy, whether it is in Vietnam, Iraq, or Afghanistan, and the terrorist suicide bomber who dies in the name of Allah, are each fighting for what they believe are righteous causes that give profound meaning to their lives—and to their deaths. In each case, the hero achieves immortality because he has sacrificed his life for a higher principle. The hero's sacrifice reinforces the values of the group and in doing so the group's identity is also re-confirmed. However different the causes may appear to be, they signify a vision of a moral society governed by a set of beliefs and ideals that provide a common identity and sense of belonging. In each case, bravery is called for to realize these ideals and the heroic act of putting one's country or one's religion above one's life is highly prized. Our human need to find meaning in our lives, expressed in terms of trying to aspire to the ideals we have of ourselves derived from our social norms, binds us to a collective identity that provides us not only with some form of security but also with the transcendent rituals that help us to accept loss and death.

Patriotism, like religious and political ideologies, constitutes a belief system imbued with a particular set of values and ideals that confers identity to large groups. I am distinguishing patriotism from nationalism here. Patriotism refers to love of the moral values and principles associated with one's country, whereas the term nationalism is used in the context of putting one's nation's interests foremost, especially at the exclusion or detriment of other nations. Durkheim recognized the structural importance of religion in unifying and providing social control and purpose for people. He writes, "Essentially, [religion] is nothing other than a body of collective beliefs and practices endowed with a certain authority" (Durkheim, 1969, p. 51). This definition can also be applied to the way in which political ideologies function within society. The principal difference with patriotism is that the group is geographically determined and takes its identity from place. Patriotism means being loyal and attached to one's homeland, one's place of birth. In this sense it is similar to being attached to one's country of origin, except that patriotism can apply to an adopted country, whereas one's country of origin remains a primary part of identity. Unlike religious and political ideologies, patriotism requires its followers to belong to one country; its borders are clearly demarcated. It is a bit like a football team that originates in a specific geographical area. Other football teams may have the same values and goals—they are after all playing the same game—but the fact that they are from different places is what distinguishes them from one another. Places come with their own characteristics and these will also color the group's identity and be used as distinguishing factors to mark the superiority of one place/group over another.

The ultimate patriotic act is to sacrifice one's life for one's country in warfare; this is a public expression not only of loyalty to one's fellow countrymen, it is an assertion that the values of one's country, or how they are at least perceived, give meaning to individual life, and because of this are of greater importance than the life of the individual. Values can be protected for posterity, whereas individual lives must end. One of the principal rationales for risking one's life to fight in a war or for a cause is that there is a clear concept of good and bad that is shared within the group. Most wars, perhaps up until the twenty-first century, have been fought on this basis, that the good of the country was self-evident and needed to be protected if not empowered. The rhetoric of the good was essential to motivate and give meaning to those who were fighting. But when the good is questioned and the delineation between good and bad becomes blurred, this produces a rift in the population and those who are fighting because what they believe they are fighting for may not necessarily conform to the reality. In recent Western history, this was most evident in the Vietnam War which, after years of failure, brought into question the whole idea of interventionist warfare, its ethics, and its effectiveness. Protests within the US about Vietnam reflected the growing distrust in government and highlighted another face of patriotism; patriotic values can also be upheld by *not* going to war. The conflict between how to best protect American patriotic values was marked by the objections to military conscription which were first voiced at this time.[1] Dying for one's country only makes sense if the cause is a righteous one. In the case of Vietnam this was far from clear and made Americans aware, for the first time since the Revolution, that patriotism, at least within a democracy, is not the same thing as blind obedience to government authority, but entails a degree of agency and conscience.

A cause worth dying for?

> I'll go to Afghanistan to prove to you that there is something exalted in life, that a fridge crammed with meat and a Zhiguli automobile aren't enough to make everyone happy. There's something more than that ...

—Alexievich, *Boys in Zinc*, p. 42

Within the United States the Vietnam War was distinct from the two world wars insofar as the rationale for US military intervention was ambiguous from the start. The end of World War II coincided with the height of Stalin's power and the communist threat to democratic institutions in countries such as Turkey, Greece, France, and Italy. The historian Max Hastings writes:

> George Kennan, head of the [US] State Department's policy planning staff and author of the famous 1946 Long Telegram from Moscow, characterised Soviet assertiveness as a "fluid stream" that sought to fill "every nook and cranny" available to it in the basin of world power. Stalin and later Mao supported revolutionary movements wherever these seemed sustainable. On 12 March 1947 America's president proclaimed before Congress what became known as the Truman doctrine: "At the present moment in world history nearly every nation must choose between alternative ways of life. The choice is too often not a free one ... I believe that it must be the policy of the US to support free people who are resisting attempted subjugation by armed minorities or by outside pressures."
>
> (Hastings, 2018, p. 28)

While, as Hastings goes on to point out, the US may be admired in asserting the need to defend democracy in the face of what was considered a real international communist threat, the Truman doctrine led the US into one political quagmire after another, Vietnam being the most contentious and ultimately disastrous.[2] The antecedents of US intervention in Vietnam prepared the political ground for the Cold War and, following US successes in World War II, enhanced the image of the US as policing and defending democracies around the world. For most Americans at this time, upholding democratic principles was in total accord with the American Dream, supporting not only the growing reputation of the US as *the* world power but its aspirations to empire. Just as the US had stepped in at the late stages of World War II to support its allies in what was considered the righteous cause of vanquishing Hitler's megalomaniac takeover of Europe, in the case of Vietnam, the US followed on the heels of the failed French colonial regime with the task of combating communist encroachment and securing democracy in Vietnam.

Every country has its own history of struggle to protect its identity and interests and to uphold certain moral values that are inextricably linked to and define patriotism within specific contexts. The historical backdrop in the United States that has determined the rationale for its military interventions was the War of Independence. The US revolution arose from the American experience of being oppressed and exploited by its English sovereign. The War of Independence can be seen in its most basic form as a response to humiliation and inequality—perhaps the two most important universal political factors behind any civil war. The basic tenet of the revolution was articulated in the Declaration of Independence drawn up by the founding fathers of the US, proclaiming that "all men are created equal" with the right to "life, liberty and the pursuit of happiness." The American Dream sprang from this principle, establishing a vision of governance that would ally the notion of freedom to prosperity, success, and social mobility. James Truslow Adams defined the American Dream in 1931 as promising a life that "should be better and richer and fuller for everyone, with opportunity for each according to ability or achievement," regardless of social class or birth. The rise of the US as the most powerful country of the last two centuries has led to a pervasive Western view that democracy is best because it promises to make individual lives better and easier. In the wake of both world wars, this ideal played a central role in US political and economic thinking.

The articulation of the American Dream within the Declaration of Independence directly expresses the collective ego ideal of the American people, applying to the country as a whole and to its individual members. It has also provided a template for the ideology of democratic governments in other parts of the globe.[3] It is an ideal that espouses concepts of justice and fairness alongside the possibility of individual success; everyone in theory has an equal start in life—a concept that was radical in the extreme when viewed against the European class structure in the eighteenth century and has become notably challenged by the changes wrought by globalization over the last twenty years or so. In order to achieve this ideal it is important that all citizens sign up to it in principle and defend it to the point of risking their lives for it.

This kind of ideological pact is no different within socialist, fascist, communist, or totalitarian regimes, representing a kind of spectrum of political systems that give decreasing valance to the rights of the individual and increasing emphasis on state responsibility for the welfare of its citizens. Even in extreme totalitarian regimes, such as North Korea, the commitment to a paternalistic leader who will take care of the people's needs is paramount and reinforces a quasi-religious ideal of worship and individual sacrifice in order to sustain the happiness of the whole. Whether the emphasis is on valuing a society of individuals, as in a democracy, or on a society in which the individual is principally valued as a cog that enables the society to function, these different ideologies rest upon the commitment and belief of large groups of people. Like religious belief systems, different ideological frameworks provide meaning and identity for different populations.

With regard to what makes us willing to die for our country, the Vietnam War is an especially interesting example as it evoked fierce patriotism in those who defended it and in those who dissented against it—to the point of risking their own lives. Supporters and dissenters were simultaneously upholding the same principles while their analysis of the real politic differed significantly.[4] What is striking about both groups is that the strength of their beliefs led some to volunteer to serve in Vietnam, risking their lives for the cause of democracy, and others to demonstrate against the war, certainly risking their freedom and future life opportunities, and for those who were killed demonstrating, their lives.

Asked why people are willing to die on a battlefront, anthropologist Scott Atran, director of research at Artis International, an institute that studies extremist violence, replied that it is "both devotion to a tight-knit group of comrades—fusion with them—and commitment to sacred values. But the values actually trumped the group, which may be the first time that was shown. Because most of the military sociology and psychology, at least since World War II, has said that will to fight is based on camaraderie and fighting for your buddies."

Atran describes sacred values as moral values that are

> immune or resistant to material trade-offs ... they generate actions because they're the right thing to do, so you're not really

worried about risks or rewards or cost or consequences ... since World War II, if you look at insurgents and revolutionary groups, they on average beat out standard police and armies with up to 10 times more firepower and manpower, because those police and armies rely on standard material incentives and disincentives like pay, promotion, and punishment. These guys rely on commitment.

When we were talking to ISIS and PKK [the Kurdistan Workers' Party, devoted fighters against ISIS], they just threw down the surveys asking about forces' physical strength and said that has nothing to do with it—it's all about what's in your heart ... Human beings are inspired by belief in apparently absurd things. Religion or transcendental ideologies, for example. This leap of faith seems to inspire others to great things, and probably is the reason we were able to form large polities. We found people were willing to sacrifice their family for these things ... Sacred values inhibit deliberative reasoning, so they're in a sense more efficient in the clutch. You don't even think about them.

(Hutson, 2017)

Atran also cites research indicating that fighters who are emotionally committed to their cause tend to have greater success than those who are less committed. In the case of terrorist groups, such as IS, their moral fervor may easily intimidate their opponents whose moral beliefs are not as powerful. While both sides risk being killed in the fighting, if a soldier believes he will become a martyr in the eyes of Allah, he is much more likely to take extreme risks, the most extreme being the suicide bomber.

Atran highlights our need to believe in what he refers to as "sacred values" that become so embedded in our psyche that "you don't even think about them." Atran equates "sacred values" with "moral values" and hence with our conscience. He is describing a collective concept of the ego ideal that synthesizes the ideal or best version of ourselves that we want to be along with a vision of the kind of world we want to live in and our responsibility to create and protect this vision. This ideal, what Atran calls "sacred values," binds us to a group and confers identity with the group but, as Atran also suggests, they transcend the group especially in the face of conflict. These collective values and ideals are also what we find in the unconscious dynamics of bravery.[5] The person who commits what is considered a brave act, such as risking his life to save another or to defend his beliefs, is similarly following moral dictates that take primacy over the ego and what might appear to be self-interest or, in the case of dissent, the apparent interest of group cohesion.

The role of sacrifice

We imagined something romantic in store for us.
—Alexievich, *Boys in Zinc*, p. 26

If we accept Atran's idea that people are willing to risk their lives in defense of "sacred values," then it is tempting to argue that there is virtually little or no difference between the religious fighter and the patriotic soldier. Both enter the battlefield risking their lives for values that represent something greater than their individual lives. However, psychologically, there may be significant differences between the two. Camus complains that he's "had enough of people who die for ideas," preferring instead to live or die "for what one loves" (Camus, 1947, p. 124). Camus is pointing to an important distinction relating to self-sacrifice and bravery. We can interpret Camus' aversion to those who "die for ideas," as referring to those who become intoxicated with their own martyrdom in a kind of narcissistic bid for love or heroism. It is unclear whom Camus had in mind here except that inevitably any cause, including patriotism, will attract people who seek recognition and love through the act of self-sacrifice. This suggests that there is a spectrum of motivations ranging from risking one's life in order to be loved by an important other to risking one's life because there are certain values that one loves and wants to preserve. Amongst the followers of IS, for example, there is a clear doctrine that encourages martyrdom as an expression not simply of devotion to Allah but as a means to ensure being loved by Allah. Loyalty to the point of death is the ultimate price to be paid in order to be loved in the eyes of God. In the Judeo-Christian tradition this summons up the all-powerful paternalistic God, who demands the sacrifice of life itself in exchange for his blessing. Abraham is willing to kill his own son at God's behest. This is the masochistic aspect of love that asserts that the loved object is not only the most important object in the world but that the subject will sacrifice life itself and all that is dear to obtain the love of the object. At the other end of the spectrum, Camus differentiates those who live and die for what they love, signifying that their sacrifice, whether it is in the way they live or in dying, is in the service of loving rather than with the aim of being loved. Within this spectrum, self-sacrifice encompasses the masochistic and the sacred, and denotes a differing relationship with the object.

In his acclaimed novel, *Silence*, the Japanese writer Shusaku Endo describes the narcissistic shadow of martyrdom. An idealistic Jesuit priest sets out as a missionary for Japan in 1640 at a time when Japan was violently uprooting Christianity, persecuting Christians to death if they did not apostatize. Despite all odds, the priest manages to land in Japan and hide from the Japanese forces tracking down Christians. He is fed and cared for by peasants who have remained faithful to their Christian beliefs, risking their lives to harbor him. Eventually he is caught, and given a seemingly impossible choice between disavowing his faith and living a useful life serving the interests of the Japanese, or choosing his faith and, as a consequence, not being killed himself but causing the death of fellow Christians who would be executed as he stood looking on. The priest is advised by an older priest who had also been given this choice years before and had renounced his faith. The older priest makes the distinction between being faithful to the Church, in other words, being a dutiful servant of God, and being faithful to the spirit of Christ. He urges the priest, saying, "For love Christ would have apostatized. Even if it meant giving up everything he had" (Endo, 1969, p. 229). As the priest recognizes that holding on to his faith is a cruelty he cannot inflict on others, the older priest assures him, "You are now going to perform the most painful act of love that has ever been performed" (ibid.). The priest's decision to renounce his faith and not to die a martyr was in fact a greater sacrifice—it was a renunciation not only of his faith but of an idealized image of himself that reflected the doctrinaire tenets of his faith. His decision to save his fellow Christians made him human; it was an act of conscience rather than an act of self-glorification. Following his act of apostasy, the priest was summoned to appear before the magistrate who had presented him with this choice. But the priest's self-hatred at his betrayal had withered along with his past faith. The priest became aware that "now he felt no sense of disgrace in the presence of this man.

Gradually he had come to realize that it was against his own faith that he had fought" (ibid., p. 249).

The Jungian analyst Rosemary Gordon points out the close connection between masochism and spiritual submission, helping to distinguish between what can be seen as narcissistically motivated self-sacrifice and sacrifice for a loved object that is valued above the self (Gordon, 1993). She emphasizes our innate need for an object to venerate or worship, whether it is in the guise of a god or of an ideology. This brings us back to Freud's idea of the ego ideal and its role in our psychic and social development, as a collective image, culturally construed, of how and who to be within one's world. But there is a further important distinction that Gordon hints at but does not elaborate upon between masochism and veneration. She refers to masochism as a shadow aspect of veneration, implying it is the negative or unseen destructive side. While self-sacrifice may be acted upon with the aim of being loved, it contains within it an act of hatred toward the object. The suicide shows the world, "Look what you [the loved object] have driven me to, I can only obtain your love through killing myself." The unconscious message in this kind of martyrdom is a very deep ambivalence toward a loved object who could allow the subject to exist in such pain and humiliation. IS, for example, typically recruit Western converts from those groups who are most alienated and denigrated within their societies—they have something to fight for; ironically, it is their experience of "not mattering" within their own societies that makes them especially vulnerable to an autocratic regime that in its demand for obeisance does not recognize self-agency. A Syrian "media organizer" explains that people get radicalized because of their experience that they don't matter (Pearlman, 2017). IS offers a narrative that provides meaning for their suffering, that provides them with a viable ego ideal, but ultimate submission to the dictates of others, as in any totalitarian system, relies on external threat to flourish.

What I have described as the masochistic sacrifice intended to obtain the love of the object can be seen at the heart of totalitarian regimes that demand complete devotion to the leader who then provides and cares for (i.e. loves) the group as a whole and the individual as a member of the group. This contrasts with democratic governments that rely on their citizens to uphold and protect the principles of democracy. The role of the leader is to ensure that these principles are applied in the political governance of the country. There is a shared commitment to an ideology that does not rest on belief in an individual leader. In writing about British soldiers suffering breakdowns at the time of World War II, Fairbairn points to the different dynamics of infantile dependence that were evident under democratic systems as compared with totalitarian regimes. Fairbairn identifies separation anxiety as the most distinctive feature of military breakdowns and writes:

> Separation-anxiety must obviously present a special problem for democracies in times of war: for under a democratic regime the dependent individual can find no substitute for his accustomed objects under military conditions (the sergeant-major proving a very poor substitute, e.g., for an attentive wife). The problem of separation-anxiety in the soldier is anticipated under a totalitarian regime by a previous exploitation of infantile dependence, since it is part of the totalitarian technique to make the individual dependent upon the regime at the expense of dependence upon familial objects. Dependence upon familial objects is what really constitutes "the degeneracy of the democracies" in totalitarian eyes. The totalitarian technique, however, has its weakness. It depends upon national success; for only under conditions of success can the regime remain a good object to the individual. Under conditions of failure the regime becomes a bad object to the individual; and the socially disintegrating effects of separation-anxiety then begin to assert themselves at the critical moment. On the other hand, it is in time of failure or defeat that a democracy has the advantage; for in a democracy the individual is less dependent upon the state, and, therefore, less subject to disillusionment regarding the "goodness" of the state as an object. At the same time, the threat to familial objects inherent in defeat (so long as this is not too devastating) provides an incentive for effort, which is lacking under a totalitarian regime.
>
> (Fairbairn, 1952, p. 80)

While Fairbairn describes clearly the types of infantile dependence fostered by these different political regimes, he does not take into account the psychological importance of the groups' collective ego ideals and the powerful impact this has on the groups' identities, especially in relation to experiencing the humiliation of defeat. Under a totalitarian regime, conditions of failure may lead to a bolstering of the leader in order to maintain the leader as a good object. We can see this reaction taking place at the moment in the refiguration of IS and the resurfacing of its leader, Abu Bakr al-Baghdadi, in the media. In contrast, the apparent defeat of democratic principles, for example, in Vietnam, led to extreme disillusionment and cynicism regarding democratic processes. This is also something we are experiencing today in the land of Trump and Brexit.

When a group with a shared ideology is under threat, regardless of how it is structured, an act of sacrifice plays a pivotal role in the reestablishment of group identity and power. In religious rites, the sacrifice would traditionally be in the form of a symbolic intermediary, such as an animal, standing in for a human, a Christ-like figure, cleansing the group of its sins by offering his life to God. The men and women who risk their lives for their beliefs, whether with the aim of being loved and sanctified or through their love of "goodness," that is, an idealized vision of the world, offer themselves as sacrificial victims in the service of war. But in war sacrifice plays a different role. It is not the scapegoat, who is weak and unclean and carries the sins of the group, who is sacrificed; it is instead largely the young and innocent, who embody the group's ideals and the group's future, who face death on the battlefield. Through their death, they restore power to the group and reinforce the group's belief system. They become the heroes and martyrs of their culture and as such sacralize the group's ideology, whether it is in the form of patriotism or religious doctrine.

Belief and reparation

He knew ideals, but he didn't know life.
—Alexievich, *Boys in Zinc*, p. 26

The following vignette is an example of a man who fought for his country, became deeply disillusioned, and yet held on to his beliefs.

I didn't know what I wanted to do with my life, I was just a kid, but I did know what mattered to me, what I believed in. I believe in the same things now and I'd still risk my life for what I believe in. But I've changed too and I wouldn't make the same choices I did in my early twenties. Beliefs can also blind you ...

John had been drafted at the age of eighteen during the last stages of the Vietnam War. He was just about to start university, but he decided, with his family's backing, to fight for what he saw then as the communist threat and to protect the principles of democracy that he had grown up with and cherished. He served just over a year in Saigon as the South Vietnamese government was virtually collapsing. Although John never fought on the front lines and was stationed as a junior officer in Saigon most of his time there, fighting within the city was intense and brutal, unexpected and shocking because of the high number of civilian deaths.

Forty-three years later, at the age of sixty-one, John contacted me for analysis. He had moved to London shortly after the war and had become a successful corporate lawyer. He immediately informed me on the phone that he had fought in Vietnam and he wasn't looking for help for PTSD. He had had some flashbacks and there were things he wished he had never seen, but he had had CBT some years ago and this had been effective. He told me it was more of an existential crisis that he wanted help with. The world had changed, and he felt lost and adrift. His wife had left him the year before, complaining that all he could think about was politics, and their childless marriage felt like "an empty shell." John had been sad at the loss of his marriage, but described a more profound sense of loss, a deeper disillusionment than he had experienced in 'Nam. He wondered what was wrong with him and how to live with what felt like a terrible loss.

John explained,

> I know this is going to sound naïve, but I can't bear what is happening in the US with Trump and I also find this business with Brexit painful and hard to bear. Like a lot of people, I can try to make sense of it all in terms of rising populism and what this is about, but this is intellectual. What really hurts is that it feels like everything I held dear has just been shoveled into the rubbish bin. It's like some awful story of a large corporation that has taken over a smaller company where the new norm is to look the other way in terms of corrupt practice. All that matters is how to raise the profits and fuck what it means to the employees.

I asked whether John's feelings of being rubbished had any resonance with his past. He thought for a while and then said,

> I actually don't think so. I think what I'm feeling now comes from some-where else in my life. It's not to say that there weren't difficulties in my family—at one point I thought my parents were going to divorce. They were fighting all the time and in the end they decided to stay together because of me and my sister. But in fact, I think they managed to work something out and had a pretty good relationship towards the end—probably because they were both so narcissistic and they knew no-one else would put up with them!

There was a long silence and John added,

> Actually, maybe that's the point. Family life was a bit rubbish and cen-tered around the attention both my parents needed in different ways. It was empty. My mother would defend every sick cat in the neighborhood but this was mainly to show what a good person she was. My father went to church every Sunday and this was his public show of goodness, while at home he taunted us all sadistically. I can see that there is a parallel here—feeling helpless with parents who are squabbling with each other and pretending it's all for the sake of the kids. But I think there's still something else. At another level I can identify with many of the Brexi-teers who feel unseen and then get caught up with a set of beliefs that become more important than anything else in their lives, regardless of the reality and the costs ... I think my parents' constant squabbling made me feel irrelevant, invisible. The only thing the family could agree on was politics—and I suppose this is where I could be the hero. I could finally be in the spotlight and get some kudos for what I was doing. And at that age risking my life for a just cause was thrilling, it gave me a sense of power and a heightened sense that everything I did had a purpose. Until, of course, I arrived in 'Nam and started seeing the reality of the place, of the war, of just what the hell we were doing there at all. Thank God I did survive, or I would never have forgiven myself!

Over the course of the next few months it became clear that John's powerful belief in democratic principles was bound up with not only the importance he set on the concepts of justice, fairness, and equal opportunities—a utopian vision of society—but as a way of setting wrongs right and creating a larger benign family in which its members were equally respected and valued. In his therapy, it was easy to link John's patriotic feelings to his unconscious desire to repair his own family. We can extrapolate that this may well be the active unconscious motivation that drives most of us to espouse any particular ideology. But I think what brought John to my consulting room was not his struggle with his failure to resolve his family conflicts. He had clearly indicated, like his dawning awareness when he was stationed in Saigon, that there were some conflicts that weren't worth fighting for or trying to repair, that were better not to engage with or to get caught up in a kind of perverse justification. What had been important to John was to test his beliefs and to act on these, to express self-agency. For many young men and women, fighting for a cause takes on vital importance because of just this reason. As we become adults, we naturally look for adventure and opportunities to prove ourselves, but we also look for a higher power outside the nucleus of the family, what Atran calls the sacred. It becomes important at this point in our lives to be able to act on our beliefs. It is not only an act of self-agency but a public validation of sacred beliefs that are timeless and universal in their reach. While John was aware of his need to escape his family and at the same time his desire for their attention and admiration, he also knew that he had to discover how to feel potent in the world in relation to his own beliefs and morality.

John's breakdown had not occurred because his belief system had unraveled and could no longer sustain him. He came to me because, as he put it, he felt suddenly "adrift" in a foreign land in which his ideals had been demoted and discarded. John's state of mind was one of existential dissonance.[6]

But, for John, what was most painful about his experience was that, at least initially, he felt that his attempts to make a better world, to repair what had been damaged, had failed. He came to me in mourning but also in hope of finding a new way of acting in the world. Paradoxically, his acceptance of what he could not achieve and his own limitations, gave him an inner confidence that enabled him to be much more effective in his relationships. His self-agency came from the freedom he experienced when he realized he did not have to fix the world.

The cost of blind belief

But people had belief! Really strong belief! Believing in something is so beautiful. It's wonderful! Then that feeling of being tricked ... Still the belief. Somehow that was a part of us.

—Alexievich, *Boys in Zinc*, p. 215

As John explained at the beginning of his therapy, his beliefs over the years had not actually changed; what had changed was the world he lived in and his experience in trying to put his beliefs into practice. John's experience is markedly different from those who, through different circumstances, either lost their beliefs altogether or defended their beliefs at great cost to themselves.

John acknowledged in his first session, "Beliefs can also blind you." In transcripts for the trial of Nuon Chea, the Khmer Rouge's chief ideologue under Pol Pot and one of three top people in the regime to be tried for crimes against humanity, Chea explained that the Khmer Rouge were convinced that the Vietnamese Communists hoped

> to conquer this country in accordance with the ambition to occupy, annex and swallow Cambodia and rid Cambodia of her race and ethnicity ... My position in the revolution [was] to serve the interests of the nation and the people ... Oppression and injustice compelled me to devote myself to fight for my country. I had to leave my family behind to liberate my motherland from colonialism and aggression and oppression by thieves who wish to steal our land and wipe Cambodia off the face of the earth.

Nuon Chea emphasizes that he sacrificed his own life and his own personal ties, leaving his family behind, to fight for "the motherland." He then adds, "We didn't kill many ... We only killed the bad people, not the good" (ECCC, 2018, Transcript of Case 002/02). With such extreme sacrifice, as in most wars, it is imperative to believe that one is in the right, that killing one's fellow man is justified and that not doing so would run the risk of being overpowered at best, and exterminated at worst. It is hardly any wonder that ambiguity and nuance, in relation to putting oneself into one's enemy's shoes, are not encouraged in warfare. Under extreme conditions, certain aspects of denial or blindness enable us to act and certainly to follow orders.

Just as it is important to be able to justify killing one's enemy, it is equally important to be able to justify the deaths of those who are fighting for their country. In his diary of opposition to the Third Reich, Friedrich Kellner observes: "Many seduced youth are drafted into the army ... at the age of seventeen. Not a few of them, by the time they are eighteen, are awarded a 'heroic death' ... Still a child and already a dead 'hero'. The Nazi bandits not only kill the children of other nations, they do not stop at their own progeny" (Kellner, 2018, p. 206). Kellner questions, "Is there anything great or heroic in this event? Can we speak here of 'devotion' or 'fulfillment'? Not at all. Yet with these terms youth is beguiled. And they die for them, not suspecting they all died for nothing" (ibid., p. 327).

Although Kellner opposes Hitler's regime and sees Germany's youth dying "for nothing," he is further appalled by his observation that as Germany begins to suffer one defeat after another, victory is increasingly extolled by Hitler and many of his entourage as sacrificing one's life for the sake of the Reich. Kellner quotes from Hitler's speech of 10th September 1943, following the betrayal of Italy:

> The fate of Italy, however, may be for all of us a lesson to never renounce, in hours of the hardest distress and the bitterest emergency, the requirement of national honor, to stand with our confederates with a believing heart, and to fulfil faithfully the obligations imposed on us. The nation that withstands this testing before divine Providence will in the end receive from the Almighty the wages of the laurel wreath of victory and thus increase the value of its existence. This must and will be, in every circumstance, Germany.
>
> (ibid., p. 280)

Kellner notes how obedience unto death is what is most revered and ensures "heroism" in the eyes of the Führer and ultimately Providence. Hitler's authority became an end in itself. "Whoever is ready to give the order to others to fight to the last bullet needs nothing other than that to become the leader—and he will easily achieve the highest military honors. The end justifies the means. The main thing is and remains blind obedience" (ibid., p. 382).

Toward the end of the war, and with the defeat of the Reich in view, "blind obedience" assumed even greater importance; what was previously allegiance to a set of beliefs and love of the Fatherland tips over into masochistic sacrifice at the cost of the people's interests and patriotic ideals.

As Kellner is increasingly aware of the atrocities being committed and sanctioned by Hitler's regime, he sees its corrupting effects on his fellow citizens, not only in their tacit or overt complicity but in the deterioration of respect for government, for the rule of law, and for justice. He bemoans the fact that the Gestapo have virtually taken over and superseded the powers of the state:

> Since we therefore do not know any way we can counter in a non-partisan way Gestapo measure, their infringement on freedom, their methods of imprisonment, their placing of German citizens into concentration camps creates a great feeling of helplessness, even cowardly fear, in the far reaches of the German people, and has greatly damaged national unity ... We demand justice. If this call remains unheard and the reign of justice is not reinstated, the German people and the German national will perish in spite of the great victories, in spite of the bravery of our soldiers; it will perish because of internal rot and decay.
>
> (ibid., p. 143)

Kellner wrote this passage in his diary in 1941 when it was unclear how the war would develop. But even in the case of eventual victory, Kellner foretells a future that has already been damaged by its history, a future founded on the corruption of fairness and justice and respect for its individual citizens that will eat at the heart of the people, eroding trust and presenting a false, and therefore precarious, ideal of what it means to be a German. As it turned out, Germany's defeat enabled the country's past ideals, guilt at having gone against these ideals as a people, and need for reparation to emerge. If Hitler's Reich had been victorious, it is hard to imagine that it would have been able to withstand and survive its own internal conflicts.

The loss of belief

While we were fighting out there the world changed.

Alexievich, *Boys in Zinc*, p. 201

What is even harder than defeat is the loss of one's world view. Through numerous interviews, the Russian journalist, Svetlana Alexievich describes the suffering and humiliation experienced by Russian soldiers returning from war in Afghanistan, a war that they could no longer make sense of and that was subsequently considered a mistake. Rather than returning to their homeland welcomed as heroes, the soldiers, as in the case of many Vietnam veterans, returned home to invisibility, if not disregard. This was not a case of dissonance, there were no conflicting ideologies at stake; it was a case of complete loss of an ideology that a whole population had lived and died for. Such widespread loss is, of course, most apparent at points of fundamental social and political change in which an old ideology is supplanted by a newer or opposing one.

In her painstaking history of Germans living through the collapse of the Reich, the divison of Germany into the GDR and the Federal Republic, followed by reunification, Mary Fulbrook depicts the experience of existential angst affecting so many as they tried to cope with ideological upheavals and what for many was an ideological void. One example is Harald J., born in 1932:

> Already (at the age of thirteen) I lay in trenches in Poland with grenades and a machine gun and then we were saved from out of there by German soldiers and after that we joined the flight with a horse-drawn wagon. And I would have died for Hitler. When he was dead, I lay in the woods and howled like a dog, because that was my life, that was my ideology, that was my faith. There was nothing else. And after the war when we saw more plausibly what had been going on here, then for me every ideology was dead. Then there was simply nothing at all any more.
>
> (Fulbrook, 2011, pp. 50–51)

For Harald J. it was not Hitler's death that created a void of meaning; he attributes his loss of belief in *every* ideology to the disillusionment he experienced when he saw the reality of "what had been going on" and saw to what extent he had been duped. No ideology could be trusted when Harald J. could not trust himself to be tricked yet again. But he also describes a crisis in faith, much as many Jews experienced in the concentration camps when they were forced to question how God could countenance such evil in the world.

Others, equally disillusioned, sought a new ideology to fill the void. Jurgen S. reveals his determination not to fall prey to depression and bitterness about what he describes as the "false ideals" of the past. Instead he turns to the future:

> I am describing my experiences of war in such detail, because this affected and influenced me so incredibly much and set my life onto entirely new tracks... ... With what sorts of *false concepts* of honour and heroism, to name but two of the so-called soldierly virtues, had we been brought up! For us youngsters, who without a valid school-leaving exam had been taken from the school benches to become soldiers, a world full of false ideals collapsed with the sad end of the war, a world to which we had committed ourselves faithfully and sincerely. Now we should not mourn what had been lost and thus fall into a state of doing nothing and waiting, but rather, with determination, we should turn to a new goal ...
>
> (ibid., p. 54)

Kurt M. writes:

> Then came, with the end of the war, gradual disenchantment and the realization that the views in which one had been brought up, and for which one had unconditionally fought, were fraud and deception on a huge scale that had to lead us to downfall ... I could no longer understand how I could have assented to such a crazy view and that I did not previously realize the impossibility of this idea.
>
> (ibid., pp. 54–55)

Kurt M.'s admission that the views with which he had grown up were "fraud and deception," adding that he could not understand assenting "to such a crazy view," indicates that he, like his peers, had been swept away by the zeitgeist of the time and had finally come to his senses. While this is an *ex post facto* explanation of Kurt M.'s revised ideology, it at least gives some recognition to the fact that belief systems are fluid and determined by many social factors. It also illustrates the importance of being able to adapt to new ideologies to maintain a sense of identity and belonging by adopting the group's new set of ideals.

It is notable in Fulbrook's accounts that it is often the older generation who have the greatest difficulty in managing the loss of their beliefs and the social structures that accompanied these beliefs. Several people painfully describe their experience and what we might understand as a form of survivor anomie in which the changed world has lost fundamental meaning. This was especially evident in accounts following the fall of the communist regime in the GDR and reunification with the Federal Republic. Reunification, which many expected would provide a better life for the ex-communist GDR residents, brought for many a stripping away of meaning and of a sense of community. There was no longer a cause to fight for and to bring people together. As the young Russian solder argues, "a fridge crammed with meat and a Zhiguli automobile aren't enough to make everyone happy" (Alexievich, 2013, p. 42). One woman after unification complained:

> But what was left from this for us? What was the perfectly normal life in contrast to the elegant and so admirably unemotional heroism of my parents? Whether intentionally or not, practically everything had to stand comparison with them and their cause, their intensive life ... I asked instead what I should become, what I should do, what was really worthwhile ...
>
> (Fulbrook, 2011, pp. 144–145)

Another woman similarly complained:

> For what did I work night and day, take on responsibility with all my might, in the most diverse areas, and in the process ruined my health, sometimes neglected my family? ... It is particularly difficult for older people to work through everything. Honest, sensitive comrades, who have never done a stroke of harm to anybody, are breaking down because of unjustified sweeping judgements

about the party. Apparently some 1st Secretaries of the District
Leadership have already shot themselves.

(ibid., p. 206)

As well as the despair and humiliation of being seen to have wasted
their lives on a defeated regime that no longer had value, many East
Germans suddenly found themselves defunct and no longer needed. As
one woman said: "Meaningless ... just vegetating along—without sub-
stance, without goals. No one needs me any more ... I am totally super-
fluous, there is no one any more who asks for my advice, or wants to
know anything from me! Who am I anyway, and why am I still here?"
(ibid., p. 213).

Being no longer needed within one's social group is perhaps the greatest blow to identity and the most difficult challenge to combat. Without
a common "cause" to fight for or without a recognizable function within
the group, one's role in society is ambiguous, if not peripheral. When
both of these roles are removed and the individual who has lived for
the state is told he/she is no longer needed by the new state, it is hardly
surprising that individual meaning and value is lost.

As in the USSR, East German allegiance to the party (GDR) superseded that of the family, providing an overarching purpose and security.
Fulbrook notes that the party assumed the role of the parental authority,
assuring a clear future that mapped out the lives of its young (see ibid.,
pp. 150 and 175). In such an authoritarian system, meaning and belief
for the individual are derived from the state and its ideology. Within this
context, self-agency for the individual is determined by the extent to
which his/her actions support the state. Agency is granted by the state to
the individual; it is not the individual who, through his/her own agency,
enables the state to exist and function.

The loss of communist ideology following unification posed a challenge in adaptation on many different levels, but for many it was a
complete negation of what it had meant to be a good citizen and, more
profound than this, what it meant to be a person at all within society.
Fulbrook makes the point that the consequences of unification for East
Germans went deeper than "merely political, economic, social and cultural" change. Unification had a deep effect on people's personal identities and sense of self. "It was, then not just a matter of anomie and not

being able effectively to play the new 'rules of the game'; nor a matter of inadequate depiction and understanding; but also of a far more fundamental challenge to identities that had been constructed over decades in a set of social relations that were now being dismantled" (ibid., p. 212). An East German describes this dismantling succinctly, "One lives, works, resides under totally new conditions and has not a clue about them" (ibid., p. 210). It is as alien as being displaced to a foreign country with no common language and no role except as an outsider with a discounted past.

Filling the void

The heroes are different now: farmers and businessmen. The ideals are different.

—Alexievich, *Boys in Zinc*, p. 216

We can recognize the anomie experienced by so many East Germans after unification in other societies that have undergone different extremes of political change, particularly throughout Eastern European countries. But what is new is the growing collapse of political ideologies across the world ranging from communist/socialist belief systems to democratic ones. The rise of globalization has had an enormous effect on our view of ourselves as belonging to a specific country and what this means in practice and what this means with respect to our identity. Globalization has overshadowed national boundaries in establishing international corporations, some with greater wealth than some countries' GDP, that have far-reaching political and social influence. Affluence and inequality have burgeoned, and we have seen a gradual shift in belief systems with the result that it is less clear what our political and national identities stand for.

The post-World War II era was marked in Europe and in the US by a forceful belief in the power of democratic capitalism and the integration of nations that needed to work together to create stability and to prosper. Western Europe experienced unprecedented economic growth with increased benefits in social welfare and a cultural renaissance that was spawned out of liberalizing political institutions.[7] In contrast, Eastern European countries suffered a series of political crises and markedly slower economic growth. Western democratic states seemed to offer wealth, growth, and stability during this period and fueled a drive amongst Eastern European countries to join the bandwagon by becoming members of NATO and the European Union and adopting economic regulations and human rights legislation within their political institutions.

However, the financial crisis of 2008–2009, causing the worst global recession in eighty years, marked the beginning of an erosion of confidence in Western democratic systems. While Europe and the US survived the recession, political threats appeared on the horizon that challenged Western supremacy. Russia attempted to influence European politics in its manipulation of public debate in Estonia in 2007. The historian Anne Applebaum notes that, following this and Russia's political engagement in the Middle East, Western Europe no longer seemed so secure.

> Europe seemed to have little ability to halt or control either the Russian invasion of Ukraine in 2014 or the wars in Syria, Libya, Yemen, and Iraq. The latter helped feed a wave of horrific terror attacks—in Nice, Paris, Berlin, Manchester—that caused a major backlash against immigration, especially Muslim immigration, not only in Europe but all across the West. After the German chancellor, Angela Merkel, unilaterally decided to let in hundreds of thousands of refugees in 2015, the backlash intensified. The election in 2016 of the first US president since World War II to harbor an instinctive dislike of Europe solidified many Europeans' fears that their institutions were not capable of coping with challenges to their security and to their borders.
>
> (Applebaum, 2019)

The result, albeit encompassing different histories and national interests, has been a growing distrust in democratic governance and economies and the consequent rise of populist movements that aim to restore stability with the enforcement of national boundaries and identities. Of course, this is not an exclusively European and American trend but a political phenomenon that we can see emerging in other parts of the world, including parts of Asia and Africa.

With perhaps the exception of China and North Korea, countries that maintain strong authoritarian regimes, there are few countries in the world in which their political ideologies have remained intact. In Russia this is particularly evident since the collapse of the USSR which has strangely mirrored the United States in its shift toward materialist ideals—it is the farmers and the businessmen who are the heroes now. These are ideals that espouse the creation of individual wealth and have become unmoored from allegiance to political ideology or moral principles. The result is the creation of aggressive policies of anti-immigration, economic protectionism, and nationalism that belies a defensive paranoia.

Alexievich captures the effect of this ideological vacuum in extensive interviews of a cross section of Russians trying to make sense of post-Soviet Russia and their place in the world (Alexievich, 2013). As one man complains, "Nobody believes in anything any more. Not in the *domovoi*,[8] and not in communism. People live without any kind of faith!" (ibid., p. 139). This vacuum of belief gives rise to a nostalgia for the USSR and for the "Motherland" of the past, just as we have seen so vividly in the US and the UK, which have both harked back to the greatness of their imperial pasts, as has Turkey in extolling the days of Atatürk. Alexievich's Russians assert:

> Russia needs a strong hand. An iron hand. An overseer with a stick. Long live the mighty Stalin! (ibid., p. 175)

> I'm a communist ... I supported the putschists, or rather, the USSR. I was a fervent supporter because I liked living in an empire. (ibid.)

> Our country has a Tsarist mentality, it's subconsciously Tsarist. Ivan the Terrible, as they call him in Europe, who drowned Russian cities in blood and lost the Livonian War, is remembered with fear and awe. The same goes for Peter the Great and Stalin. While Alexander II, the Liberator ... the Tsar who gave Russia freedom, who abolished serfdom ... he was murdered. The Czechs can have their Vaclav Havel, but we don't need a Sakharov in charge here, we need a Tsar. The Tsar, the Father of the Russian people! Whether it's a general secretary or a president, it has to be a Tsar. (ibid., p. 195)

These voices reflect not only the loss of belonging to a powerful country that engendered respect, if not fear, but the loss of an explicit social hierarchy and sense of place. Under the communists, and under the Tsars, people had prescribed roles and functions and knew who or what ideological belief they were living—and dying—for. At the heart of this nostalgia, any ideology is better than none, and the clearest recovery of an ideological framework can be found in the past—a past that is at least familiar and that offers the illusion of a known identity rather than the disruption of alienation and recreating a social identity.

Another Russian longs for the days when she wanted to prove her love for her country by sacrificing her life for it. She explains,

> My greatest dream was to die! To sacrifice myself. Give myself away. The Komsomol oath: "I am prepared to give up my life if my nation should need it." These weren't just words, that's what we were really taught ... "I am prepared to devote all of my energy, and if necessary, to give my life to my Motherland." (ibid., p.153)

But with the loss of the socialist dream, just as with the loss of the demo-cratic dream, comes a loss of identity, both for the individual and the group. The social norms and aspirations are altered irrevocably as the ideal of what is important and to be admired becomes outmoded. When the ego ideal of a nation loses its potency the threat arises of the disin-tegration of national identity—a large-group sense of self. At this point, the group tends to seek to restore its identity through creating an illusion of its position in the world; the group looks for a leader who will carry this illusion, rather than a leader who can bear the anxiety of the group and help the group adapt to a changing reality.

The French psychoanalyst Chasseguet-Smirgel warns us that when a group's identity is under threat, and there is too much dissonance between its ideals and reality, the group defends itself by finding a leader who signifies total power and creates a new ideology in his/her image. The leader then represents for the group an amalgam of the ego and the ideal ego—they are one and the same and symbolize the omnipotence of the group, an omnipotence that is by affiliation bestowed on each of its members. We have examples of such leaders in Putin and Trump, as well as Duterte, Assad, Erdogan, Kim Jong-un, and others. These are leaders who stand for total power and have no need to unify the group by means of a shared set of moral values. Instead the leader assumes the role of a

Midas figure who will magically make the group rich and promote what Chasseguet-Smirgel refers to as a "phantasy of narcissistic assumption" (ibid., p. 82).

The danger of what we are experiencing as an ideological vacuum is that it creates fundamental existential anxiety amongst large groups and entire populations. A kind of pseudo-ideology in the guise of an all-powerful leader can be found that maintains the unity of the group but is based on a narcissistic illusion. This pseudo-ideology is by its nature precarious because it relies on the leader to embody it. It cannot ultimately sustain itself without the leader. On the other hand, the anxiety caused by failure of one's belief system can be intolerable.

In her account of the Special Operations Executive (SOE) agent Vera Atkins, the journalist Sarah Helm quotes from a conversation between Atkins and another SOE agent who had recently been released from Buchenwald concentration camp. Robert Sheppard remembers:

> The first morning they asked me to beat a prisoner in front of the others. He was a Russian. And I refused. And the SS officer, he took the stick and he went and he did it. And we had to adjust but many didn't. I saw people who died within three or four days because they stopped believing. People committed a kind of suicide because they could not believe this world.
>
> (Helm, 2005, p. 94)

It is only too easy to think that people died in these circumstances because "they could not believe this world" of depravity. However, depravity can also come into being without cruelty or sadism, in the very negation or absence of belief. The patriotic beliefs that so many of us live and die for give shape to our identity and the moral principles we live by within society. Patriotism, like religion, binds us together through our belief in higher ideals, or what Atran describes as "sacred values"—the beliefs that fill the void and give our lives meaning. In times of corruption and anomie, it is the "sacred values" embedded in patriotism that bear the seeds for repair.

In the recent re-release of the 1968 Kartemquin documentary film, *Inquiring Nuns*, two young nuns ask people they meet at random on the streets of Chicago whether they are happy. Most of the people interviewed respond positively with the recurring exception that the war in Vietnam makes them unhappy. Nearly fifty years later, the nuns, both of whom have left their order, are interviewed and asked the question of what makes them happy. Catherine Rock (formerly Sister Mary Campion) replies, "This election has been so inspiring—the way it was when Kennedy and Bobby and Martin Luther King were alive." Kathleen Westing (formerly Sister Marie Arne) adds,

> They have captured the next generation ... that is the most excit-
> ing thing to me because there was a cynicism and an unhappiness
> with where we were going and who we were and you feel you
> can bequeath the principles of our country to the next generation
> because they're ready to work for it and have a leader who will
> engender that. I'm excited. I'm ready to pass it on.

Over this fifty-year span, the disillusionment arising from the Vietnam War and the resurgent power of "the principles of our country" are recurring threads for these two women that are instantly associated with personal happiness. These "principles" are the sacred values that affect our identities and our hopes for the future.

Notes

1. Military conscription ended in the USA in 1973 and marked a profound change in American attitudes and the scope of patriotic obligations. With voluntary enlistment, the armed forces became more overtly careerist, while continuing to attract individuals who feel the importance of militarily defending their homeland.
2. Hastings comments on the "grievous injustices" committed by the US under the Truman doctrine. He writes: "For almost two generations Washington acquiesced in the fascist tyranny of Spain's Gen. Francisco Franco, and also sustained Central and South American dictatorships whose only merits lay in their protestations of anti-communism. In southern Africa, the British and Americans indulged white minority rule for decades after its indefensibility had become apparent. And in Indochina the French persuaded the West's Croesus-state that the cause of colonialism was also

that of anti-communism. After Mao Zedong's forces swept China, conservative Americans appalled by the 'loss' of their favourite Asian nation demanded stern measures to ensure that such an outcome was not repeated elsewhere. Henry Luce, proprietor of *Time-Life* and a passionate supporter of the Chinese Nationalists, threw the weight of his empire behind the anti-communist cause in Vietnam, for which it remained and advocate through two decades" (Hastings, *Vietnam*, p. 28).

3. The US Declaration of Independence (1776) predated France's Declaration of the Rights of Man and of the Citizen (1789) by thirteen years and was far more radical in its interpretation of equality of men as encompassing not only equality under law but equality of opportunity.

4. Patriotic conflicts over military foreign interventions, whether they be in Kosovo, Afghanistan, Ukraine, or elsewhere, are not new and are often only clarified when failure is evident. Nevertheless, the conflicts consist of disagreement on different levels about the pros and cons of intervention, including whether intervention stems from imperialist or protective motives. These are not conflicts about fundamental political ideals. In this respect, populist movements today signify underlying differences in political ideals.

5. See Chapter Two.

6. I have described this state of dissonance and its painful consequences in Chapter Four, "My country, my self."

7. In a review essay of Ian Kershaw's book *The Global Age: 1950–2017*, Applebaum writes: "In the early years, this gigantic and unprecedented experiment in democracy and integration brought immediate benefits for all of the members of the West. What the French called *les trentes glorieuses*— the thirty years of steady growth and expansion of social benefits from the 1940s to the 1970s—had its echo elsewhere in the bloc. Germany had its *Wirtschaftswunder*, led by Adenauer's finance minister, Ludwig Erhard; Italy had its *boom economico*, an extraordinary transformation that saw incomes double and triple within a generation. Even in the dictatorships of the Iberian peninsula, which did not join European institutions until the 1970s, postwar growth was remarkable: in Spain, GDP per capita rose by a factor of ten between 1960 and 1975. Growth and industrialization were accompanied by a parallel growth in social benefits: universal health care, free education, and government safety nets became the norm everywhere

in Western Europe" (Applebaum, A. (2019). The Lure of Western Europe. *New York Review of Books*, 6 June).

8. In Slavic *domovoi* means the household god or ancestors of a given kin.

References

Alexievich, S. (2013). *Second-Hand Time*. London: Fitzcarraldo Editions.

Alexievich, S. (2017). *Boys in Zinc*. London: Penguin.

Applebaum, A. (2019). The Lure of Western Europe. *New York Review of Books*. 6 June.

Camus, A. (1947). *The Plague*. London: Penguin, 2001.

Chasseguet-Smirgel, J. (1985). *The Ego Ideal: A Psychoanalytic Essay on the Malady of the Ideal*. London: Free Association Books.

Durkheim, E. (1969). Individualism and the Intellectuals. *Political Studies, 17*: 14–30.

Endo, S. (1969). *Silence*. London: Picador Classic.

Extraordinary Chambers in the Courts of Cambodia (2018). *Transcripts of Trial of Nuon Chea*. Phnom Penh: ECCC.

Fairbairn, W. R. D. (1952). *Psychoanalytic Studies of the Personality*. London: Routledge & Kegan Paul.

Fulbrook, M. (2011). *Dissonant Lives: Generations and Violence Through the German Dictatorships*. Oxford: Oxford University Press.

Gordon, R. (1993). Masochism: the shadow of veneration and worship. In R. Gordon, *Bridges: Metaphor for Psychic Processes*. London: Karnac.

Hastings, M. (2018). *Vietnam: An Epic Tragedy, 1945–75*. London: William Collins.

Helm, S. (2005). *A Life in Secrets: The Story of Vera Atkins and The Lost Agents of SOE*. London: Abacus.

Hutson, M. (2017). Why do people die fighting for a cause? Interview with Scott Atran. *Science*. 5 September.

Kartemquin Films (1968). *Inquiring Nuns*. Film.

Kellner, R. S. (Ed.) (2018). *My Opposition: The Diary of Friedrich Kellner, A German against the Third Reich*. Cambridge: Cambridge University Press.

Pearlman, W. (2017). *We Crossed a Bridge and It Trembled: Voices from Syria*. New York: HarperCollins.

CHAPTER SIX

Defying mortality: the shadow of bravery

Who does not fear death is almost omnipotent.
—Alexander Mikhailov, *Road to Revolution*, 1957

A British surgeon is being driven into a war zone in a foreign country to set up an operating theater for the wounded in the local hospital. Although he knows his transport is in danger of being gunned down by snipers, he is not feeling frightened, he is concentrating on what he needs to do when he arrives, his checklist of procedures and equipment, and wondering about the skills of the other doctors who will be assisting him. His mind is entirely focused on the task ahead of him and a passing anxiety about whether he will ever be able to fall asleep again. The surgeon is experiencing what soldiers and journalists at the front lines say they feel, the immediacy of the moment, the urgency of absorbing everything they need to do their job, and the sense that they are intensely alive and immune from death.

Because bravery entails risking one's life, the act itself can be intoxicating because it pushes us beyond our limits. The challenge of defying the odds in extreme situations can be enticing and exhilarating. Even if there is no conscious experience of fear, the adrenaline rush of acting against adversity and defending a deep-seated belief can be very powerful. Alongside the physical state of excitement, the act of bravery is experienced as untarnished by doubt—the dictates of the self and reality are at one. It is a moment of pure self-actualization that is experienced as both immensely powerful and as a transcendence of self; one's mind has taken over completely to determine what needs to be done for the maximum chance of survival. These extreme experiences bring us beyond the boundaries of what we know as "normal" life and can imbue us with an intoxicating sense of immortality that can also become highly addictive, to the point of self-destruction. Bravery, even in its triumphs, leaves its scars.

The glorification of bravery in war

Sasha Solianin

FOURTEEN YEARS OLD. NOW A FIRST-DEGREE WAR INVALID.

I really didn't want to die … I especially didn't want to die at dawn …

We are being led out to be shot. We walk quickly. The Germans are in a hurry somewhere, I understood it from their conversation. Before the war I liked German lessons. I even learned several poems of Heine's by heart. There were three of us—two first lieutenants, prisoners of war, and me. A boy … I was caught in the forest when I was gathering weapons. Several times I escaped, the third time they got me.

I didn't want to die …

I hear a whisper: "Run for it! We'll attack the convoy, and you jump into the bushes."

"I won't …"

"Why?"

"I'm staying with you."

I wanted to die with them. Like a soldier.

"We order you: run for it! Live!"

(Alexievich, 2019, p. 195)

When the shooting began, Sasha Solianin did run but was so terrified he forgot the address he had been given of a safe house to go to. Although he wanted to die with the soldiers, to be one of them, he was ordered to escape, to live. If he had not been given this order, it is doubtful he would have tried to escape. It seems clear that fourteen-year old Sasha was identifying with an ideal in his mind; he wanted to be "like a soldier," bravely sacrificing his life to defend his country. For Sasha, running away, at least in his perception, might have been considered an act of cowardice had it not been that he had been ordered to run away. This final order enabled Sasha to save himself and his conscience. However, his desire to stay and die "like a soldier" may not have been driven purely by his conscience but also by the promise of glory given to those who die for their country. A hero's death. Sasha may have also realized that, despite his idealized vision of glory, there is a difference between being brave and throwing one's life away, given the choice.

There are countless examples within literature and history of the glorification of a soldier's death in the service of protecting his country. The soldier's death, at its most idealized, is associated with immortality. The Vikings, for example, believed that only by dying could a warrior reach Valhalla and join the gods. Although our concept of immortality today is more nuanced, we nevertheless promote the idea that dying for one's country immortalizes the soldier in our collective memory. Public memorials such as Arlington Memorial Cemetery and the numerous memorialized sites of World War I and II give testimony to these deaths. As I have written in the previous chapter, dying for a cause or a belief system that unites a group and provides meaning strengthens the identity of the group by what is perceived as an act of immortality—the belief system transcends the life of an individual and lives on forever. The act of sacrifice is not only intended to protect the group in the present, but also to preserve its identity and beliefs in the future. This is as true of the self-sacrificing soldier who dies in defense of his/her country as it is of the suicide bomber who is martyred for the glory of Allah.

However, such acts of bravery are only as meaningful as the value system they support. If a war is seen to be for a just cause, even in the instance of defeat, its losses remain sanctified. But if defeat occurs and brings with it the demise of an ideology that is no longer tenable, as happened in the fall of the German Reich, it inevitably leaves the surviving population to question whether its losses were all for nothing. As starkly evident at the end of the Reich, there are other numerous examples of doomed wars, notably Vietnam and Afghanistan, in which as defeat became increasingly clear the pressure mounted to continue fighting—so as not to expose the failure of their strategic underpinnings and belief systems but, alongside these, the terrible waste of life left unjustified in the wake of these defeats. Bravery only exists within the context of a righteous cause; otherwise it becomes folly and fanaticism resulting in suicide.[1] Returning to Sasha, if he had not aspired to the ideal of being a brave soldier, willing to risk his life for his country, he would not have hesitated to try to escape the firing squad.

The glorification of bravery in war is not only a powerful motivating force to go into combat and to make sense of what might otherwise be seen as senseless acts of violence, it also serves to mitigate the guilt of war—guilt concerning the murder of enemy troops and civilians and one's own countrymen. At the end of the Reich, for example, faced with defeat and publicized atrocities committed by the Germans during the war, it became increasingly important to create and uphold an image of the Wehrmacht as highly principled and honorable. Fulbrook comments on the re-writing of historical narrative at the end of the war as a way for people to purify their own involvement and to dissociate themselves from its criminal shadow. Fulbrook writes:

> In West Germany the Army was widely portrayed as "clean," untainted by "excesses" that were increasingly associated with the SS. This became effectively the "alibi of a nation"—the scapegoat that was the really criminal organization. In this way, a positive notion of patriotic heroism could be retained, and the bereaved could still feel proud of those who had "fallen" for their country (now omitting Hitler from the previous formula of "Führer, Volk, and Fatherland"). Prisoners of war returning from Soviet camps to West Germany were treated as war heroes—and even those perpetrators who had served sentences for war crimes were now seen rather as victims of communism.
>
> A few individuals explicitly developed the myth of the "clean Wehrmacht" in self-serving autobiographical accounts. As Kesselring put it, in the closing paragraph of his memoirs, his aim was to "contribute something towards a truthful record of a good piece of German history, to the raising of a monument to our magnificent soldiers and to helping the world to recognize the

face of war in its grim totality." ... Distancing himself from "the mistaken racial policy of Hitler and his associates," Kesselring managed to describe the war against the Soviet Union in 1941 without any mention of the murderous Einsatzgruppen or the assistance given to them by the Wehrmacht ... [Kesselring also accused] "sabotage troops" who "increasingly violated the laws of humanity."

(Fulbrook, 2018, pp. 224–225)

Like many others, Kesselring pointed to the atrocities of the enemy as a justification for German army violations such as the murder of civilians. The "crimes" committed by the Wehrmacht were portrayed as motivated by self-defense, as opposed to the actions of the partisan "sabotage troops." As more information was revealed over time about German atrocities, this myth could not be so forcefully sustained. Nevertheless, as Fulbrook notes, "The image of the patriotic Wehrmacht, contrasting sharply with the demonized SS and Gestapo, persisted for several decades, providing succor to those who had lost loved ones at the front" (ibid., p. 225).

Such attempts to de-criminalize extreme forms of violence within the context of war are, of course, endemic to the way in which warfare, and atrocities in particular, are depicted and justified in public discourse. In psychological terms, "criminality" is projected into the enemy. In this way, the enemy becomes the evil perpetrator, while one's own side takes on the mantle of the innocent victim, defending the righteous cause. Without this defensive splitting and an appropriate rationale for the loss of lives, the guilt and the trauma of war is intolerable. While extolling the bravery of the soldier at war is correct, insofar as the soldier believes in the cause at stake, its glorification can also be used to mask and exonerate its opposite—the inherent sadism and violence of war.

The perversion of bravery

In his autobiography, the psychoanalyst Wilfred Bion describes the British ideal of manliness that was prevalent during both world wars and continues to be a powerful meme in the British psyche for success (or in some cases failure) achieved through endurance and deprivation. Bion describes his initiation into army culture:

Part of the pretension of manliness was to turn up for the day without any good—being indifferent to hardship and food was manly. In my soft way, nurtured on the luxuries of Colman's boat on the Broads, I thought—but did not say—that it was not manly, merely incompetent. Years later, when I read a book describing the dreadful winter of the South Polar exploration, I felt I knew it all—the manliness, the incompetence, the utter futility, contrasting so nobly with the sneaking, unmanly clockwork precision and success of a rival team. In my soft feminine way I preferred success.

(Bion, 1982, p. 101)

Bion ironically depicts a culture in which the brave man transcends his physical needs and conquers the elements and his own fear through sheer willpower. Comfort is eschewed as "feminine," with the suggestion that it breeds compliance and passivity. Deprivation and sacrifice become virtues in themselves and, as such, distinct signifiers of bravery and manliness. Here, as Bion reveals in his reference to the South Polar expedition, is another face of the shadow of bravery in which foolhardiness is mistaken for bravery. As we have seen in the interviews of rescuers during the Holocaust, although bravery is an act of spontaneity, it is also a highly calculated act in terms of its chances of success. If it means getting killed in the process, so that it effectively means not being able to rescue anyone else, then it is not an act of bravery, but of foolishness. The British ideal of "manliness" is a solitary, narcissistic image that basically turns hardship, caused by lack of knowledge and resources, into a good.[2] What is important is not winning or failing, but how the battle is fought—often the favored argument of the losing side. Perhaps, as in the case of public acclaim for the brave soldiers who lost their lives in the course of a war doomed to fail, Scott's disastrously incompetent expedition to the South Pole could only be made palatable subsequently through this lens of manly bravery.

Hemingway notably extols the virtues of courageous manhood through perseverance, even in failure. In his novel *The Old Man and the Sea*, the hero, Santiago, spends his life fighting to live "correctly," with "honor, courage and endurance," despite the pain this may cause him. After eighty-four days at sea without any catch, Santiago finally hooks a huge marlin, but as he reels it in the fish is destroyed by sharks, and the struggle wrecks Santiago's hands. When he finally hoists the mangled fish on deck, Santiago tells the marlin, "I am sorry that I went too far out. I ruined us both. But we have killed many sharks, you and I, and ruined many others ... I'll fight them until I die" (Hemingway, 1952, pp. 89–90). The declaration to go on fighting in the face of defeat signifies for Hemingway "grace under fire," the stoicism that makes man ultimately the victor in life. But is this a stoicism founded on life-giving heroism or on deathly pride?

Just as an ideal can inspire for the good, it can equally be perverted for the bad. The ego ideal of being "brave" can serve to bring out the best in a person in relation to his behavior toward others and his commitment to certain values within society, or it can serve to enhance a person's narcissism and self-aggrandizement. The distinction is in the motivation and aim of bravery—whether a person commits an act of bravery out of adherence to a higher ideal that is external to the self, or whether a person's ideal is to be someone who is seen to be brave and therefore admired and superior to others.

Purnell makes this distinction clear in her biography of the American spy, Virginia Hall, who worked for the British SOE during 1941 to 1944, primarily assisting the French Resistance (Purnell, 2019). Purnell emphasizes that Virginia Hall's remarkable acts of espionage and sustained bravery were motivated by her desire to fight injustice and tyranny, to struggle against the persecution of others, and not out of a need for personal recognition. At the end of the war, in a conversation with other agents speculating on whether they would receive honors, Hall insisted "that we hadn't fulfilled our missions for medals, honours or official recognition," but for more noble motives (Purnell, 2019, p. 305). Hall approached her work as a vocation in which saving as many lives as possible was her own measure of success. By and large it was the agents who were attracted to the glamour and danger of the role, along with the reward of recognition, who tended not to fare so well. In her preface, Purnell quotes from the chief of MI6 who claims to look for recruits "who do not shout loud and show off but who have had to 'fight to get on in life'" (ibid., p. 5). Purnell also makes the important point that bravery is often invisible and goes unrecognized. She refers to the prostitutes in France, some of whom Hall worked with, who deliberately spread infection to their German clients. As Purnell comments, "most people were interested only in clearly defined acts of heroism rather than these more complex displays of courage" (ibid., p. 319).[3]

Like other agents, Hall's bravest achievement may have been her endurance of years of unrelenting fear. Purnell writes:

> All agents are scared. Most suffered from chronic insomnia. "There are endless nightmares of uncertainty," said one. "The tensions, the nerve strain and fatigue, the all-demanding alertness of living a lie, these are [the agent's] to meet, accept, and control. They are never, really, conquered." But even if not vanquished, the fear had to be controlled without the prop of alcohol, gambling or sleeping around. Agents had to find the strength to go on from within themselves, but there were precious few who could do so.
>
> (ibid., p. 149)

Hall's endurance, however, is a far cry from Bion's lesson in "manliness" or Scott's stalwart deadly mission in the Antarctic. Paradoxically, it was Hall's awareness of the reality of danger and her own fear that kept her and the agents working for her safe. If she had been lured by the narcissistic appeal of the hero, she might have stepped into the trap of omnipotence and jeopardized her life and those of others.

Dissociation and reenactment

> A bullet had spattered, missing my head. I had not heard it or been aware. The near miss they said, unlike the whining more distant bullet, made a loud crack—or killed you.
>
> As I looked at my map and hands in the tank I felt I was floating about four feet above my self, Allen [a fellow soldier] an interested and unfrightened spectator. This dis-association, depersonalization was a way of achieving security—spontaneous, automatic, but potentially costly as it involved not knowing of the imminence of death.
>
> (Bion, 1982, p. 132)

Bion describes his experience of being under attack in his tank. As he understands it, the disassociation and depersonalization that take him over automatically give him some sense of safety, however illusory. The "imminence of death" is whitewashed out of the picture, obliterating fear and mortality at the same time. This is what enables Bion to go on functioning and, as it turns out, to save most of his crew.

Dissociation is a defense against events that threaten our existence, whether they be physical or mental. On high alert, the endorphins in our nervous system are triggered with the effect of giving us a surge of adrenaline that both heightens our sense of awareness and disconnects us from the physical reality of being within our own bodies. This disconnect does not simply quell our sense of fear, it also stimulates a sense of invincibility and omnipotence—the high that is such a prevalent experience of those who have served on the frontlines. A high that can easily become addictive, both on an actual physical level and psychologically.

The lethal addictiveness of a dissociative high appeared unexpectedly in a session with a twenty-seven-year-old foreign student, Madeleine, who was in analysis with me. Madeleine had originally come into analysis because she was suffering from panic attacks. After a few months it became clear that Madeleine's panic attacks occurred when she was angry with her mother and, terrified of expressing her anger openly, she became gripped by anxiety and a strangling sensation in her throat that made her gasp for air. Madeleine's brother was seven years older, and when she was two years old her father suddenly walked out of the family home, never to appear again. No one knew what had happened to him. Her mother was so distraught and anxious that any small complaint or demand on Madeleine's part would result in her mother becoming furious and blaming her daughter for her father's disappearance. In the course of her analysis, Madeleine could see that her mother was most probably having a breakdown at the time, and that it was possible for her to have a different relationship with her as an adult. Madeleine's panic attacks ceased, and she said she felt much happier and less anxious in her everyday life. She was also much more aware of her anger toward friends and her employer when conflicts arose.

Madeleine said, "When I feel very very anxious, I now have some clue that it's because I'm feeling angry and I can't quite trust it's going to be all right. I take a big breath and try to think what it is that's making me angry."

I commented, "When you can breathe and create a space inside of you, you can create a space to think as well. You don't have to shut everything down."

Madeleine then became silent and it seemed as if her body, lying on the couch, had become paralyzed.

She said,

> A strange thing happened to me. It might have been last night or the night before—I can't honestly remember ... I was walking home and I walked down the same street where I had been raped. Normally I do everything to avoid the area. But that night I felt I *had* to go there. I wasn't afraid, if anything I felt excited and I think this is what made me go there again. I felt this rush of excitement, not exactly sexual, but close to it. Nothing happened but I don't recall seeing anything very clearly, just feeling like I was on a massive high. I got home and everything was normal again. I then had a dream that it was a very cold wintry night and I was skating on a lake covered by ice, like I used to do as a child. There was a group of people standing on the shore watching me and looking very anxious. The ice was thin in parts and I knew it wasn't safe. But I also knew it was different for me—that bad things didn't happen to me and I felt euphoric as I twirled on the ice showing off in front of the people on the shore. I suddenly woke up just as the ice was beginning to crack beneath me.

Madeleine had been attacked and raped on a small side street one night as she was going home several years ago when she had been at university. It was a brutal attack, leaving her with serious injuries that took some time to recover from. She had told me about the attack at the beginning of her analysis and described having an out of body experience while it was happening. She watched herself being attacked, and then walked away in her mind to the shore of a lake where she had often retreated as a child when it was too painful to be at home. Madeleine assumed that during the attack she had dissociated and psychically retreated to a place of safety as a way of distancing herself from how terrified she was.

After Madeleine told me her dream, I noted, "A relief not to have to have to go on skating on thin ice, but not so exciting."

Madeleine, wiping some tears from her face, replied,

> I couldn't resist walking down that street again. I wanted to feel like I did when I was dissociated. It was two days after I found out about my brother's cancer and I felt so helpless. I think in some way I wanted to go back to the lake and freeze time. I wanted to feel powerful again and the only way to do that was to risk something dangerous, to risk my own life.

Although Madeleine had spent considerable time going over the details of what she could remember of her rape and her feelings of rage and impotence at the time, it was only by re-experiencing her physical excitement through the reenactment of her trauma that she was able to understand her compelling need to put herself at risk. The news of her brother's cancer had made Madeleine feel as helpless as she had during the rape, and as helpless as she felt when her father disappeared, and her bewilderment at being blamed for this. Replaying these events in her life had enabled both of us to see how powerful dissociative states can be in offering to alleviate what is in reality too frightening and painful to be able to experience and to think about. Omnipotence takes the form of a safe haven that defies reality and helplessness.

In the documentary film *Storyville: Under the Wire*, about the journalist Marie Colvin's final assignment covering the siege of Homs in Syria, the narrator, Paul Conroy, who accompanied Colvin as her photographer, observes Colvin watching, enraged, as a baby dies in the field hospital. Conroy states, "I knew that this was now her story and she was going to take this story and go for it whatever the cost, whatever the cost." Colvin had, throughout her career as a war journalist, emphasized the importance of bearing witness and being the mouthpiece for the victims of war. Taking on this role enabled her to allay her own sense of helplessness in the face of extreme violence. What the photographer could see at this point was that her defiance against her own limits in her struggle to help had won. Her insistence to stay in Homs in order to cover the attacks on civilians and the hospital itself ultimately led to her death.

Although Colvin did not intend her acts of bravery to draw attention to herself, she had a history of defying her limits from childhood (see Hilsum, 2018). Her naturally defiant temperament, coupled with her survival of so many close calls with death, would have certainly encouraged her to take what many other journalists would see as dangerous risks. It may have been her lack of fear, or her repeated experiences of escaping fear in an adrenaline rush, that made Colvin reckless. Her act of selfishness was to extend her stay in the hospital in Homs, encouraging her fellow journalists to stay on by example—but in doing so, as the shelling worsened, Colvin was killed along with a colleague, and several others, including Paul Conroy, were seriously injured, becoming a burden to the Syrians they were trying to help. Colvin had made it clear amongst the small number of journalists in Homs that this was *her* story (of the dying baby) and possessively staked her claim. Her drive to get the most powerful story, to change the course of events, seemed to have taken on the qualities of an addiction, most notably as a way of anesthetizing her frustrations and anger and of defying her own limits. Death is embraced as an act of defiance. Colvin's bravery is in stark contrast to the unseen bravery of the spy, Virginia Hall, who could never identify herself without risk and who was keenly aware of her responsibility for the lives of others and the dangers of taking risks that would jeopardize them or the cause they were fighting for. Rescuers, as we have seen, often deny feeling fear, explaining that they felt compelled to act by their conscience. This is not the same thing as overcoming fear. Although both Hall and Colvin must have felt fear at different times, they both knew the risks of dismissing it.

The addictive ideal of bravery

David Nott, a vascular surgeon, describes the allure of power that attracted him to working in war zones. Nott points to two experiences that were instrumental in shaping what was to become a vital mission for him, as well as an ideal to aspire to. The first epiphany happened when Nott saved a woman's life. He writes, "I was amazed that a simple act of surgery could pull a patient back from the brink of death. It was above all a sense of power … the saving power of surgery if you have acquired the necessary techniques to resolve or prevent the effects of a particular physical problem" (Nott, 2019, pp. 46–47). Having experienced this new sense of power, Nott then watched the film *The Killing Fields*. He writes,

> There is even a scene set in a hospital in Phnom Penh, overrun
> with patients, where a surgeon has to deal with a shrapnel injury

and complains about the lack of blood to infuse—I wanted to be that surgeon. I wanted to be a humanitarian doctor, in severe and stressful situations, using my knowledge to intervene and make a difference ... I began to feel a very strong sense of mission, an urge to work in war zones where my surgery could be put to good use in hospitals like the one in the film ...

(ibid., p. 49)

Here we see the progression within Nott of realizing he had the skills to save lives, and the power this gave him, to being able to imagine himself in a besieged environment in which everyone's life was in danger. He could not only save a patient's life, he could risk his own in the process. It was as if his ego ideal had latched on to yet a more intense challenge that would test not only his professional skills to their limit but that would push his own physical and emotional resources to their limit.

Nott recalls,

Every night I watched the news from Sarajevo in a state of high anxiety, transfixed by the horror of what was happening. I could feel my heart pounding and my breathing getting faster. It was as if I were being physically drawn in. It felt very strange to have such a powerful physiological reaction to events happening far away, in a country I'd never visited, but a flame had been lit ... [I] had a sleepless night before we flew down to Sarajevo. But the sleeplessness was due as much to excitement as anxiety (and the cold—it was freezing). Also, I was a young man. I felt immortal.

(ibid., pp. 52–53)

Swept away by the enormity of the task ahead, Nott points out that it was his excitement that was preventing him from sleeping and from being aware of anxious feelings—an excitement that fueled his sense of omnipotence in the face of danger.

Nott goes on to describe his experience in arriving at the Kosovo Hospital and how quickly he became attuned to the different levels of threat in being under constant bombardment. He writes,

That first night I shivered again in my sleeping bag, but this time was kept awake by the sheer noise of the gunfire all around.

It was constant, although the snipers tended to be quieter at night because they couldn't see their targets. But the shelling went on, and over time I would be able to distinguish between the sound of incoming fire from the Serbs and outgoing missiles being fired back at them. There was a subtle difference in pitch, and we got to be quite blasé about the sound of a rocket we knew was heading away from us.

(ibid., p. 57)

Nott's attunement in this situation was the opposite of dissociation; it was a natural adaptive response that enabled him to discern when he was in imminent danger and to disregard peripheral alarms that could distract him from his work.

Nevertheless, Nott's dedication to his work became tinged to a fault with his omnipotence. Nott describes suddenly finding himself in the operating theater, in the dark, abandoned by his medical team while the hospital was being shelled. Despite Nott's valiant efforts, the patient, a young boy died. As Nott admits, "this experience taught me two things: first, I'd have to toughen up; second, I also had to take care of myself. Not just because there was no one else there who was going to do that for me, but because I wouldn't helping anyone if I was dead" (ibid., p. 64). Nott was learning the lesson that Virginia Hall had been all too aware of and that Marie Colvin had, in her determination to brave anything in order to succeed, failed to heed.

However, taking care of himself flew against Nott's sense of omnipotence. He knew he had been "bitten by the bug of adrenaline," and explains, "The danger was a buzz. I felt that nothing could touch me. I was invincible" (ibid., p. 67). In this heightened adrenalin state, ordinary signals of pain and fear are dulled so that even our most basic needs to sleep and eat become remote in our awareness. Fighting fear in order to survive or to ensure the survival of others is paramount. It is hardly surprising that those who have been in the frontlines of battle find ordinary life lackluster. As Nott admits, "The endorphin rush of hearing and feeling bullets and missiles whizz overhead was like nothing I'd encountered before, and everyday life seemed humdrum by comparison" (ibid., p. 70).[4]

Nott makes it clear that the experience of living on a knife edge and the heightened awareness of power it brings can be highly addictive.

Escaping death while others around you are dying provokes a sense of immortality. At the same time, with the sense of immortality comes that of responsibility and guilt when not everyone can be saved. Both the high of defying fear and death and the guilt about inevitable failures provide a strong pull to return to the frontline. Nott is particularly aware of his own vulnerability to power. He describes riding in an ambulance and being shot at by snipers:

> I felt righteously angry about it. Ever since that day, the cause of ensuring the sanctity and free passage of medical personnel in war zones has been very close to my heart, and not just for my own self-preservation.
>
> But once the initial shock had faded, I had to confront another emotion that was more surprising, even a little disturbing. I felt elated, exhilarated, euphoric. I had never felt more alive; it was as if I had been reborn. I had come close to being killed, but that only made it more exciting. If I could cope with this, I thought, I could cope with anything.
>
> Sarajevo was my first taste of this, and I knew I wanted more. It was a strange mix of altruism, wanting to help others, and pure selfishness—chasing the high of intervening to save lives, but also of living my own life close to the edge.
>
> (ibid., p. 69)

During another bombardment of the hospital where Nott was working, he states: "As the alarms went off a strange feeling would come over me—everyone could hear the sound of mortars landing and sometimes they were extremely close, but I always felt that one would never land near me or cause me any harm. It was like, *This is happening, but it won't happen to me*" (ibid., p. 87).

Being devoid of fear, anything becomes possible—even immortality—as long as one continues to be dissociated from reality.

Nott inevitably continues to be haunted by the violence and deaths he has witnessed, counterbalanced to some degree by the triumphs. He is also fully aware of the addictive aspect of repeatedly placing his life at risk. Rather tellingly, he admonishes, "The trick is knowing when to stop, as any ex-junkie will tell you" (ibid., p. 151). But as any ex-junkie will know, it is not a question of knowing when to stop; the only answer is total abstinence.

Fear and submission

A Russian soldier recounts his experience of fighting in Afghanistan:

> We were suspended between life and death, and someone else's life and someone else's death was in our hands too. Is there anything stronger than that feeling? We made whoopee there in a way we'll never make whoopee again anywhere else. Women loved us there in a way they'll never love us again anywhere else. Everything was heightened by the closeness of death: we were always spinning and sparkling, right there alongside death. We had lots of different adventures. I think I know the scent of danger, the way it smells when you see the back of your own head through someone else's eyes ... Your third eye opens up ... I tried everything there and I came out unscathed. It was a man's life there. I feel nostalgic. The Afghan syndrome.
>
> (Alexievich, 2017, p. 106)

This soldier, like the surgeon, describes in similar terms the intoxication of being "suspended between life and death" and having the power over someone's else's life and death. They were gods who could not be touched by fear or death. In this immortal twilight zone, they could transcend themselves and their vulnerability. The experience of self, of "*me*," becomes hugely powerful one moment and insignificant the next. Another soldier explains: "Something happens to time when you think about death and see it. Close to the fear of death—the attraction of death" (ibid., p. 17).

While omnipotent states enable us to transcend the self and its boundaries, death is the ultimate negation of self, a final submission to a higher force in which the self no longer exists. The attraction of death described by the Russian soldier is, however, complex as it bears the promise of complete release from life with its struggles and limitations and freedom from fear itself. Unless death is the result of suicide, it is something outside our power to determine. In this respect, death highlights our acts of self-agency. Through our mortality we are reminded of our need to feel powerful, to exert self-agency, and our desire to submit to a greater power.

Power and submission are inextricably linked, two sides of the same coin. Taken to their extreme, they become destructive. A contemporary example of this is the suicide bomber who sacrifices his/her life for a higher cause with the reward of honor on earth and perpetual love in the hereafter. This is not so far away from the soldier who is martyred in fighting for his country. But in the case of what it means to be brave, martyrdom has little value and lacking fear has even less currency. Acts of bravery are primarily motivated by individual conscience and shaped by one's ego ideal;[5] their effectiveness rests centrally on a calculation of risk, often made in the moment of crisis, that is founded on fear. Without paying attention to our fear, or at times our lack of fear, we cannot judge the effect of our actions. Rather than protecting or saving others from harm, we may become reckless and destructive, to ourselves and others. This is not an expression of self-agency; it is instead a complete disregard for self. Without our fear, paradoxically, we become like the gods, indifferent to our fate and to the power of mortals.

In his novel *Island of the Doomed*, written in the aftermath of World War II, Stig Dagerman describes the terrifying anxieties of seven castaways facing inevitable death on a deserted island. Dagerman warns against the loss of fear, as it is fear that guides us and brings our conscience to light:

> [W]e know thanks to the most wide-open of all the world's wide-open eyes that, as often as not, the goal is an illusion, and the important thing is the direction, because that and that alone is what we have control over. And awareness, oh yes, awareness: the open eyes which fearlessly scrutinize their dangerous position must be the stars of our ego, our only compass, the compass which decides which direction we take, because if there is no compass, there can be no direction ... we need to sharpen our awareness until it becomes as sharp as a sword-blade, and sharp as an arrow-head supplemented by the brutal strength of a drill. Then our conscience operates in our consciousness, which is after all just an idyllic description of our fear, for our fear reminds us

constantly of the right direction ... That's why we must keep our fear alive within us, like an ice-free harbor which can always help us to survive the winter. The bubbling undercurrent beneath the winter floods.

(Dagerman, 2012, pp. 333–335)

Notes

1. It is striking to note here that within a week of the fall of the Reich and Hitler's suicide, Germany experienced an "epidemic" of suicide across the population as their vision of the future and the structural meaning of their lives was destroyed (see Huber, F. (2019). *Promise Me You'll Shoot Yourself: The Downfall of Ordinary Germans in 1945*. London: Allen Lane).
2. It is notable that the retrogressive Brexit battle cry, "Let's Make Britain Great Again," harks back to the patriotic spirit of post-World War II, a time in which widespread hardship is seen to have brought the country together.
3. During war women have traditionally played important parts behind the scenes that remain largely unrecognized. Women who take on traditional male roles that require bravery, who are, for example, engaged in espionage or war reporting, face the further obstacle of challenging societal expectations of women's roles. Their bravery is twofold. Commenting on her experience as a war reporter, Zahra Hankir writes, "To be a woman war reporter in this part of the world [the Middle East] can sometimes mean you are defying not only the state but also your society, family, and the role you are expected to play within your home" (see Hankir, Z. (2019). *Our Women on the Ground: Essays by Arab Women Reporting from the Arab World*. London: Penguin).
4. Medical staff working in emergency rooms of hospitals often experience a similar addictive attraction to their work, explaining that it pushes them to their extreme limits, they have no time to think or to get bored, and it gives them an adrenaline rush that is hard to beat in ordinary life.
5. See Chapter Two for a full discussion of what it means to be brave.

References

Alexievich, S. (2017). *Boys in Zinc*. London: Penguin.
Alexievich, S. (2019). *Last Witnesses*. New York: Random House.

Bion, W. R. (1982). *The Long Week-End: 1897–1919*. Abingdon: Fleetwood Press.

Channel 4. (2019). *Storyville: Under the Wire*. Documentary film narrated by Paul Conroy. Channel 4 Productions. 11 February.

Dagerman, S. (2012). *Island of the Doomed*. Minneapolis: University of Minnesota Press.

Fulbrook, M. (2018). *Reckonings: Legacies of Nazi Persecution and the Quest for Justice*. Oxford: Oxford University Press.

Hemingway, E. (1952). *The Old Man and the Sea*. London: Arrow Books.

Hilsum, L. (2018). *In Extremis: The Life of the War Correspondent Marie Colvin*. London: Chatto and Windus.

Nott, D. (2019). *War Doctor: Surgery on the Front Line*. London: Picador.

Purnell, S. (2019). *A Woman of No Importance: The Untold Story of WWII's Most Dangerous Spy, Virginia Hall*. London: Virago.

CHAPTER SEVEN

Belief and dissent: whistleblowers, conscientious objectors, and saying no

> [T]here always comes a time in history when the person who dares
> to say that two and two make four is punished by death. The school-
> master knows this quite well. And the question is not what reward or
> punishment awaits the demonstration; it is knowing whether or not
> two and two do make four.
>
> Camus, *The Plague*, p. 101

Unlike a state of war in which a country is defending itself against a
foreign threat, dissent is a signifier of internal conflict within a nation,
a community, a family, or within oneself. It has the potential to divide
groups along sectarian lines marked by the belief systems that form the
basis of our identity. We inevitably absorb the belief systems of those
around us, but we also make emotional choices that are in tune with
how we perceive the world, what kind of world we want to live in, and
how we see ourselves as actors within the world. These are psychological processes that establish our identification and belonging with certain
groups and our personal identity. Our internal moral compass also relies
on our sense of identity, and binds us to social norms and collective
morals. While as humans we may be able to survive physically in certain

conditions, we cannot survive psychically without a sense of who we are, and this is derived from our relationships with others, starting with our mother who gave birth to us. Within this context, dissent is an essential component of our relationships; it gives us the freedom to question our beliefs and to differentiate what may be "right" or "wrong" in the way we want to relate to the world and others. Our ability to dissent is critical in protecting our identity on many levels and in helping us to ensure a healthy society.

The person who dissents is expressing a fundamental disagreement that reflects his or her own psychic "truth"—a truth that contests a reality that is misperceived or distorted. This is the bravery of being true to oneself, voicing or acting on what one believes is right and moral, often at the risk of endangering one's life or well-being. These are the whistleblowers, the conscientious objectors, the investigative journalists, and the ones who do not watch or comply with group corruption or abuse but who act on their principles. The person who acts in opposition to the group and its norms is either vilified or ostracized. Stories of the "Me Too" campaign highlight not only the pressure to remain silent but some of the consequences of exposing institutionalized systems of abuse against women. Dissenting against the status quo or exposing falsehoods or tyrannies that oppress large groups of people may be suppressed in other ways, for example, by total censorship and eradication of the dissenters, as we see in totalitarian societies such as North Korea and China, or by playing down the evidence of corruption either by disregarding it outright or by claiming it is false. We tend to see this latter stratagem in democratic societies, such as the USA and the UK, where whatever is contrary to the politics of the ruling party is debunked as insignificant or "fake news." This was vividly apparent in the way in which the US impeachment proceedings against Donald Trump (December 18, 2019 to February 5, 2020) were broadcast by the media; a brief glance at news reporting between CBS and Fox News revealed clearly different views of reality and what were considered the "true" facts. Just as political dissent may be suppressed in a variety of ways, we also suppress our internal dissenting views, our inner voice, in similar ways—through denial, dismissiveness, and disbelief. Most of us are aware at some point in our lives of believing in something we later discover is not true, and how much our beliefs are emotionally tailored to the way we want our world and ourselves to be. If we look in the mirror of our individual psyches, we can see how our belief systems are formed and the dynamics of dissent clearly reflected.

Being true to oneself—the whistleblower

The whistleblower who exposes corruption committed either by an individual or an organization risks ostracism, excommunication, imprisonment and in some cases death. It is a highly dangerous position to be in and while in some instances, such as sexual harassment, it is fueled by personal grievance, it is more often triggered by a sense of what is right and wrong and the importance of protecting a system of moral values. Like the bravery of those who rescued Jews and others persecuted in Nazi Germany, the whistleblower acts on his/her own conscience. It is not a heroic act intended for self-glorification or stemming from a narcissistic need for attention,[1] it is an act intended to bring to light an abuse of power either between individuals or within a group and an attempt to reassert moral order.

With the huge advances in modern technology and worldwide social media, whistleblowers in the field of information gathering and intelligence have received notable public attention. Edward Snowden, working for the CIA, began raising ethical concerns about the use of developing technology to no avail. In 2013 Snowden then released extensive classified NSA documents to journalists exposing a global network of surveillance programs run by the National Security Agency (NSA) and the Five Eyes Intelligence Alliance with the cooperation of telecommunications companies and European governments. As a result of this action, Snowden was charged with violating the Espionage Act of 1917 and his US passport was revoked. He secured asylum in Russia, where he continues to live. His recent memoir, *Permanent Record* (2019), provoked the US Justice Department to file suit against Snowden for breaching non-disclosure agreements with the US federal government. As a result, Snowden's book sales have skyrocketed, and *Permanent Record* was listed as No.1 on the Amazon bestseller list the same day.

Five years after Snowden's disclosure and in the wake of the UK Brexit referendum, two whistleblowers, Christopher Wylie and Shahmir Sanni, employees of the media firm Cambridge Analytica, exposed the widespread manipulation of social media, and Facebook in particular, conducted by Cambridge Analytica in influencing the referendum vote. Further information pointed to interference in the Trump election in the US. Wylie's disclosures about the illegal role played by Cambridge Analytica resulted in a parliamentary inquiry into fake news held by the Parliamentary Digital, Culture, Media and Sport Committee in 2018; the resignation of Alexander Nix, CEO of Cambridge Analytica; the effective shut down of Cambridge Analytica; and, in the US, a congressional hearing with Mark Zuckerberg about Facebook's use of personal information, leading to a maximum fine of £500,000 (which Facebook is appealing).

Many believe that Wylie's exposure of the manipulation of data acquired through social media to undermine democratic processes and the abuse of power manifested by the largest social media organization, Facebook, has had a more profound effect on public awareness and the way in which politicians think about and use technology than Edward Snowden's disclosures. However, the striking difference is that while Snowden has become a political refugee and continues to be attacked by the US government, Wylie's whistleblowing has more or less vanished in the wind. Wylie complains,

> I feel like the whole story is a lesson in institutional failure. Because although Facebook paid the price in its share value, there have been virtually no consequences for people who have committed unlawful acts ... When you look at how, for example the NCA [National Crime Agency] has just sat on blatant evidence of Russian interference in Brexit ... When you look at how you can go and commit the largest infraction of campaign finance law in British history and get away with it ... the consequence of this is an irreversible change to the constitutional settlement of the country.
>
> (Cadwalladr, 2019)

Both Snowden and Wylie revealed institutional abuse and subsequent failure to acknowledge and rectify this. Snowden breached confidentiality and was outlawed to a foreign country (as it happens, a country that is heavily implicated in media interference of the US). Wylie has been outlawed through inaction. One of the most effective methods of

Western democratic social control to quell dissent when it has raised its head is to absorb and normalize it, thereby neutralizing it. In the case of Cambridge Analytica, the press, Parliament, and the US Congress have all found various parties guilty of wrongdoing but, perhaps because there are no individual victims to insist on justice, the consequences can be put to one side and the dissent silenced.[2] Just as is the case within a family when one of its members protests about unfair treatment, within large groups, governments, or organizations, hearing the dissent and doing nothing about it maintains an illusion of democracy while reinforcing the power of the oligarchy.

Both Snowden and Wylie, like other whistleblowers, acted according to their conscience and a deep-seated belief in constitutional rights and due process—they were also both highly aware of technology's invasive power into the lives of private citizens and both reached a point in their work of what might be called "revelation." For Snowden, the question of ethics first arose when he was introduced to XKEYSCORE, the NSA's tool used for intimate electronic surveillance. He describes a pivotal moment in his work when he was observing an Indonesian man whom the NSA was interested in. Snowden writes,

> He [the Indonesian man] was sitting in front of his computer, as I was sitting in front of mine. Except that in his lap he had a toddler, a boy in a diaper.
>
> The father was trying to read something, but the kid kept shifting around, smacking the keys and giggling. The computer's internal mic picked up his giggling and there I was, listening to it on my headphones. The father held the boy tighter, and the boy straightened up, and, with his dark crescent eyes, looked directly into the computer's camera—I couldn't escape the feeling that he was looking directly at me. Suddenly I realized that I'd been holding my breath.
>
> (Lethem, 2019, p. 27)

In this chance one-way encounter with the little boy on his father's lap, Snowden suggests a moment when he felt found out and, perhaps because of this, he was able to identify with the one who is watched and experience the invasiveness of what he was doing. This was a moment of self-professed personal insight, but it was also linked to Snowden's patriotic fervor following the September 11 attacks, which he describes as a "totalizing moment." Discharged from the army after an injury, Snowden offered his computing skills to the intelligence community in his wish to protect his country from further attack. He was also what Lethem, reviewing Snowden's book, describes as a "Constitution dork"—*Permanent Record* was published on 17 September, Constitution Day (ibid., p. 28). Snowden explains to his readers that he *liked* to read the Constitution, "partially because its ideas are great, partially because its prose is good, but really because it freaked out my coworkers" (ibid., p. 29). Lethem chalks up Snowden's flippant last line as a way of detracting from his pain and understands Snowden's attachment to the Bill of Rights as "a kind of lonely companion, or perhaps something like a rescue animal that only he cares for sufficiently." Lethem continues to write, "In the period in which he's struggling to understand whether it is incumbent on him to destroy his life in order to protect the Constitution, Snowden is diagnosed with epilepsy. Though he himself never quite goes there, it's hard not to interpret these chapters allegorically: cognitive dissonance as a slow-motion brain seizure. Secrecy as disease" (ibid., p. 29).

Wylie also seems to have experienced a process, if not a moment, of revelation in his work with Cambridge Analytica. As Wylie became increasingly cognizant of illegal activity from misuse of funds to misuse of data, he realized he was operating within a "culture of total disregard for the law." Wylie was a fervent believer in British sovereignty and, like Snowden, in the principle of constitutional rights. During the Parliamentary committee hearings, Wylie stated,

> It makes me so angry because a lot of people supported Leave because they believe in the application of British law and British sovereignty ... And to irrevocably alter the constitutional settlement of this country on fraud is a mutilation of the constitutional settlement of this country. You cannot call yourself a Leaver, you cannot call yourself somebody who believes in British law and win by breaking British law in order to achieve that goal.
>
> (Casalicchio, 2018)

Most significantly, however, Wylie, like Snowden, experienced shame when he began to realize what he was complicit in. He states, "I felt huge amounts of shame for having been part of it. And I don't think I could have forgiven myself for it until it was stopped" (Cadwalladr, 2019). For Wylie, the cognitive dissonance of working within a culture of deceit became untenable because it produced too much shame. We return to the brave actor who puts himself in the path of danger in order to be true to his moral principles, not out of altruism but out of a need to adhere to beliefs that form an integral part of his identity. As we saw in the story of Neoptolemus, he ultimately disobeyed Odysseus' orders when he realized he could not live with himself if he were to betray what he knew was the right way to act.

The internal whistleblower

For many people, the decision to embark on psychoanalysis is the greatest act of bravery and dissent they will make in their lives. Psychoanalysis endeavors to expose and challenge the defense mechanisms developed by the psyche to survive in a dysfunctional environment. These defenses inevitably take their toll in inhibiting development and the ability to think for oneself. Psychoanalysis, as distinct from other forms of psychic healing, is an act of dissent against a collective belief system that has become toxic and harmful to the individual. Entering psychoanalysis is an acknowledgment that something is not working. Usually the patient thinks that he or she is the square peg that needs to be re-shaped in order to fit into the round hole of his/her life. It is only after some time that patients begin to be aware that the misfit can be understood and approached differently. Despite the patient's conscious narrative of what is wrong, there is also the presence of an unconscious rebel that is creating havoc in the patient's life and that is often desperately trying to be heard and seen.

Samantha, a young woman of twenty-six, arrived for a consultation, wearing a somber black suit, dark sunglasses, and black painted fingernails. She wore her austerity like a suit of armor. She announced that she had already tried therapy a couple of times but hadn't felt the therapists understood her and had quit early on. I felt immediately I was being tested and my heart sank with the thought that I would also fail the test. I then wondered whether Samantha, Sam for short, might be a lost cause, determined to destroy whatever relationship was on offer. I also wondered whether perhaps Sam had felt she had in some way failed the test in her life and asked her about this. I managed to hit a nerve; Sam took off her sunglasses and started to tell me about her struggle with her parents. She explained that she had set up her own business to support herself but really wanted to be a writer— something which she was also struggling with. She also explained that a few years ago she had joined a very strict religious group in the hope that this might help her to, as she put it, "overcome myself," but this too had failed, and she left the group feeling more hopeless and conflicted than ever.

I soon began to realize that behind Sam's tough exterior was a frightened and exhausted little girl who had been living under a harsh regime in which the only thing that mattered was what she achieved and never showing any weakness. Her mother had emigrated from a communist country and gave up a menial job after her marriage. She had failed to train as a nurse and instead devoted herself to helping others and charity work, complaining about how badly organized everything was and how undervalued she felt. Faced by her mother's continual complaints, Sam saw herself as the hero who was meant, by her achievements, to rescue her mother from her own sense of failure and frustration, and at the same time she was reminded of her inadequacies by her workaholic and absent father. Sam had spent much of her childhood caught between these impossible demands, living in a regimented way devoid of affection and comfort, and often feeling she had to be the "man" of the house in the absence of her father. When she first contacted me, Sam complained that she had virtually stopped sleeping and admitted, "Something has to give."

In the course of our work together, it became clear that Sam had survived her parents' impossible expectations of her by idealizing their values of utter strength, self-reliance, and perseverance. Her twenty-four-year-old little sister had similarly high expectations of herself, fueled by her older sister's stellar example, and had unconsciously expressed her protest in becoming anorexic and at one point needing hospitalization. Sam, however, continued to perform well until her twenties when she began to have persistent insomnia and to experience writer's block.

She also started to have severe pain in her jaw as she discovered she was clenching her teeth in the night.

As I began to question the "rules" that governed Sam's life and suggested they were a way of trying to please her parents and at the same time imprisoning her within their world, Sam began to be less harsh on herself; she allowed herself to have breaks from her work, and acquired a kitten to keep her company. She also began to sleep better.

Sam came to a session in an excited state, eager to tell me of her dream from the night before.

> I hardly ever dream and this really makes me feel like something's happening inside of me—that I have an inside! I'm not just empty inside. I've had this dream before and have always felt it was a kind of warning, but I didn't know what it was warning me about. I dreamt that I was crossing a railway track and my shoe had gotten trapped in a siding somehow. I could hear in the distance the sound of a train coming towards me and I couldn't free my foot. I then saw that my parents were standing on the track far ahead and weren't moving. I stepped out of my shoe and ran to the side of the tracks just in time. I yelled to my parents but they couldn't hear me and were oblivious to the train approaching. The train killed them both. I woke up feeling both shocked and elated—it felt like a huge relief that it was all over.

Sam told me her first thought about the dream:

> I had started to write last night—I've been able to do a bit of writing every now and then when I don't think about it too much—I have to catch myself unawares as it is. I then remembered a conversation on the phone with my mother earlier in the day when she was complaining that nothing was going right with her committee work. It made me feel I should have found a way to help her, but I couldn't. I was useless. Of course, after this, I couldn't do any more writing. I think I felt really pissed off—I can't bear hearing her complaints. I ended up hanging up on her and kept shouting, "Stop it, stop it, stop it!" I think the train in the dream is this unrelenting pressure to perform and make everything all right—a pressure that is going to kill me. The only way to escape is to step out of my shoe—probably like stepping out of my life! And that's what saves me. But my parents can't do that and they're killed.

I commented,

> When you're angry with your parents for putting you under such extreme pressure, you feel murderous toward them. And maybe you also want to kill off this couple who rule your world, who make you feel that you can only fail and who drive you to exhaustion. Stepping out of your shoe is an admission that you can only save yourself if you allow yourself to be vulnerable. It is also your rebellion against your parents' rules that you must always wear strong shoes to protect yourself.

Sam replied,

> Yes, that's right! Such a relief to step out of my shoe and to get rid of *them*! I don't even feel guilty about it. It makes me feel hopeful. I'm sick of my heavy shoes. I want to wear delicate shoes—shoes that are not meant just for work.

Sam's dream marked a turning point in her analysis and in her growing awareness that she had choices about her actions and some degree of agency over her future. In the beginning of her analysis, she had likened her state of mind to being in a kind of Stalinist regime, in which all that mattered was production levels and basic survival. Everything was done for the glory of the Fatherland, and every sacrifice was honored. Sam recounted an incident before she started analysis when she was trying to tell her mother that she hadn't slept in days and was at her wit's end. Her mother interrupted her, saying that she had to leave for a committee meeting, at which point Sam had a panic attack. Her mother chided her for being histrionic, and left her writhing on the floor. Sam's protest fell on deaf ears, as she felt had happened many times in the past. By the time Sam started her analysis with me, she found it hard to imagine a world outside her family's communist collective. Feeling understood in her analysis opened the possibility of living in another world. As Sam later said, "It doesn't have to be this way."

After a year or so of analysis, Sam had dinner with her sister, Louise. They rarely met, as Louise lived in another city. Sam had encouraged her sister to start therapy, especially as she was still struggling with her eating problems. At dinner, Sam reported that she had tentatively tried to discuss her parents with Louise and suggested that the family dynamics had been destructive to them both as children. Sam said,

> I remember when we were teenagers and there was a big drama because my mother had collapsed from exhaustion and, of course, my father was away at work. We were left to look after my mother. My sister would not leave my mother's side and I knew she was throwing up whenever she ate anything—she was stick thin. I said to my sister, "This is all so screwed up—they are both killing themselves by their obsession about being productive and we're the ones who are suffering and keeping Mother alive." My sister simply looked at me as if I was speaking a foreign language and said I shouldn't say such negative things, that I had no sympathy. I felt like I had blown the whistle on our family and there was no one to hear me. At dinner, now that my sister is in therapy, I thought she might have changed. But when we started talking about our parents, she said how important it was to try to understand them and not to be angry with them. She said she is beginning to understand her eating problem and can see that it is her need to control everything but she insisted that it has nothing to do with her feelings about our parents. She actually said, "It's my fault, I feel such a failure and I just have to be stricter with myself."

Sam stayed silent for a while and then said,

> She's given up. She wants to go on thinking it's all her fault. I had hoped she would become a kind of ally—that she would dissent as well—but she won't. She's like a prisoner who has given up hoping she will be released from prison. She thinks she just has to make do with her prison cell. I remember how hopeless I felt when I first came to see you and how long it took to begin to think that things could be different. I'm not sure if she will get there.

Sam described how despairing she had felt as a teenager when her dissent, her whistleblowing, had not been heard. She withdrew further into herself and felt even more isolated. When she spoke about her sister, she could see how her sister had lost hope of being heard (even within herself) and could only cope by strengthening her defenses of being strong and persevering and in this way dissociate from her pain. Sam's description of the trajectory from dissent to dissociation is reminiscent of John Bowlby's writings on stages of attachment and separation in the development of young children. Bowlby writes:

> Whenever a young child who has had an opportunity to develop an attachment to a mother figure is separated from her unwillingly he shows distress; and should he also be placed in a strange environment and cared for by a succession of strange people such distress is likely to be intense. The way he behaves follows a typical sequence. At first he *protests* vigorously and tries by all the means available to him to recover his mother. Later he seems to *despair* of recovering her but none the less remains preoccupied with her and vigilant for her return. Later still he seems to lose his interest in his mother and to become emotionally *detached* from her.
>
> (Bowlby, 1978, p. 46)

Bowlby concludes with the reassurance that, "Nevertheless, provided the period of separation is not too prolonged, a child does not remain detached indefinitely. Sooner or later after being reunited with his mother his attachment to her emerges afresh" (ibid., pp. 46–47).

In Sam's case, although she had not been physically separated from her mother, she told me that her mother had first started her regime of training her to be self-reliant and "grown up" when she was a toddler. I suspected this regime change, albeit gradual, had nevertheless been experienced as a painful deprivation and that Sam's attempts at protest had not been successful, as indeed her later panic attack had failed. When she began analysis, Sam was in a state of despair verging on detachment. Bowlby describes these emotional states in relation to a child's experience of dependency that has been disrupted and threatened. We can extend this analogy to our experience of changes in our physical or social environment in which what is familiar and offers some sense of security, of "going on being," as Winnicott describes, is taken away or lost, and is accompanied by feelings of impotence and futility.

Silencing dissent

If we substitute the word "dissent" for "protest" we can apply Bowlby's stages on a wider scale to political dissent that either fails or remains unheard. This process is vividly described in Sebastian Haffner's well-known memoir, *Defying Hitler*, focusing on the year 1933 and the gradual encroachment of fascism in the early days of the Third Reich (Haffner, 2003). Haffner's discomfort in the face of increasing Nazi power was, he claims, shared by many Germans.

> As for the Nazis, my nose left me with no doubts. It was just tiresome to talk about which of their alleged goals and intentions were still acceptable or even "historically justified" when all of it stank. How it stank! That the Nazis were enemies, my enemies and the enemies of all I held dear, was crystal clear to me from the outset.
>
> (Quoted in Sunstein, 2018, p. 65)

The possibility of protest was weakened if not virtually disabled by the fact that, as Haffner states, the opposing forces were divided. "'We' ... had no alternative party, no banner to carry, no programme and no battle cry. Whom could we follow?" (Haffner, 2003, p. 75).

The lack of a strong, unified liberal party that Haffner describes is as relevant today as it was in the 1930s. Divided opposition has markedly hampered effective protest, most notably in the UK and the US, in fighting the populist groundswell.

Haffner, like other Germans, points to the Night of the Long Knives (Kristallnacht) as the turning point in Hitler's seizure of power and widespread acceptance of what Haffner described as the "inevitable." Haffner describes

> the slow approach of the dreaded event; the confusion of the forces opposed to it and their hopeless adherence to the rules of the game which the enemy daily infringes; the one-sidedness of the "civil war" (there were no barricades, but every day meaningless and childish brawls and gunfights, attack on party offices, and regularly also killings). The mindset of "appeasement" was

also apparent. Powerful groups were in favour of rendering Hitler "harmless" by giving him "responsibility".

(ibid., p. 76)

Citizens' rights and the rule of law were, insidiously, being gradually eradicated.[3] This process took place in incremental stages and, often, in seemingly insignificant ways, for example, a blind eye turned against the boycotting of Jewish stores that was eventually to be extended to racial extermination. As a result, there was time for people to adapt to the new reality and to accept it as the "new normal."

Referring to an incident resulting in the brutal killing of Social Democrats in the Copenick area of Berlin by the SA, Haffner explains,

> This form of terror had the advantage that, according to the circumstances, one could either shrug one's shoulders and speak of "the unavoidable, if regrettable, side effects of any revolution"— using the justification for revolutionary terror—or point to the strict discipline and explain that public law and order were being maintained and that these actions were required to prevent revolutionary disorder overwhelming Germany—the justification for repressive terror. Both excuses were used in turn, depending on the audience being addressed.
>
> (ibid., p. 105)

Through these rationalizations, terror was "normalized" to the point that it could be accepted as a part of everyday life. State censorship further suppressed dissent about what was in effect licensed violence.

Haffner continues: "only a few weeks after the atrocities began, a law was passed that forbade anyone, under pain of severe penalties, to claim, even in the privacy of their own home, that atrocities were taking place" (ibid., p. 105). With this, censorship was not only imposed publicly but reached into the heart of private life. Protest, if it was expressed, had to be made in secret and locked away.

The danger and despair experienced by those who were in opposition to the Third Reich ultimately led to a state of futility and resignation followed by political detachment and dissociation. Like Bowlby's child forcibly separated from his mother for too long, the citizen who is suddenly bereft of a belief system that has defined his/her social norms and expectations will similarly experience protest, despair, and detachment. The gradual acclimation to this kind of traumatic rupture and the impotence it instills creates a slow psychic death that is largely unseen at the time, and yet leaves its mark on the future. Seemingly insignificant aspects of daily life were gradually taken over and molded to reinforce the power of the Reich, the obligatory gesture of "Heil Hitler" being one of the most apparent.[4]

Haffner witnesses his own growing numbness,

> I felt, intensely, the choking, nauseous character of it all, but I was unable to grasp its constituent parts and place them in an overall order. Each attempt was frustrated and veiled by those endless, useless, vain discussions in which we attempted again and again to fit the events into an obsolete, unsuitable scheme of political ideas ... Daily life also made it difficult to see the situation clearly. Life went on as before, though it had now definitely become ghostly and unreal, and was daily mocked by the events that served as it background ... Strangely enough, it was just this automatic continuation of ordinary life that hindered any lively, forceful reaction against the horror.
>
> (ibid., pp. 113–114)

In this "ghostly and unreal" life, the truth is not only silenced but the distinction between true and false is transgressed. The propaganda, what would today be called "fake news," produced by Nazi Germany to support its aims ultimately proved its most effective weapon in undermining and dismissing dissent—and in prolonging its disastrous war policy.

When dissent cannot be silenced

Dissent can succeed within systems that are stable and resilient enough to recognize internal conflicts and to use them as indicators that something needs to change. In this respect, political dissent has been a function of democratic process since the time of Socrates and the founding of the Athenian city-state. Voting is a direct expression of conflicting views that paves the way for political reform. This is not the same as neutralizing dissident elements in order to render them politically ineffective. In the case of my patient, Sam, she was able to dissent against her internal psychic regime not only because her protest was validated by someone else/an "other" but because in this process of affirming her psychic reality, her ego—her head of state—was able to acknowledge that she needed to change, her old defense system was no longer working properly, and she couldn't sustain the ideals she had for so long aspired to. Sam had been exhausted by years of struggling against her parents' belief system and unconsciously had risked her life in this struggle, as her dream of being stuck in the railway track indicated. She underwent a bloodless, if not painful, revolution. On a political level, we can see this kind of successful, bloodless dissent in the Climate Crisis movement in which protestors, such as Greta Thunberg most notably, have made a widespread impact in raising consciousness about the need to change the way in which we use and develop our natural resources. When dissent is stifled, or it is perceived as too threatening, it rears its head in violence. Referring to the American civil rights movement, Martin Luther King Jr. observed, if "repressed emotions do not come out in nonviolent ways, they will come out in ominous expressions of violence. This is not a threat; it is a fact of history" (Anderlini, 2019). Violent dissent comes about when there is a basic disjunction between two or more realities that brings the survival of the predominant reality—and group identity—into question. The protest that asserts two and two make four, as Camus writes, then becomes a fight to the death.

While there are numerous historical examples of political dissent that has turned into violent revolution, the recent example of protestors in Hong Kong is particularly striking. The protest is exceptional in comparison with other political protests around the world, insofar as it has had no single leader. While there have been individuals who have taken a lead amongst some small groups, the protest has appeared like a powerful generational wave overtaking the island. The fact that there has been no identifiable single leader may indicate that the protest is largely coming from the generation of young Hong Kong citizens whose future is most at stake—as a group, they all have something to lose, and this binds them together in action.

As the protest has escalated, with eruptions of violence from both police and protestors, it has fomented intense patriotic loyalty to the values and "freedom" Hong Kong represents since the Handover to mainland China in 1997. Although the Handover agreement ensured that Hong Kong would retain its own legislative system along with people's rights and freedoms for fifty years, this has been widely contested, as rights such as universal suffrage have yet to be achieved. The 2019 extradition law sparked a new wave of protests that has brought to the surface the underlying dissonance in handing Hong Kong sovereignty over to China. This unhappy marriage was essentially an attempt to graft a state governed along democratic principles, giving central importance to individual rights and freedoms, onto a communist system of governance that has emphasized the state's supremacy over the individual. The extradition law marked the first significant threat to control the Hong Kong population. Young people who had grown up with the values and expectations of due process and individual rights became acutely aware that their beliefs and their future were at stake. When the identity of a large group is threatened, the group response is most often to assert its sovereignty, and to resist outside or what is perceived as foreign influence.[5]

While the extradition law has been formally withdrawn as a result of the protests, universal suffrage, guaranteed by Hong Kong's constitution, known as the Basic Law, remains in dispute. Recent elections in Hong Kong have resulted in a pro-democracy landslide, bolstering young people's hopes to protect democracy within Hong Kong and maintain the "one country, two systems" rule. In the meantime, mainland China seems to be taking a long view and is not actively intervening to quell the protest as yet, perhaps wary of another Tiananmen Square. Nevertheless, Beijing described Hong Kong protestors actions as "near terrorism" and their demands for democracy a "malignant virus," accusations which do not bode well for the future in defining protestors as outlaws, threatening the health of the nation.

The journalist Anderlini quotes the Chinese saying, "Birds born in cages think flying is an illness" (Anderlini, 2019). He makes the point that for the Hong Kong protestors to succeed, they need to dispel the image of protestors as being canaries who mistakenly think they can survive outside the safety of their cage. Anderlini argues that the Hong Kong protestors need a visionary leader who can inspire a different view of the future and mitigate the anxieties surrounding widespread change—of surviving outside the cage of communism. Mainland Chinese will be far less sympathetic to protestors depicted as terrorists or as carrying a "virus" than to a leader who represents a higher moral argument and advocates non-violence in affecting change.

The reactions of young people in Hong Kong provide a striking contrast to those of Haffner and his peers in Nazi Germany. The significant difference in these instances is that Hitler was promising to restore Germany as a leading power, if not *the* leading power, in the world, along with prosperity and supremacy in aspects of social life. The Germans were being offered a Faustian pact in which the benefits could be seen to readily outweigh the drawbacks. In Hong Kong, Beijing's attempts to gradually erode Hong Kong's independent constitutional protections threaten the political identity of Hong Kong. There is no Faustian trade-off from the Hong Kong point of view, only increasing restrictions on its governance and its freedoms. Young Hong Kong citizens are highly aware of the threat to their future identity and the potential loss of being able to have a political voice. Some of the protestors have made it clear that this is a fight worth dying for, if need be.

An interview on Channel 4 News conducted by newscaster, Matt Frei, with Hong Kong student protestors illustrates their unflinching courage to protect their future and their beliefs:

> Matt Frei: So you think that this violence—you might get shot, you might get run over, you might get beaten—how much does that scare you?
>
> Joy Siu: I guess we are very frightened, not only the free office but also the protestors in Hong Kong. We know it is the end game of Hong Kong and we know that it is the fight for freedom and our autonomy, so I guess we're all very prepared for this.
>
> MF: And are there students amongst you who are saying to you, "Actually, I don't want any part of this, I'm so scared for my own personal safety I will stay at home as my parents are asking me to?"
>
> JS: I guess the majority are very prepared and they would like to use their lives to defend Hong Kong.

MF: You mean that … to use your lives to defend Hong Kong?

Sunny Cheung: Actually I can give you another example which is many protestors who at the front line they actually prepare a letter—their will.

MF: Have you done that?

SC: Actually I did and put it in my pocket but the point is that we know we have a difficult position in the movement and we try to facilitate and foster and help them.

MF: [Looking at JS] So have you prepared a letter?

JS: Yeah.

MF: You have?

JS: Yeah.

MF: Which you keep on you only when you're demonstrating in case you get killed or you get imprisoned or you keep it at home?

JS: No, I sent it to my little brother.[6]

MF: You did. Have you done that too? [Looking at Kex Leung]

KL: Yes. I would keep it in my pocket when I was out there and I informed my friends that I have such a letter prepared in case I have my untimely death out there on the streets.

While these young people seem to be fully prepared to die for their liberty by continuing to demand that their rights are recognized and enforced, a more subtle and powerful form of dissent is also apparent within the protest in the form of artistic memes that have spread hope and courage across the city. Wall murals, public music, performance art light up the devastated sections of Hong Kong that have seen the greatest destruction. One of the most powerful memes is the image of "Pepe the Frog," taken from a 2006 American comic book and subsequently adopted as an alt-right symbol of hate. The image of "Pepe" can now be seen on t-shirts and banners, with the backstory of being slowly cooked alive. It is an image that has two sides, of Hong Kong being slowly killed and, in contrast, of the alt-right being killed. In combining these opposite meanings, the symbol captures the life and death struggle for the city perfectly (Khong, 2019).

A performance artist, Kacey Wong, well-known for protesting against mainland intrusion, walked through the streets in August 2019 dressed as Moses, holding the tablets inscribed with the five demands of the protestors.[7] The playfulness of the performance alters the impact and the meaning of the protest. As Wong explains, "People not only see it, but they enjoy it … My existence is to provide a moment of relief, to remind us that art can play a humanistic role even in the worst moments" (ibid., 2019). The artistry of dissent emphasizes that culture and beauty and the human need to be creative lie behind the need to protest. Without an open mind, art and the expression of emotion are stifled within the individual and the group.

The patriotic fervor of these students to a democratic Hong Kong is not only a fight for their autonomy; more fundamentally it is a fight to retain their identity and not to be subsumed within the body of communist mainland China. Democracy is the unifying feature for the protestors, coupled with loyalty to place, the island with its clear geographical boundary separating Hong Kong from the rest of China. Paradoxically, Hong Kong's history of British rule, since it became a colony in 1841 during the First Opium War, instilled certain democratic principles from British governance and at the same time created an antipathy to being governed by foreigners. While British rule was considered relatively benign and assured prosperity to the region, it is hardly any wonder that many Hong Kong youth don't want to be governed by "foreign" China, especially at this crucial time when they are establishing their own separate identity. As long as Hong Kong protestors make no substantial headway with Beijing, and without a strong leader to create a sympathetic position, the protest may turn into a war of attrition. The moment the protest begins to die out will, Anderlini predicts, be the most dangerous point; if the more radical protestors feel abandoned they may try to alleviate their anxiety and frustration by provoking violent confrontation and this could, ultimately, lead to quashing the protest altogether and the extinction of a self-governing Hong Kong. Beijing would be wise to adopt a more laissez-faire attitude to Hong Kong that would allow for a continuing benign co-existence. For the young Hong Kong the fact that the Basic Law was established with a time limit and was never envisaged as a permanent arrangement has set up a kind of political reprieve at the end of which certain limited freedoms will be withdrawn, killing off any hope of a democratic future. By beginning to encroach on Hong Kong's self-governance with a view to gradual take-over, Beijing is only fomenting anxiety and unrest within much of the Hong Kong youth. Ironically, it is the paranoia that characterizes totalitarian regimes that so often fosters dissent.

Loyalty, conscience, and bravery

Fighting for one's country is very different from fighting for a cause abroad. During the period of US empire building over the last century or so, the US has intervened and been involved in scores of foreign wars across the world. The justification for foreign intervention has nominally been to protect the principles of democracy in countries where this is under threat, including, more recently, the war against terrorism. Other countries, notably Russia, also have lengthy track records of foreign intervention with parallel ideological rationales, whether it is in Afghanistan or Ukraine or the middle east. Political causes may be the expressed reasons for going to war abroad, but inevitably these are colored by, if not founded on, economic interests and the drive toward colonialization. No matter what motherland sends its sons to war, and no matter what the rationale may be, fighting on foreign ground which soldiers have no affinity with and for a cause that may seem nebulous at best necessarily creates conflicts of interest and of conscience. As we have seen in the history of both world wars, conscientious objectors in the US, in Europe, Russia, and Japan were commonly vilified as unpatriotic cowards, treated as unmanly, and ostracized.[8]

While conscientious objectors are most often those whose religious beliefs conflict with going to war and killing other human beings, there is a different level of complexity when a conscientious objector refuses to go to war on the grounds of patriotism. This latter conflict ran throughout the course of twenty years of US involvement in the Vietnam War (1955–1975) and directly impacted American citizens with the obligatory draft imposed in 1969 that confronted young men with the question of what it was they would be fighting and dying for. This was a particularly acute question given the ultimate French defeat in 1954 by Viet Minh forces, backed by China and the Soviet Union. US engagement was ostensibly to defend democratic rule and to combat the spread of communism, but the already attenuated history of battle in Indochina did nothing to encourage the hopes and aspirations of foreign soldiers.

The documentary filmmaker Ken Burns illustrates the personal conflict that young men faced as they were drafted to fight in Vietnam. Tim O'Brien, a soldier in the US Army, describes his own internal conflict:

I grew up in a small farming community in southern Minnesota, called Worthington. Everybody knows everyone else's business and their faults and what's happening in their marriages and where the kids have gone wrong. I remember the day my draft notice arrived. It was a summer afternoon, maybe June of '68. I remember taking that envelope into the house and putting it on the kitchen table where my Mom and Dad were having lunch. And they didn't even read it; they just looked at it and knew what it was. And the silence of that lunch—I didn't speak, my Mom didn't speak, my Dad didn't speak. Just that piece of paper lying at the center of the table is enough to make me cry to this day—not for myself, but for my Mom and Dad who both of them had been in the Navy during World War II, had believed in service to this country and all these values. On the one hand, I didn't think the war was less than righteous. On the other hand, I loved my country and valued my life in a small town and my friends and family. And so the summer of '68 I wrestled with what to do. It was for me, at least, it was more tortuous and devastating and emotionally painful than anything that happened in Vietnam. In the end I just capitulated—but it wasn't a decision, it was a forfeiture of a decision. Turning a switch in my conscience, just turning it off. So when (inside me, there is) barking at me, saying, "You're doing a bad and evil and stupid and unpatriotic thing."

Do you go off and kill people if you're not pretty sure it's right? And if your nation isn't pretty sure it's right and there isn't some consensus? Do you do that? I was at Fort Worth, Washington and Canada was a ninety-minutes bus ride away. What prevented me from doing it? I think it was pretty simple and stupid, it was a fear of embarrassment, a fear of ridicule and humiliation, what my girlfriend would have thought of me and the people in the Gobbler Café in downtown Worthington, the Kiwana [Kiwanis] boys and the country club boys in that small town I grew up in. The things they'd say about me—what a coward, what a sissy for going to Canada. And I would imagine my Mom and Dad over-hearing something like that. I couldn't summon the courage to say no to those nameless, faceless people ... And I had to live with it now for forty years. It's a long time to live with a failure of conscience and a failure of nerve. And the nightmare of Vietnam for me is not the bomb or is in the bullets, it's that failure of nerve that I so regret.

(Burns, Series 1:7, "Chasing Ghosts" (June 1968–May 1969))

O'Brien continued to suffer from what he called his "forfeiture of a deci-sion" which was in effect a betrayal of his own conscience. The disap-probation of his family and his community and the fear of being cast out swayed O'Brien to "turn the switch" in his mind. It was clear, neverthe-less, that his parents and his community, who upheld the patriotic values of loyalty and service, had not experienced anything like the conflict in values presented by Vietnam. Ironically, it was these same values, inher-ited from his family, that created O'Brien's own conflict.

In contrast to O'Brien were the young men who acted on their con-science. Jack Todd describes his experience:

There were only two choices—it was go to jail or go to Canada. And for me going to jail was just ... that one I couldn't face. So I went to Canada. And I remember after we crossed the border, it was a breeze—they just sort of waived us through and, looking in the rear view mirror, thinking there goes my country. I'll never see it again. I get called a coward all the time. It took me a long time not to feel that what I had done was cowardly because I still had that military ingrained feeling inside. That was the bravest thing I ever did. It was the bravest thing I ever did.

(Burns, Series 1:8, "A Sea of Fire" (April 1969–May 1970))

Todd's bravery was to choose to dissent in order to follow his conscience and what he determined was his own patriotic choice, risking not only the condemnation of others but also, and perhaps most importantly, losing his country forever. Being true to his idea of his country meant forfeiting his right to belong to that country. The sacrifice was conscious and enabled Todd to go on living with himself, very much like Neoptolemus, who ultimately defied Odysseus' orders to betray Philoctetes for the greater cause of victory, choosing instead to follow his own moral principles.

As greater losses accrued in the Vietnam War, US involvement became increasingly questionable and was voiced in violent domestic protests, most notably Kent State. The combination of faulty motives, incompetent leadership that was to some extent due to political manipulation, and massive loss of lives[9] fueled bitterness and undermined trust in political leaders. Both Johnson and Nixon had prolonged the Vietnam War in order to secure their stay in office, and as this came into the public consciousness it brought with it the realization that it was the old men who were sacrificing the next generation in order to remain in power.

Rudyard Kipling, a staunch patriot during the First World War but too old to fight, reviled the fact that it was effectively fathers who sent their sons to die in war. After his own son, John, went missing in action at the Battle of Loos in northern France, wracked with guilt, Kipling wrote, "If any question why we died/Tell them, because our fathers lied" (Kipling, 1919).

When John had been rejected as an army recruit because of his poor eyesight, Kipling pulled strings for him to be commissioned in the Irish Guards and was painfully aware of his role in his son's death.

Similarly, the historian Marc Bloch, in his devastating analysis of the fall of France in World War Two, questions this sacrifice, asking, "What, after all, is a 'civilian' in time of war?" He further questions why older men should be exempt from battle only to submit their sons to death:

> He is nothing more than a man whose weight of years, whose health, whose profession (if it be judged essential to the well-being of his country) prevents him from bearing arms effectively ... My sons will take my place. Am I, therefore, to conclude that my life has become more precious than theirs? Far better, on the contrary, that their youth should be preserved, if necessary, at the cost of my grey hairs. Herodotus said, a long time ago, that

the great impiety of war is that it forces fathers to consign their children to the tomb ... For the nation at large there can be no worse tragedy than having to sacrifice those very lives on which her destiny reposes.

(Bloch, 1969, p. 13)

Both Kipling and Bloch, along with many other writers, point to the tradition of authorized filicide on the part of political leaders, who as fathers are responsible for declaring war and for the sacrifice of the country's young men and future leaders.[10] These writers decry the sacrifice of youth in war but this tradition is more profoundly objectionable in the case of corrupt leaders. In this situation, as we can see in the Vietnam War, an oedipal dynamic is enacted whereby the fathers who are anxious to maintain power eliminate the strong men in the younger generation. In being sent to war, a younger generation is spawned who carry their own murderous guilt toward their fathers. In order to maintain the unity of the group (or loyalty to the country), the younger generation must then displace their murderous feelings by finding enemies in the form of other groups or nations and so wars continue. In this way, the unity of the group is preserved and the nation is cleansed of its guilt. This kind of cycle is essentially a perverse defense against feeling guilt, related to destructiveness against members within the group. Protests against the war in Vietnam pointed to just such corruption; the lies of the fathers and the deceit of patriotism.

In the final episode of Ken Burns' documentary, we see the shame of those who survived and bear the memory of needless deaths. Burns interviews Phan Quang Tue, a South Vietnamese who emigrated to the US:

"Through the whole thing [I thought] this is crazy, you know, why do we have to live under these conditions? It was so humiliating and I carry that humiliation with me to the United States where I get in line to sign up for job ... I remind them of the war in Vietnam which the Americans hate. You have to lose a nation and a dream to feel that humiliation."

(Burns, Series 1:10, "The Weight of Memory"
(March 1973 onward))

Protest and the surge of populism

In the various examples I have given of dissent, whether in whistle-blowing, protesting against political encroachment and loss of identity, defecting from an intolerable psychic regime or staying true to one's conscience, each act of dissent is in the service of defending reality or truth, the truth that two and two make four. The concept of reality and how we determine what is real is complex. In psychoanalytic thinking it is signified by the congruence between our perception of the world around us and our internal psychic reality, that is, what we feel. Returning to Sam, although she felt like a failure because she could never live up to the extreme ideals of her parents, she was at the same time aware that there was something amiss in her parents' belief system that was crippling her and them. Their Stalinist regime was imprisoning the family, crushing them physically and mentally to the point where Sam could no longer continue to suppress her feelings in order to conform to the ideals that had been set for her. Freedom, in other words, Sam's ability to make choices for herself, came when she could connect how she felt in the world with the kind of world she was living in. Although it was painful to become aware of the dysfunctionality of her parents' world, it was a relief to be able to recognize the reality of this and not to have to mask it by believing it was her failing.

Sam's dissent against her family's belief system arose from cognitive dissonance; her perception of herself and her idealized self became increasingly at odds with one another and unrealizable. On a large group level we are seeing a wave of populism and nationalism spreading across the world in reaction to political cognitive dissonance, or what many see as the false promises of globalization and liberal democracy that have not been realizable. Instead of raising the standard of living for people across the world and fulfilling the promise of a melioristic future, there is growing economic inequality, increasing immigration, and profound existential anxiety due to climate change. Local identities are under threat or being eroded with the demise of certain industries either already happening or looming ahead. Climate change is also effectively making certain parts of the world uninhabitable and giving rise to climate change refugees and a new class of dispossessed poor.

A common initial reaction to identity anxiety is to retreat to a nostalgic powerful past, to make the group "Great Again!" and to rebel against the system that has failed to fulfil its promises. When one belief system fails, groups, like individuals, tend to turn to a belief system that appears to offer greater security. This is what Sam did when she first rebelled against her family's belief system, replacing it with what she perceived was a safer community in the religious group she joined. She soon realized she had replaced one prison for another. Similarly, the group's need for security opens the way for a charismatic, powerful leader who promises a rosy future in return for loyalty and obedience. The pact is, "Follow me, believe in what I tell you, and it will all turn out well." Any ambivalence toward the leader is dispelled through the psychological defense of splitting in which an outside enemy is targeted who carries the negative projections of the group. In this way, group cohesion is strengthened, and a narrative of group purity is created to enhance identity. The "other" embodies all that threatens the existence of the group and as such needs to be kept out, if not, under extreme circumstances, exterminated altogether. The paranoia that results from this dynamic can be seen clearly in the recent spate of walls being erected in various countries across the world. The political scientists Krastev and Holmes comment on this phenomenon:

> When the Berlin Wall was toppled, there were only sixteen border fences in the world. Now there are sixty-five fortified perimeters either completed or under construction ... The three decades following 1989 turned out to be an "inter-mural period," a brief barricade-free interval between the dramatic breaching of the Berlin Wall, exciting utopian fantasies of a borderless world, and a global craze of wall-building, with cement and barbed-wire barriers embodying existential (if sometimes imaginary) fears.
>
> (Krastev and Holmes, p. 2)

The difficulty about this anxiety-driven political dynamic is that it is essentially regressive in nature and does not encourage thought or dissent leading to a new awareness and the possibility of adaptation. The retreat to fantasy in a time of crisis may help us to deny the reality of what is going on, but it does not help us to imagine a way forward. We can see this process unfolding before us in the strikingly parallel politics of the US and the UK. Both countries have blamed internal socio-economic problems on other countries as well as their own liberal elite[11] and have elected leaders who promise a greater future, a clear identity, and protection against foreign, and therefore undermining, influence. In their bid for greatness, both Trump and Johnson have shown they are above the law, both are well-known for their lies and, like autocratic leaders elsewhere and in the past, their strong-arm tactics have swelled the numbers of their followers, especially those who have felt impotent and blocked in the face of their own life opportunities.[12]

Although there has been a wave of dissent in the US against the erosion of the rule of law, protectionist and isolationist trade policies, human rights infringements, culminating in the House of Representatives vote to impeach Trump. These protests have failed so far to make a significant impact because they are not addressing, and perhaps cannot address, the massive existential anxiety that is threatening our everyday way of life. In the UK, the protests to reverse the decision to leave the EU following the referendum have largely been quashed with the majority vote for Johnson's Conservative government (in December 2019). However, the relief of certainty and short-term stability after three years of what was experienced as futile debate, often uninformed and based on fearful fantasies of the EU/other, may serve to anesthetize the reality of loss, not only of the UK's membership within the EU but of the internal conflicts and losses the UK has been facing for the last ten years or so as some of its industrial communities have struggled to stay alive. As the anesthesia gradually wears off, the pain of these losses and our attempts to deny them will undoubtedly surface into consciousness. Just as we need to deny reality when we are facing extreme loss in order to protect ourselves emotionally, we also eventually need to accept reality, that two and two make four, in order to adapt and survive.

Our ability to dissent ensures that we protect our capacity for thought and do not succumb to lies and the denial of reality. The pact with an autocratic leader who offers safety to the group is a pact to retrench into the mother's body where no thought is required and hence no anxiety felt. In rocky times, totalitarianism is appealing for this reason. Lies are also appealing, as they support the fantasies we want to believe. The difficulty in distinguishing between truth and lies in turn subverts our ability to exercise moral judgment and leaves us mindless. Because there is no accommodation for individual thought—everyone is subsumed within the system and it is the leader who determines the truth—there can be no dissent. There can be no individual mind to pass judgment or determine action (self-will), no one has responsibility for what happens, or for the actions taken. Arendt describes the principal traits of the totalitarian leader:

> total responsibility is the most important organizational aspect of the so-called Leader principle, according to which every functionary is not only appointed by the Leader but is his walking embodiment, and every order is supposed to emanate from this one ever-present source ... The leader ... cannot tolerate criticism of his subordinates, since they act always in his name; if he wants to correct his own errors, he must liquidate those who carried them out; if he wants to blame his mistakes on others, he must kill them. For within this organizational framework a mistake can only be a fraud: the impersonation of the Leader by an imposter.
>
> (Arendt, 2017, p. 490)

The consequence of conferring total responsibility to the leader and the movement, supported by its functionaries, is that it removes responsibility from the individual.

Clearly referring to Hitler, Arendt goes on to explain how dissent—and any form of internal conflict—is magically erased under totalitarian leadership. She writes:

> The real mystery of the totalitarian Leader resides in an organization which makes it possible for him to assume the total responsibility for all crimes committed by the elite formations of the movement and to claim at the same time, the honest, innocent respectability of its most naïve fellow-traveler.
>
> (ibid., p. 491)

This blanket blessing not to have to think, to pass judgment, or to take responsibility is appealing under extreme conditions and, as long as these conditions continue, they bolster the human need for escape, denial, and protection. Individual morality is extinguished and supplanted by collective subjugation: dissent is no longer conceivable when there is no mind to judge what is right and wrong and the individual has become a means toward an end, a tool of the collective.

In the face of global anxiety for the future, when it is no longer possible to deny reality or rely on others to determine our fate, dissent appears on the threshold and beckons us forward. The words of the songwriter, Stephen Stills, protesting against the Vietnam War, are as much of a warning now as they were then, not to be detached from "what is going down":

> There's something happening here
> What it is ain't exactly clear
> There's a man with a gun over there
> Telling me I got to beware
>
> I think it's time we stop, children, what's that sound
> Everybody look what's going down
>
> There's battle lines being drawn
> Nobody's right if everybody's wrong
> Young people speaking their minds
> Getting so much resistance from behind
>
> It's time we stop, hey, what's that sound
> Everybody look what's going down...
>
> —Stephen Stills, "For What It's Worth," 1966

Notes

1. Snowden differentiates between "leakers" and "whistleblowers," arguing that "a leaker only distributes information for personal gain" (interview with Amy Goodman on *Democracy Now!* on 26 September 2019).

2. The UK Parliamentary Committee investigating Cambridge Analytica, citing Russian links to UK paid-for propaganda, called for an independent inquiry into foreign interference in the UK referendum. This has been ignored by the government and the leader of the opposition.

3. There are now a host of examples of Donald Trump in the US and Boris Johnson in the UK defying constitutional rights and the rule of law. Although there is open dissent in both countries regarding these infringements, there is nevertheless a worryingly large constituency that applauds them.

4. Even with foreigners there was an expectation that they used the greeting "Heil Hitler." In her book, *Travellers in the Third Reich*, Julia Boyd describes an English woman, eighteen-year-old Joan Tonge, who attended an SA rally and stalwartly refused to salute. Boyd writes, "Within seconds 'several squat and ugly Brown Shirts came galloping up, shouting ferociously and wind-milling their arms' until 'Helmut [her companion] stamped over with his ankle-length overcoat swirling, shouting even louder at them that I was an Englander'" (Boyd, J. (2017). *Travellers in the Third Reich*. London: Elliot & Thompson).

5. This is a worldwide phenomenon that is evident within the EU, the UK, the US, South America, and parts of Asia.

6. Some young protestors entrusted their wills to their siblings for fear of their mothers finding out that they were involved in the protests. They admitted they were more afraid of their mothers than of the police, suggesting that dissent within the family is taken even more seriously than against the state (Channel 4 News).

7. The five demands are: (1) withdrawal of the extradition bill, (2) the release of protestors from prison, (3) repealing the classification of the protests as riots, (4) an independent investigation of police violence, and (5) recognition of universal suffrage.

8. The US is no exception in disapproving of, if not condemning, conscientious objectors to war. There is an extensive history of conscientious objection in most countries. Conscientious objectors have been punished for failing to fight since ancient times. Maximilianus, the first recorded conscientious objector, refused to be conscripted into the Roman army in 295 due to his religious beliefs and was duly executed, resulting in his subsequent canonization as Saint Maximilian.

9. US Defense files record 58,220 US military fatal casualties in Vietnam. Nearly two million civilians on both sides and 1.1 million North Vietnamese and Viet Cong fighters were killed. US military estimated that between 200,000 and 250,000 South Vietnamese soldiers died.

10. It is only recently that women in some countries have been conscripted as soldiers to serve at the front of war. See Svetlana Alexievich's *The Unwomanly Face of War* for personal accounts of Russian women serving at the front in World War II (Alexievich, S. (2017). *The Unwomanly Face of War*. London: Penguin).

11. The so-called liberal elite in both the US and the UK can be accused of ignoring growing economic and social disparity but they also represent the promise of liberal capitalism, albeit in its excess, in contrast to the imagined safety of political capitalism (e.g. China). See Milanovic, B. (2019). *Capitalism Alone: The Future of the System that Rules the World*. Cambridge, MA: Harvard University Press.

12. In a CNN interview, Bill Clinton commented, "When people feel uncertain, they'd rather have somebody that's strong and wrong than somebody who's weak and right" (CNN, "Democrats Pull Together to Take Aim Against Republicans," 3 December, 2002).

References

Anderlini, J. (2019). Hong Kong's protestors need a leader now more than ever. *Financial Times*. 12 December.

Arendt, H. (2017). *The Origins of Totalitarianism*. London: Penguin.

Bloch, M. (1999). *Strange Defeat: A Statement of Evidence Written in 1940*. Oxford: Oxford University Press.

Bowlby, J. (1978). *Attachment and Loss: Volume 2. Separation, Anxiety and Anger*. London: Penguin.

Burns, K. (2017). *The Vietnam War*. Film documentary.

Cadwalladr, C. (2019). Cambridge Analytica a year on: "a lesson in institutional failure." *Guardian*. 17 March.

Camus, A. (1947). *The Plague*. London: Penguin, 2001.

Casalicchio, E. (2018). Cambridge Analytica whistleblower: Vote Leave mutilated UK constitution by cheating to Brexit victory. *PoliticsHome*. 27 March.

Haffner, S. (2003). *Defying Hitler*. London: Phoenix.

Khong, E. L. (2019). Hong Kong and the art of dissent: how viral images have inspired and sustained opposition to Beijing. *Financial Times*. 6 December.

Kipling, R. (1919). Epitaphs of the War, 1914–18, Common Form. In R. Kipling, *The Years Between*. London: Methuen.

Krastev, I. and Holmes, S. (2019). *The Light that Failed*. London: Allen Lane.

Lethem, J. (2019). Snowden in the Labyrinth. *New York Review of Books*. 24 October.

Snowden, E. (2019). *Permanent Record*. New York: Macmillan.

Sunstein, C. R. (2018). It can happen here. *New York Review of Books*. 28 June.

CHAPTER EIGHT

Braving the new: the struggle from loss to agency

... as the Odyssey knows, to live well in the world, nostalgia must be resisted: you must stay with your ship, stay tied to the present, remain mobile, keep adjusting the rig, work with the swells, watch for a wind-shift, watch as the boom swings over, engage, in other words, with the muddle and duplicity and difficulty of life. Don't be tempted into the lovely simplicities that the heroic past seems to offer.

Nicolson, A., *The Mighty Dead*, p. 6

Our lives are marked by loss from the moment of birth until our death. It is also our experience of loss that enables us to let go of what is familiar and to be open to new experiences and to change. In his study of Homer's Odysseus, Adam Nicolson describes the nostalgic lure of the Sirens' song that promises to restore Odysseus' heroic past as an escape from the pain and losses of the present (Nicolson, 2014). Odysseus' crew know that he cannot resist and tie Odysseus to the mast, ensuring that they continue their voyage as they face an unknown future. The lure of an imaginary, idealized past is something we all know, and becomes especially power-ful at times of change and loss. The current rise of populism around the world is underpinned by just such nostalgic fantasies of a secure past, untouched by loss. This is often a turning point in psychoanalysis when a person becomes aware, for example, that distorted beliefs and images of the past can no longer be sustained and need to be shed. Stepping out of familiar behavior patterns and venturing into new ways of relating—to oneself and others—may feel as frightening as entering a foreign country with no common language. This is the ordinary challenge of living for us all but for those who have been living in isolated or severe conditions or those who face extreme loss, it is a challenge that requires bravery—a bravery that is often unseen but nevertheless palpable.

Exile and starting again

In his first meeting with me, Harry, a tall gaunt man in his early forties, exiled from his country of origin for political crimes, said, "It has taken me a year to contact you. I have had your number the whole time but I was too frightened. Everything has been taken away from me, everything has changed in my life and I am frightened that I will have to change, that I won't know who I will be, that I will become a foreigner to myself." Harry was clenching his fists, not in anger, but from trying to control his pain and his tears. He began to tell me his story, a story of a glorious past in his country where he was a well-known and much revered dissident, fighting for justice and democratic values. He was the leader whom everyone turned to for help, and the "fixer" during a crisis. He had adopted this role since childhood when, at a young age, he became the family "hero." His much older, successful father was often away on business and Harry readily stepped into the shoes of being the man of the house, helping his mother, who was bedridden with depression for long periods of Harry's childhood. As the eldest, Harry took care of his four younger siblings, three girls and a boy, making sure they went to school, did their schoolwork, went to bed at the right time at night, and did not get into scrapes with their friends. Although there were nannies looking after the children, Harry made the important decisions about his siblings and looked after them as a surrogate father. His favorite make-believe game was to play the king with his siblings as his courtiers and vassals, coming to him with their problems to solve. Harry created a magical kingdom of justice and plenty in which there was no hunger or poverty, everything was shared equally, and, because of this, there was no crime or suffering. Harry's parents praised their little king, his father glad that Harry was taking over for him during his many trips away and his mother glad that Harry took care not only of his siblings but of her when she felt too depressed to do anything but sleep. For Harry, too, this was an ideal solution as he was admired and loved as the hero-king and he did not have to be aware of his absent parents who failed to care for their children.

Harry's empire seemed to grow from strength to strength. He was a natural leader and, even when he came to the UK for his university education, he quickly established his own following on political issues. On returning to his own country, having qualified as a lawyer, Harry resumed his political activities in the face of a government that was rapidly turning into an autocracy. Nevertheless, Harry was an able politician, was known for his diplomacy in dealing with his opponents, and held a respected ministerial position in the government that allowed him certain limited influence and privileges. As Harry accrued a larger power base, many "power-hungry" women, as he called them, began to pursue him. It was Harry's strengths as a leader that became his downfall in his personal life. Harry's face had become ashen as he referred to his downfall and he sat silently facing me with a pleading look on his face. I commented that Harry had experienced a lot of tragedy in his life, and we were both left in suspense until our next meeting.

Harry arrived a few days later for his session and asked if he could lie on my couch, explaining, "I'm exhausted; I don't think I can even manage to sit up today." He started to describe the past year as a time when he been so broken that all he could do was stay in his little flat and sleep, like his mother had done throughout his childhood. Harry told me, "The morning when I decided to contact you, I woke up and thought, 'No, I am not going to turn into my mother, I am not going to be defeated by this.'" At the same time, Harry said he felt lost when there was no one to help and the only thing to fix was himself. He also said that he had lost his trust in his own judgment and this was the most difficult and disorienting problem in his life.

Harry then went on to explain that he had gotten involved with a very beautiful woman from a rich family who had earmarked him as her future husband. She was intelligent and seductive, and was the first person who had expressed a desire to care for him and who, it seemed, was making no demands of him. However, as the relationship developed, Harry began to feel increasingly claustrophobic. Maria wanted to know where he was at any given time of day and was constantly trying to anticipate his needs; she was also anxious to be married and have a child. Before the end of the year, Harry had broken their engagement and, in retaliation, Maria had spread various false political stories about him amongst his opponents, who then leaked these to the national press.

With a civil war looming, Harry was forced to escape from his country or face indefinite internment and possibly torture. Harry curled up on the couch and began to sob, "What have I done? I have tried so hard to help others, to be just and loving, to do what is right and what is it for? I have only once said 'no' to someone, to Maria, and now I am being punished."

I reflected, "It isn't fair that life has not honored the deal you made with it."

Harry replied, "No, that's just the problem, it wasn't meant to turn out like this and now I'm really on my own. The deal has been broken and I don't know how to live or who to be."

Over the next few months Harry's disillusion took on devastating proportions—everything he had believed and worked for had been swept away and destroyed, no one could be trusted, and at the same time he berated himself for being so foolish as to allow himself to be vulnerable to this poisonous woman. Harry's fury and confusion when his world toppled around him was like a toddler's rage when he becomes painfully aware that he cannot control the world around him and is not always at the center of it. In the case of the toddler, this experience of impotence is normally mitigated by a mother who can comfort her child. Through this action, the mother demonstrates her child's impact on her and helps to restore some sense of self-agency to the child. In his analysis, I thought Harry needed to use me as a mother who could understand his fall from grace and help him to recover, not only through venting his rage but through experimenting with his limits in his new life. Like learning to walk, this proved to be both exciting and frightening.

A large part of the reason that Harry experienced his fall from grace as overwhelming was because it wasn't only his present but his past that had unraveled. Harry's loss of his kingly status confronted him with the reality that he had used this persona to mask the fact that there were effectively no parents in his home. As Harry exclaimed,

> It would have been better if we had been orphans—at least that would have been real. Instead, we all held on to the belief that everything was fine because our parents were there, even when we weren't actually there in their minds. I've been living this charade most of my life. It makes me think that maybe the deal for me was that if I played my part as best as I could, they would then play their parts. But they didn't. That was not the deal for them … When S came into power in my country at first I thought, 'Good, he will be a real father to his people, he will tell everyone what they need to do and in return he will look after everyone.' But now I can see that this is the father I had been trying to be to my siblings and later on to my colleagues. This kind of deal means that the king is the only one with power because no one has to take responsibility for himself, no one can develop or grow up. It's only now that I'm away, that I can see some of my sisters and my brother beginning to figure some things out for themselves and to wise up to their reality—both in our family and in our country.

Giving up his position as hero-king was a painful process for Harry; he likened himself to a snake shedding its skin for the first time. For several weeks Harry fluctuated in his thoughts about the future. One day he would tell me excitedly about his plans to resurrect his empire by transplanting it to the UK, and how he would essentially set up an alternative government here, where he could once again be the shadow leader. He explained that this setback had taught him a lot and he could be even stronger now with more resources than ever before to help his oppressed countrymen. These manic episodes made Harry feel hopeful, but they also made him feel precarious, as he could not completely deny that things had changed radically in his life and it might not be so easy to recreate his lost kingdom. During this time Harry dreamt that he was back with his family and his closest colleagues at his family house, but they were all under house arrest and couldn't leave without severe consequences. Harry thought the dream was telling him that this was in fact what would happen if he tried to return to his past; he would be imprisoned by it.

He then became despondent, recognizing that he was also desperately trying to retrieve a sense of belonging somewhere. Hoping to find a foot-hold, Harry announced that he thought he would train as a psychothera-pist. I understood Harry's wish as primarily his attempt to be accepted and belong to a group rather than a wish to identify with me specifically. He was knocking on doors where he hoped to be allowed in.

These highs were followed predictably by Harry telling me about his despair and fear for the future—he had lost everything in his life, and he could see no way forward. At one especially low point, I voiced my con-cern that Harry's despair might tempt him to kill himself. He paused for a long time and then admitted, "I've been thinking of suicide for weeks now—every time I wake up in the morning I have this idea that at least I can do myself in, at least that is the power I have left in my life when I have no other power."

I compared Harry's thoughts of suicide to an internal revolution he was planning:

> It's a bit like a coup that you're planning, an assassination of the leader who has failed you and who doesn't listen to you either, who just keeps harping on about the past and how great it was. When you can't get the leader to change, the only way to have any power is to kill him. Is the problem that you're angry with this stubborn, short-sighted, omnipotent leader and really want to do him in? This could be S [the autocrat], your father, or the you who wants to remain king? They've all had their day.

Harry suddenly sat up and said, "I'm not going to allow these tyrants to win! If I killed myself, I'd be just as omnipotent as they are—and just as pathetic. It's a bit like the snake deciding to kill itself rather than to change into a new skin."

This realization turned out to be turning point for Harry. He had only overtly asked for help twice in his life. In the first instance Harry sought help from a wealthy uncle living in the UK to help him secure residency. The second instance was when he contacted me for treatment, fearful of becoming like his mother trapped in a lifetime depression. Without his old skin, Harry was acutely aware of his vulnerability and a deep sense of shame caused by years of denying his need to be cared for by others. He had received care by using others as proxies for himself while starving inside. His old way of relating was no longer sustainable and, materially, the funds he had managed to exist on were running out. He was beginning to feel that he might create a new future for himself but was also frightened that he would lose his connections to his past and become uprooted. Faced with having to find a way of continuing to survive in his adopted country, Harry decided he would go back to his university law degree to qualify as a lawyer and approach his uncle for a loan to tide him over. Harry explained,

> I'm not going to be king anymore, but I can still work to help others and I can take care of myself better now. I can't go back to my country anymore. I will always miss it and my family and friends but I can't stand still—I want my own family and maybe all these changes that I have been so afraid of are also because I've been afraid of being myself—of discovering what I really feel and what I can and cannot do. I haven't lost my principles but I have to find a different way of living by them.

Identity and the rise of populism

Harry's actual physical and political dislocation triggered a psychic dislocation that fundamentally challenged his ideal image of himself and stripped him of his social identity. This cataclysmic loss initially fueled an impulse to regress to his past self in order to mend the rupture that had occurred in his life and to create even greater defenses against future threats. When this strategy failed, Harry's rage about the loss of the better world he had expected nearly provoked him to take his life. When he realized that such an act would only imitate the destruction of what he valued most, he had to think hard about how to survive his losses and how to forge a different identity that was nevertheless true to the basic values by which he had lived.

Harry's struggle to make sense of the losses in his life provides a kind of microcosm of what we can see happening on a global scale in the wave of populism[1] occurring in countries across the world as local economies, boundaries, and the concept of the nation-state are under threat. Liberal democracy is in decline if not under outright attack and we are seeing the resurgence of the nation-state with the rise of strongman leaders, such as Trump, Putin, Erdogan, Orban, Duterte, Modi,

Xi, and Johnson in the UK. This is no coincidence but clearly the result of globalization's growing threat to national power bases and national identity with inequality and immigration on the rise and international corporations increasingly owning mass amounts of wealth, even greater than individual nations. In response to the erosion of national political authority, there is a backlash of "apocalyptic nationalism" that has come into vogue, characterized by "machismo" leadership, xenophobia and wall-building, theories of racial purity and, above all, spectacular promises to restore these nations' glorified pasts—often pasts that were never that glorious or, like the British Empire, ended well over fifty years ago (Dasgupta, 2018). The waves of nostalgia for a time representing a secure powerful identity echo Harry's longing to turn the clock back to the time when in hindsight he had felt loved and powerful, although he admits that in reality his position was always precarious. As the identity of nation-states, and therefore their survival, is increasingly under threat, uncertainty and fear about the future take hold, leaving citizens vulnerable to emotional manipulation and false promises.

Preying on these fears, politicians at both conservative and liberal extremes present themselves as the true defenders of their country by maintaining safe borders that will keep the "enemy" out, cultivating an "us and them" mentality. As we have seen in the impeachment proceedings, Trump does not hesitate to declare his opponents "treasonous" and "un-American." A similar divisive antagonism against the "elites" is also promoted, as evident in slogans adopted by the liberal left, for example, Bernie Sanders in the US and Jeremy Corbyn in the UK, advocating "for the many, not the few." In writing about Cold War liberalism, Jan-Werner Müller warns us that the narrative of the "other" has been dangerously extended. Müller observes:

> In a speech he gave in Warsaw, Trump's rhetorical question— "Do we have the confidence in our values to defend them at any cost?"—could be mistaken for a soundbite from the height of the cold war, but tellingly, he followed it with another: "Do we have enough respect for our citizens to protect our borders?" With this, he conjured a world in which real Americans are constantly threatened by caravans of Middle Eastern terrorists and people

from Latin America who can pass for citizens but might be enemies within.

(Müller, 2018)

Trump's message also raises the question as to who qualifies as a citizen
and how we identify a "real American," questions that hark back to Nazi
Germany's concerns with racial purity.

On the liberal end, Müller also points to "Hillary Clinton's cynical
call for Europe to stop aiding refugees, since, in her view, the migration issue just helps populists. Her underlying idea appears to be that
one can defeat one's political adversaries by imitating them" (ibid.).
The fallback position at both ends of the political spectrum seems to
be to win votes by fostering mass paranoia and populist fantasies of
a future protected by isolationism. Change is perceived as dilution of
identity and ultimately a threat to survival. Retreat is the safest line of
defense.

In writing about the use of xenophobia as a means of bolstering
nationalism, Martin Wolf points out that a citizen's passport has become
emblematic of identity; it confers belonging and membership, it signifies
national characteristics and, most importantly, it stands for sovereignty
of the group. Wolf comments:

> The more economic outcomes diverge within a nation state, the
> more easily cynical politicians can persuade anxious citizens that
> their interests are being sacrificed to those of a "globalist"—that
> is, treacherous—elite and its foreign associates and servants. The
> view that those who think globally are traitors is not surprising.
> It is a natural result of national feeling. Since the middle of the
> twentieth century, nationalism has gone global. In China, for
> example, we see the creation, for the first time in its history, of
> a Chinese nation state. It is no surprise, then, that it cannot deal
> well with its minority communities. In highly complex societies,
> such as India, creation of an overarching national identity is
> even harder.[2] Today, we are witnessing the resurgence of malign
> nationalism across the west and, most significantly, in the US.
>
> (Wolf, 2018)

Like pouring money into a bankrupt business to save it, the immediate solution to waning nationalism has been to reinforce nationalist values and to protect the nation-state from invasion. The surge of fake news and interference with the press serves both to enhance the power of the state, while diminishing that of foreign states, and at the same time to increase paranoia. In this way, populist politicians become even more powerful as they can readily capitalize on what people want to believe is true, what politicians want their constituencies to believe, and the illusion that the nation-state is largely self-sufficient or, in the case of Trump's stance in the US, can call the shots on international trade and cooperation. In order to save nationalism, paradoxically, the values of liberal democracy, those same values that have been nurtured under nationalism, have to be sacrificed, as the history of the rise of the Third Reich in Germany has so vividly demonstrated.

Over the past two hundred years or so, nationalism has not only served as a powerful secular religion, binding individuals and communities together, but because it has served this function, it has also become an intrinsic part of our identity. While this may be especially so in the West, modeled on the Ancient Greek city-state, it has also been a powerful force in Eastern countries that have shifted from imperial rule to different forms of totalitarianism that remain circumscribed and defined by national boundaries. Increasing globalization and increasing economic development have brought in their wake vast increases in economic inequality. The American Dream that held the promise of both moral and material amelioration blossomed dramatically after World War II, only to reach a tipping point with the financial crash of 2008. The American Dream, at least in terms of its materialistic manifestation, was becoming a nightmare as its byproduct, economic inequality, was becoming the new threat.

The scourge of inequality

In 2014 Thomas Piketty's ground-breaking treatise, *Capital in the Twenty-First Century*, was published and quickly rose to No. 1 on Amazon's bestseller list. Its success was attributed to the fact that it constructs a well-documented frontal challenge to the inequality debate in economics and politics. Prior to this, leading politicians on both sides of the Atlantic have extolled free trade policies, and tax benefits for corporations and inheritance, both of which generate inequality. In 2000, the CEO of Louis Vuitton boasted: "Businesses, especially international ones, have ever greater resources, and in Europe they have acquired the ability to compete with states ... Politicians' real impact on the economic life of a country is more and more limited. Fortunately."

According to Robert Wade, a leading UK economist, most economists either don't think about inequality or believe in the self-adjusting market system—a view that has fundamentally supported political policies for decades. Poverty and wealth tend to be viewed as part of the natural order.

Obama, during his presidency, declared inequality "to be the defining challenge of our time." Pope Francis has also echoed this. Both have been accused by the wealthy of persecuting the rich. As predicted by Obama, rage against the rich (and the elites) has taken hold since 2008 and has prepared the ground for populism to take root. The rage was not unfounded. Wade points out, "In the period 2009–2012, 93% of the increase in the US national income accrued to the top 1%—and this in a stable democracy rather than a kleptocracy such as Equatorial Guinea" (Wade, 2014, p. 1076).

In a report published in 2014, IMF researchers challenged the idea of a self-adjusting market system. They found that "countries with a higher inequality tend to experience lower and more volatile growth; countries with lower inequality tend to experience higher and less volatile growth ... in short, inequality is a drag on growth and fosters financial instability." Wolfgang Münchau of the *Financial Times* reported, "The most likely trajectory is a long period of slow growth, low inflation, and a constant threat of insolvency and political insurrection" (Muchau, 2014).

Carol Graham, a US economist who studies inequality, has demonstrated that it is not simply the poor in the US who are being affected by economic changes, it is also the middle classes. She describes a "black box of no hope" that now characterizes much of middle-class experience in the US. Graham makes the point that inequality is tolerable as long as people are optimistic about their opportunities to be upwardly mobile. When these opportunities disappear, inequality can no longer be accepted (Graham, 2017).

On the other end of the scale, amongst the rich and stemming from the financial crisis of 2008, there is increasing resistance to government regulation. In the US and UK libertarian views that support the idea of a self-regulating market system and individual sovereignty are gaining strength and encouraging the dissembling of government institutions.

The threat of the Other

Although immigration figures in many European countries and in the US have fallen over the past few years since increased restrictions have been put in place, the prospect of future immigration, whether it is economic or climate change refugees, looms large. Immigrants are perceived either as leeches, bleeding limited local resources or, on the other hand, as representing a new wave of upwardly mobile foreigners that are being given opportunities and help that are not available to the indigenous population. If immigrants do well, they evoke envy; if they remain dependent and poor, they evoke resentment. Either way, they represent a threat.

Immigrants are also seen to threaten local identities and culture. Timothy Garton Ash, writing about Germany, ironically points out,

> There is a striking inverse correlation between the number of immigrants (or people of migrant origin) in an area and the populist vote: East Germany has the fewest immigrants and the most AfD voters. As one participant in a demonstration organized by the far right, xenophobic movement Pegida (the initials stand for Patriotic Europeans Against the Islamization of the West) told a reporter: "In Saxony today there are hardly any immigrants, but there is a danger of the Islamization of Germany in fifty or a hundred years." An urgent matter, then.
>
> (Garton Ash, 2017)

Garton Ash cites that

> 95 percent of AfD voters said that they were worried that "we are experiencing a loss of German culture and language," 94 percent that "our life in Germany will change too much," and 92 percent that "the influence of Islam in Germany will become too strong."

Feeding this politics of cultural despair—to recall a famous phrase of the historian Fritz Stern—is a milieu of writers, media, and books whose arguments and vocabulary connect back to themes of an earlier German right-wing culture in the first half of the twentieth century. This is a new German right with distinct echoes of the old.

Garton Ash also emphasizes that the AfD "is not a party of the economically 'left behind'. This strong presence of the educated upper middle class distinguishes populism from many other populisms" (Garton Ash, 2017).

This phenomenon is not only evident in Germany but can also be seen across Europe and within the UK.

Immigrants not only threaten to "dilute" and "contaminate" indigenous cultures but, fleeing from disasters in their own countries, they are harbingers of the global dangers that defy borders. The increase in climate refugees is a case in point as it is often linked with problems of economic inequality. The political scientist, Ronald Inglehart, describes a "tipping point" in democratic societies in which social and economic inequality reaches an intolerable level and creates a backlash that paves the way for authoritarian governance (Inglehart, 2018). Although climate change is not usually named as part of this process, it is an important factor. It is the poor who can't afford rising costs in food, oil, and housing. It is the poor who are vulnerable to becoming climate refugees. It is the poor who can't escape the path of the hurricane and, if they manage to, can't rebuild their demolished houses. It is also the poor and, for that matter, the middle class who will turn to populist leaders who acknowledge their need for a better life. As climate change affects us more and more, large-group anxiety is bound to intensify and, from our experience so far, this is likely to provoke greater authoritarianism. We can, for example, anticipate an increase in migration due to dwindling habitable land mass.[3] If we are not quick in developing alternative methods of food production, due to climate change and isolationist trade policies, we can also expect much greater competition for food and rising starvation. If we consider these conditions together, they constitute many of the factors that have led in the past to war and genocide—as a means of maintaining group identity in the threat of extinction.

Security in autocracy

As we saw in the case of Harry, when an individual is stripped of his belonging to a group and his function within that group, he loses an essential part of his identity. In this state of vanishing identity, the individual becomes highly susceptible to powerful authority figures who offer membership, security, and the eradication of conflict. When basic trust is broken, blind trust in a "totalitarian object" takes over (see Volkan, 2004). On a larger scale, the shift toward autocratic leaders indicates increasing levels of conflict and insecurity within national boundaries.

Despite polls that show the Z generation as largely supporting liberal elites, amongst millennials in Western countries there is greater support for autocratic leadership. The American journalist Sasha Polakow-Suransky writes:

> Those who believe millennials are immune to authoritarian ideas are mistaken. Using data from the World Values Survey, the political scientists Roberto Foa and Yascha Mounk have painted a worrying picture. As the French election demonstrated, belief in core tenets of liberal democracy is in decline, especially among those born after 1980. Their findings challenge the idea that after achieving a certain level of prosperity and political liberty, countries that have become democratic do not turn back.
>
> In America, 72 percent of respondents born before World War II deemed it absolutely essential to live in a democracy; only 30 percent of millennials agreed. The figures were similar in Holland. The number of Americans favoring a strong leader unrestrained by elections or parliaments has increased from 24 to 32 percent since 1995. More alarmingly, the number of Americans who believe that military rule would be good or very good has risen from 6 to 17 percent over the same period. The young and wealthy were most hostile to democratic norms, with fully 35 percent of young people with a high income regarding army rule as a good thing.
>
> (Polakow-Suransky, 2017)

It is not surprising that it is the young and wealthy who are reported as "the most hostile to democratic norms" as they are the ones under attack and who have the most to lose.

Political anomie

In psychoanalytic terms, we can understand the retreat of different countries into narcissistic isolationism as a regression into an illusory omnipotent past. The strongman, narcissistic leader who is above the law belies the fragility of his position. Behind the carapace of postured strength, we find what Inglehart aptly refers to as the "existential insecurity" that has beset nations around the world, and will only increase with the challenges of climate change (Inglehart, 2018). Ideology and political ideals are scrapped in the scuffle for survival. When there is so much anxiety and uncertainty about the future and when facts are not reassuring it becomes hard to think clearly about the dangers ahead. The vacuum of ideological meaning is evident in the lack of political vision amongst many leaders who are preoccupied with staying in power and keeping their countries afloat. Suddenly, it seems that the idea of progress and what that means for individuals has turned sour. In an interview with the French writer, Roger Errera in 1974, Hannah Arendt percipiently warned, "The law of progress holds that everything now must be better than what was there before. Don't you see if you want something better, and better, and better, you lose the good. The good is no longer even being measured" (Arendt, 1978). In our anxiety to survive within our own countries, are we becoming inured to the destruction that is being wrought in the name of nationalism?

Globalization has been central to the widespread belief in melioristic capitalism, that people's material standard of living will get better and better with the promise that poverty along with many associated social problems can be eradicated. Rather than wealth being shared in this utopian vision, it has increasingly come into the hands of large corporations and an elite few with the gap between rich and poor ever widening. The drive toward economic prosperity, starting in the 1990s, has spread like an infection—under Deng's premiership in China huge billboards saying, "Get Rich!" were erected over the highways, Putin has also made it clear the two aims for Russia are wealth and power, and other leaders, notably Trump, have followed suit. The "good" has become immediately aligned with power and stripped of ideological value, measured by wealth alone.

In her analysis of the new totalitarianism that has been inculcated by Putin in Russia, Masha Gessen refers to Yuri Levada's observation, based on research in Russia and China, that "every totalitarian regime forms a type of human being on whom it relies for stability. The shaping of the New Man is the regime's explicit project, but its product is not so much a vessel for the regime's ideology as it is a person best equipped to survive in a given society" (Gessen, 2017, p. 59). In fact, ideology may get in the way of survival as it creates political inflexibility and dissent. Levada argued that the totalitarian system produced a certain kind of person, without self-agency and subject only to the rules of survival, and that this non-individuality led the way for authoritarian government. While Levada's theory has been widely criticized by social scientists (Sharafutdinova, 2019), he underlines the importance of the ideological vacuum that occurred with the implosion of the USSR at the end of the Cold War. The necessity to survive within the collective, especially toward the end of the Cold War when Russia's economy was suffering, morphed into the aim of materialist progress under Putin's capitalist autocracy. As Svetlana Alexievich so powerfully illustrates in her interviews with a cross section of the Russian population during the early 2000s, the political ideals of the past, under Lenin, Stalin, Gorbachev, and Khrushchev, regardless of their differences, had died, leaving a painful vacuum in their wake (Alexievich, 2013).

In such a vacuum political identity is not informed by a set of beliefs and values so much as loyalty to a powerful autocracy. A whole generation of Russian youth, now in their twenties, have grown up with Putin as their only leader. Eduard Ponarin, professor of sociology at Russia's Higher School of Economics, describes this generation as, "Happy, apolitical and nationalist, to generalise ... and that is why politics is nothing to worry about, for most" (Foy, 2020). Politics is nothing to worry about when elections are pre-determined and there is essentially no political choice, leaving nationalism as the only framework for belonging. Without an ideology that carries with it an image of the ideal citizen or member of the group, there is little to aspire to, and little to bring people together in a common purpose—except anxiety for the future. Despite Ponarin's positive spin, Putin's failed promise of economic growth and state corruption are giving rise to protests led by Russian youths promoting citizens' rights. Without the foundation of political ideals, it is not surprising that these protests lack any sense of a cohesive world view.[4]

In the West, the ideals of democratic liberalism have been similarly eroded due to economic inequality along with corruption and mistrust in authority and institutions of government. We can understand the development of populist groups as an attempt to fill the ideological void, to restore former nationalist ego ideals and to re-establish group identity. However, populist beliefs as they are manifest today portray a vision of the past, not the future. They are retrogressive by their very nature; while they may provide a sense of security through familiarity, they cannot facilitate imaginative discourse and thinking in terms of a creating a new future. The historian Timothy Snyder uses the phrase "the politics of eternity" to describe "the seduction by a mythicized past [that] prevents us from thinking about possible futures" (Snyder, 2017, p. 123). We use this mythicized past to obliterate the pain of loss. This was the conflict Harry experienced when his world fell apart. It was only when he was able to acknowledge that he could not replicate what he had lost that he was able to imagine a different life.

Adapt or die

The greatest threat to our identity is when the beliefs we have lived by have been overturned and we are left with no markers to point the way forward. When groups experience fundamental changes in their everyday life and expectations of the future, for example, through modernization, displacement, or political upheaval, their response to these changes is vital to their identity and to their survival.

The most tragic response to massive change is that of suicide, whether of the group itself or of its members. This is the suicide brought on by humiliation and defeat in the face of an overwhelming force that has destroyed one's way of life and one's most important beliefs. At the end of the Reich, following Hitler's own suicide on 30 April 1945, a suicide epidemic swept across all of Germany. As the war was nearing its end and German losses were indisputable and severe, the prospect of suicide rose within the collective consciousness. The Reverend Gerhard Jacobi, perhaps aware of the anger and despair of his parishioners, preached in early March from his lectern at the Kaiser Wilhelm Memorial Church in Berlin on the evil of suicide. In an interview with a journalist at the time, the vicar said, "I have regular visits from parishioners who confide in me that they have procured ampoules of cyanide. They see no way out" (Huber, 2019, p. 77).

The journalist had also noted that the congregation expressed "no surprise" at their vicar's warnings. He then spoke to a fellow journalist, loyal to the Nazis, who exclaimed, "I can't carry on … Everything I believed in is turning out to be madness and crime" (ibid.). Suicide featured

> in newspapers, on state radio, and even in the Nazi leadership's rhetoric. "Goebbels has changed his tune: he is talking of suicide as a last resort." In a radio broadcast dripping with pathos, Goebbels had invoked the example of Frederick II, who had believed only in death or victory. Goebbels offered up the Prussian king as a martyr because he had once, at a time of military crisis, toyed with the idea of taking poison. Rarely had the propaganda machine appealed so heavy-handedly to the self-sacrificing spirit of the German people.
>
> (ibid., p. 79)

By early March, just as the Reverend Jacobi had feared, the suicide epidemic had begun, costing thousands of lives. While fear of brutal reprisals from the invading Russian soldiers was rife, fueled by German propaganda, it did not explain the extent and nature of the suicides that occurred. Many felt intense loyalty to Hitler and the Nazi regime, exacerbated by the scores of lives lost fighting to defend the Reich and the daily sacrifices made by those who survived. There was also shock that the beliefs that they had lived and died for had been destroyed along with their vision of the future. Others were shocked when they discovered the dark reality of the Nazi war crimes and the sudden disillusionment of their ideals.[5] There was also the murderous rage of being defeated, a rage that was turned inwards in the act of suicide. Without their leader, German identity was suddenly left vulnerable. At this point of crisis, mass suicide, as in the case of religious groups under threat, can restore a group's identity and illusion of omnipotence. Volkan writes,

> Identity enhancing massive suicides occur in religious groups when the members develop a shared conscious or unconscious fantasy that through death they join a divine power. Members of such a group physically die when they kill themselves, but, paradoxically (and illogically), just before their death they contaminate their group identity with omnipotence and believe that an omnipotent group identity will survive.
>
> (Volkan, 2004, p. 69)[6]

Even those who had not been Nazi supporters may have been susceptible to what was a form of mass hysteria.

For others still, the excitement and hope in building a new and better life had made them feel important for the first time in their lives. The Austrian novelist Peter Handke, in *A Sorrow Beyond Dreams*, describes the postwar depression of the narrator's mother, leading to suicide. Handke writes, "Personal life, if it had ever developed a character of its own, was depersonalized except for dream tatters swallowed up by the rites of religion, custom, and good manners; little remained of the human individual, and indeed, the word 'individual' was known only in pejorative combinations" (Handke, 2019, p. 40). The humiliation of defeat, of poverty and of the loss of what it meant to be an individual could also lead to despair. The narrator see the changes in his mother's face, "gradually, in its daily effort to keep up appearances, her face lost its soul" (ibid., p. 48).

Sudden changes in our lives present huge losses that are painful and difficult to overcome, especially when they affect the world we live in and depend upon. The struggle to manage and adapt to these changes may in certain circumstances either be impossibly loaded or actually counter to the culture's belief system. The forced transition to modern life amongst undeveloped tribes, such as the Inuit in Arctic Canada, is a case in point. In his research on suicide amongst the Inuit, Michael Kral interviewed scores of young Inuit men who had attempted suicide and found that about 70 percent of suicide attempts occurred after romantic break-ups. This raised the question as to why Inuit young men seemed so much more likely to attempt suicide in this situation compared to other groups. Kral came up with an important finding reported by an Inuit government official. She explained,

> The theory I have is that [Inuit] who commit suicide are doing it to protect the community … When we lived in small groups, we had a contract for survival. You lived for the collective, not for yourself. We're in this together. Children are conditioned to be calm. If someone explodes, that person is a threat to everyone. Then [the one who explodes] thinks, "Everyone will be better off without me. I'm a problem because I can't handle my emotions." It's hard to get that out of your head, because we're conditioned not be a burden to others.
>
> (Epstein, 2019, p. 18)

Coming from a culture in which the harsh physical conditions required emotional strength and rationality for survival, any slip from this could endanger the group. The traditional ego ideal of the group that had ensured survival within their own native environment was, ironically, the greatest obstacle in preventing its members from adapting to the changes in their new way of life. By continuing to adhere to their old ideals, the Inuit have remained trapped in a past that can no longer provide them with a sense of self-agency.

Our traditional ego ideals guide us in our social behavior and are instrumental in inspiring how we see ourselves in the future. But what happens when these ideals are no longer helpful or even in some cases viable? A nineteenth-century story of two native American tribes and how each dealt with modernization elucidates the role of the ego ideal and whether it can be perform a destructive or creative function in group survival.

By the end of the nineteenth century, the Crow Indians in Montana were facing extinction, like many other Indian tribes (Lear, 2006). As a young boy, the Crow Indian chief, Plenty Coups, had a dream foretelling the disappearance of the buffalo and the extinction of the Crow way of life. Not only did the Crow depend on the buffalo for their material survival but their identity, or their ego ideal, centered on being strong and brave hunters. Facing despair about the future, some years later Plenty Coups had another dream. In this dream, a little bird called the chickadee told Plenty Coup that the tribe needed to be like the chickadee to survive. For the Crow, the chickadee was a bird known for its ability to adapt to different conditions within its environment; it listened carefully and learned to adapt from what it heard. With this new vision, the tribe was able to shift from its traditional ideal of hunting and fighting to adopt a new ideal of listening and learning—a shift that enabled the Crow to maintain their identity as a group while adapting to the new world introduced by the white man. As a result, unlike many other Indian tribes, the Crow have been able to keep the majority of their land.

In contrast to the Crow Indians, the Sioux Indians became extinct. Their leader, Sitting Bull, insisted that continuing to fight and to fight even harder was the only way to win. His failure to accept their changing reality and to relinquish the tribe's ideal of themselves as warriors proved disastrous. What is vividly portrayed in the stories of these two tribes is the psychological devastation wrought within a group when their ideals cease to be realizable and "they cannot find ideals worthy of internalizing and making their own" (ibid., p. 140). In facing up to reality and recognizing forces beyond their control, Plenty Coups enabled his tribe to accept loss and to create a new ideal that could be internalized and sustain the tribe's identity in a new form. Sitting Bull tried to short-circuit reality by reinforcing his tribe's ideal as fighters with a disastrous result. The parallel here with modern-day populist responses to the massive social changes that are already affecting us is only too clear. The lure of the past ultimately beckons us toward self-destruction.

Bravery and facing the new

Returning to Odysseus, we can see that, despite his pleasurable sojourns on various islands with seductive goddesses and nymphs, he never abandoned his aim to reach Troy and then to return home. Odysseus' journey is a metaphor of life's struggles and how these shape our sense of ourselves and, ultimately, give meaning to our death. Driven off course by the fates and by his own failings, Odysseus overcomes each new challenge, resisting the temptation of the oblivion of immortality and resisting the temptation to cut his journey short and return to the human safety and warmth of Penelope's arms. Nicolson describes Odysseus as

> no victim. He suffers but he does not buckle. His virtue is his elasticity, his rubber vigour. If he is pushed, he bends, but he bends back, and that half-giving strength was to me a beautiful model of a man. He was all navigation, subtlety, invention, dodging the rocks, story-telling, cheating and survival. He can be resolute, fierce and destructive when need be, and clever, funny and loving when need be. There is no need to choose between these qualities; Odysseus makes them all available.
>
> (Nicolson, 2014, p. 3)

Just as Odysseus may have been "a beautiful model of a man" to the Ancient Greeks, he remains so today. The quality that is not mentioned, and conspicuous in its absence, is bravery. Odysseus' elasticity, his "rubber vigour," enables him to adapt and survive and yet, as Nicolson points out, he is "no victim." Odysseus is a heroic figure because he makes his own choices, often in defiance of the gods, according to what he knows he has to do. Although he is waylaid by sybaritic pleasures, he continues to be responsible for others, for his crew and for his countrymen, and he continues to face danger and uncertainty by binding himself to the mast of his principles. This is the binding required by bravery to face the changes of the future, both the losses and the new.

In a famous debate on the definition of courage, led by Socrates, one of the Athenian generals, Nicias, proposes that "courage is the knowledge of the grounds of fear and hope" (Plato). Socrates picks apart the meaning of knowledge, concluding that this is a virtue that encompasses courage and therefore cannot stand as a definition of courage per se. What Socrates fails to grasp is the meaning of Nicias' revealing juxtaposition between fear and hope. Nicias is making the point that courage is necessarily comprised of both fear and hope, the mortal fear that characterizes every act of bravery, but also the hope that guides every act of bravery. Fear tempers the action that can be taken—there is always an assessment of risk in bravery—but without hope of a good, that is, life-preserving, outcome, there is no point in acting bravely. Our hope in facing the future rests within our capacity to be true to ourselves and to the ideals that will light our way through the darkness ahead.

Notes

1. I am defining populism as political movements or groups that claim to represent the people and are characterized by anti-establishment, anti-elite attitudes, opposition to liberal economics and globalization, anti-immigration (xenophobia), protectionist economic policies, and nationalism. Populist groups tend to favor authoritarian governance.
2. At the time of writing, India has been overrun with protests about banning Muslims from citizenship.
3. Climate refugees are often portrayed as displaced immigrants in spite of the fact that within large countries such as the United States the most vulnerable populations live within the country.
4. This lack is not only apparent in Russia but it is apparent in protests across the world from India to Turkey to the US. For example, in Hong Kong, referred to in the last chapter, protestors want what they have been promised under the Basic Law, but there is little vision of what is sought for when this agreement expires and Hong Kong is fully absorbed into mainland China.
5. There is increasing evidence that most Germans had some awareness of at least some instances of war crimes that were being committed within Germany and abroad. Repudiation and outright denial were also common.
6. Robert Jay Lifton's study of the Japanese cult of Aum Shinrikyo refers to "totalistic communities" as characterized by an emphasis on purity, ideological totalism, continual self-confession, spiritual truths, and the "dispensing of existence" in which those who are not pure do not have the right to live. Ultimately, the self-annihilation of the cult ensured its immortality (see Lifton, R.J. (1999). *Destroying the World to Save It*. New York: Holt).

References

Alexievich, S. (2013). *Second-Hand Time*. London: Fitzcarraldo Editions.

Arendt, H. (1978). Hannah Arendt: From an Interview. *The New York Review of Books*. 26 October.

Dasgupta, R. (2018). The rise of the nation state. *Guardian*. 5 April.

Epstein, H. (2019). The highest suicide rate in the world. *The New York Review of Books*. 10 October.

Foy, H. (2020). Generation Putin: how young Russians view the only leader they've ever known. *The Financial Times Magazine Life & Arts*. 9 January.

Garton Ash, T. (2017). It's the Kultur, Stupid. *The New York Review of Books*. 7 December.

Gessen, M. (2017). *The Future is History: How Totalitarianism Reclaimed Russia*. London: Granta.

Graham, C. (2017). *Happiness for All? Unequal Hopes and Lives in Pursuit of the American Dream*. Princeton: Princeton University Press.

Handke, P. (2019). *A Sorrow Beyond Dreams*. London: Pushkin Press.

Inglehart, R. (2018). *Cultural Evolution: People's Motivations are Changing and Reshaping the World*. Cambridge: Cambridge University Press.

Lear, J. (2006). *Radical Hope: Ethics in the Face of Cultural Devastation*. Cambridge, MA: Harvard University Press.

Müller, J-W. (2018). What Cold War liberalism can teach us today. *The New York Review of Books Daily*. 26 November.

Münchau, W. (2014). Europe faces the horrors of its own house of debt. *Financial Times*. 16 June.

Nicolson, A. (2014). *The Mighty Dead*. London: William Collins.

Piketty, T. (2013). *Capital in the Twenty-First Century*. Cambridge: Harvard University Press.

Plato. (2017 [380 BC]). Laches, or Courage. In Plato, *The Dialogues of Plato*. London: Oxford University Press. Translated by B. Jowett.

Polakow-Suransky, S. (2017). Is Democracy in Europe Doomed? *The New York Review of Books Daily*. 16 October.

Sharafutdinova, G. (2019). R.I.P. 'Soviet Man': Scrapping Homo Sovieticus in the Spirit of Yuri Levada. *Woodrow Wilson: The Russia File*. 29 April.

Snyder, T. (2017). *On Tyranny: Twenty Lessons from the Twentieth Century*. London: The Bodley Head.

Volkan, V. (2004). *Blind Trust: Large Groups and Their Leaders in Times of Crisis and Terror*. Charlottesville, Virginia: Pitchstone Publishing.

Wade, R. (2014) The Piketty Phenomenon. *International Affairs*, 90(5): 1076.

Wolf, M. (2018). The Faustian bargain of nationalism. *Financial Times*. 18 December.

Epilogue

In these chapters I have tried to show that every act of bravery is an act of self-agency and, as such, a political act. When we defend someone else's life, we are defending our own and, more importantly, we are defending what Camus describes in his novel, *The Plague*, as "decency." Camus stresses that resistance to destructiveness, in this case the plague, is not to do with heroism, it is to do with decency, with our responsibility toward one another and toward ourselves to preserve "goodness" in life. It is this responsibility that binds us together in our beliefs, in our belonging and in our patriotism; it is our belief in "goodness" that shapes our identity, that guides our action and gives voice to our dissent. Camus writes, "It may seem a ridiculous idea, but the only way to fight the plague is with decency" (Camus, 1947, p. 125).

Tarrou, a visitor to Oran, has joined the fight against the plague and describes his moral position to Dr. Rieux, the narrator of the story, explaining that the greatest evil is to enable murder. He confesses:

> "For a long time I have been ashamed, mortally ashamed, of having been—even at a distance, even with the best will in the world—a murderer in my turn ... Yes, I have continued to feel

ashamed, and I learned that we are all in the plague, and I have lost my peace of mind … All I know is that one must do one's best not to be a plague victim and this is the only thing that can give us hope or peace or, failing that, a good death. This is what may give relief to men and, even if it does not save them, does them the least possible harm and even sometimes a little good."

(ibid., p. 194)

While most of us may not have actively enabled or been complicit in murder or other acts of extreme harm, we know the shame of not intervening. It is these acts of cowardice that stay to haunt us because we have betrayed ourselves and allowed ourselves to become pawns in a dehumanized world.

At the end of Tarrou's notebook, after the worst of the plague is over, he reminds himself that, nevertheless, he needs to keep in readiness. In questioning whether "he was, in fact, ready," Tarrou replies, "that there was always an hour of the day or night when a man was a coward and that he was afraid of nothing but that moment" (ibid., p. 216).

The plague is once again amongst us, spreading across continents in different guises. World leaders, from Trump to Netanyahu, Erdogan, and Putin, transgress the laws of their countries with impunity, Xi suppresses public information about the outbreak of coronavirus from his country and from the world, and at a time when we are beginning to experience the devastating effects of climate change, the Paris Climate Agreement is failing. As populist autocracies gain ascendency in the world and truth and dissent are silenced, we need to be especially vigilant in guarding against the cowardice of inaction and complicity that costs us our conscience, our countries and, ultimately, our lives.

30 December 2019

Reference

Camus, A. (1947). *The Plague*. London: Penguin, 2001.

Index